The State and the Soldier

In memory of Tim Gray
January 16, 1962 – August 29, 2019

THE STATE AND THE SOLDIER

A History of Civil–Military Relations in the United States

Kori Schake

polity

Copyright © Kori Schake 2025

The right of Kori Schake to be identified as Author of this Work has been asserted in accordance with the UK Copyright, Designs and Patents Act 1988.

First published in 2025 by Polity Press Ltd.

Polity Press Ltd.
65 Bridge Street
Cambridge CB2 1UR, UK

Polity Press Ltd.
111 River Street
Hoboken, NJ 07030, USA

All rights reserved. Except for the quotation of short passages for the purpose of criticism and review, no part of this publication may be reproduced, stored in a retrieval system or transmitted, in any form or by any means, electronic, mechanical, photocopying, recording or otherwise, without the prior permission of the publisher.

ISBN-13: 978-1-5095-7053-9

A catalogue record for this book is available from the British Library.

Library of Congress Control Number: 2025930829

Typeset in 11.5 on 14 pt Adobe Garamond
by Cheshire Typesetting Ltd, Cuddington, Cheshire
Printed and bound in Great Britain by CPI Group (UK) Ltd, Croydon

The publisher has used its best endeavours to ensure that the URLs for external websites referred to in this book are correct and active at the time of going to press. However, the publisher has no responsibility for the websites and can make no guarantee that a site will remain live or that the content is or will remain appropriate.

Every effort has been made to trace all copyright holders, but if any have been overlooked the publisher will be pleased to include any necessary credits in any subsequent reprint or edition.

For further information on Polity, visit our website:
politybooks.com

Contents

1 Introduction — 1
2 Origin Story — 14
3 Bad Examples — 38
4 A Standing Army — 64
5 Dogs That Mostly Didn't Bark — 91
6 The Modern Military — 119
7 How Worried Should We Be? — 156
Epilogue: Disputing the Canon — 190

Acknowledgments — 207
Notes — 210
Selected Bibliography — 244
Index — 250

President Franklin Roosevelt reviewing troops in Casablanca, Morocco, January 18, 1943

mccool / Alamy Stock Photo

> In pleasing contrast to the noisy, ever-changing management, or mismanagement, of blundering, plundering, money-making vote-sellers who receive their places from boss politicians as purchased goods, the soldiers do their duty so quietly that the traveler is scarce aware of their presence.
> John Muir[1]

> The President said that he believed that in a future nuclear war the chief task of the U.S. ground forces would be to preserve order in the United States. God only knew what the Navy would be doing in a nuclear attack.
> Memorandum of Discussion at the 277th Meeting of the National Security Council, Washington, DC, February 27, 1956[2]

> The weird thing with being a veteran, at least for me, is that you do feel better than most people. You risked your life for something bigger than yourself. How many people can say that? You chose to serve. Maybe you didn't understand American foreign policy or why we were at war. Maybe you never will. But it doesn't matter. You held up your hand and said, "I'm willing to die for these worthless civilians."
> Phil Klay, *Redeployment*[3]

Chapter 1

Introduction

How is it that a country founded in fear of a standing army would come to think of its military as a bulwark of democracy? That is the animating question of this book.

There is no other country in which the military is so proficient, so respected, so influential in policymaking without becoming a threat to civilian governance. Standard models of civil–military relations would predict a military so constituted to be tempted by coups or state capture.[1] Yet, for over 250 years, there has never been an organized attempt to overthrow the US government by its military. It is a precious, anomalous history.

Why that is the case isn't simple. It's partly the political culture of the colonies that would become the United States devising a government of distributed and counterbalancing power. It's partly the restraining example of an extraordinary individual during state formation, giving time for civilian institutions and military norms to form and strengthen. It's partly structural factors such as geographic expanse, rival and dispersed urban and commercial centers, and a benign international security environment coupled with urgent domestic insecurity (the "insider threat" of conflict with Native Americans) resulting in a weak federal army and strong militia. It's partly adroit politicians demonstrating the skills that make them successful and simply outplaying ambitious military aspirants. Which is to say that the American experience has proven beneficial and durable but difficult for other states to emulate.

This book isn't a comprehensive military history of the United States. Many important events that shaped the country and its forces go unrecorded in this account. Many themes that frame understanding of events do not appear here. This history focuses on only one of the five sets of interdependent relationships that comprise civil–military relations, that between civilian elites and military leaders.[2]

INTRODUCTION

What this book attempts to do is look at the evolution of relations between the American military and its civilian leadership, elected or appointed by those elected to determine national policy. To do so, it focuses on consequential instances of friction between those civilians with authority over the military and military leaders' response to that authority. What emerges from that interaction is a system of rules and norms of behavior that scholars term civil–military relations.

This book focuses on the military side of the equation: what are the constitutional, legal, and normative standards? What cases help understand appropriate military comportment? While civil–military relations are interactive, we predominantly police the military rather than the civilian leadership, for two reasons. First, because there are no qualification requirements political leaders must meet beyond election or appointment to merit their structurally superior position over the military. And, second, because it is the military that has recourse to violence.

My colleague Frank Gavin describes civil–military relations as the most boring subject in academia. He is woefully mistaken. The arc of the story is inherently interesting – George Washington inspiring mutinous soldiers to instead be the first army in a thousand years not to become a threat to democracy, the terrible dilemma of Ulysses Grant having to choose which constitutionally prescribed civilian source of authority to obey during cataclysmic feuding between the president and Congress, struggles to understand fighting limited wars in the nuclear age, the glittering success of professionalization after ending conscription, the unbalancing of the system when public trust in everything but the military collapses, and the maneuverings by civilians to pull the military into political partisanship that will delegitimize the military with the American people.

Where Frank Gavin is correct is that most of us who write about civil–military relations write at the postgraduate level, and for each other. We political scientists who comprise most of the scholars working on the subject mostly wrestle with theory, which I think it's fair to say is seldom of general interest even to other scholars and certainly not to policymakers living the issues, historians recounting and assessing them, or people who don't spend their professional lives thinking about these issues. So, while I do examine the canonical literature addressing civil–military relations, with apologies to all the smart people writing on the issue, I put the literature at the end of the story so as not to frighten off the Frank Gavins of the readership.

What I'm trying to do with this book is invite general readers into an understanding of the subject by telling the story of the evolution of a unique relationship of a powerful military comfortably subservient to elected leaders. Or at least a military that is at nearly all times mostly principled and placid in that subservience, because there are numerous bad examples – incidents where military officers traduce law or norm or, more recently, where political leaders attempt to goad the military (sometimes successfully) into a more politicized role. But those bad examples are exclusively individual actions, not the mobilization of a restive military in insurrection.

The most important thing I learned researching and writing this book is that the Founding Fathers had it wrong – they worried that a standing army would be a threat to civilian governance, but what actually happened is that the creation of a professional military dramatically reduced the challenges to civilian control of the military in the United States.

The main tenets of civil–military relations as established in the United States are that the military:

- owe their loyalty to the Constitution;
- are subordinate both to the president as commander in chief and to the Congress;
- can only either faithfully carry out civilian orders or resign their commission.

There are almost no incidents of military insubordination during the nation's actual wars. Whether the US is winning or losing, it is deeply engrained in the American military tradition that civilians determine the strategy and resourcing of wars, for better and for worse. The only example of wartime insubordination is that of General MacArthur during the Korean War, and President Truman's firing of him rings down through the decades uncontested.

The US experiences more friction in the aftermath of wars, as civilians and the military argue over reduced forces and budgets. Those instances are hyperbolized as dangerous rebellions – the Admirals' Revolt! – but are mostly the earnest actions of both civilian and military leaders, struggling to understand changing technologies and geopolitical developments, acting within the bounds of a political system designed for Congress to contest executive control by the president. The understanding of how nuclear weapons affect risk calculations and uses of conventional forces was particularly challenging, as civilian leaders came to think quite differently from most military leaders of the time.

Creation of a volunteer force and the military becoming small relative to the population created another turn of the kaleidoscope. In those circumstances, the military has become a main source of public understanding about warfare in ways with which civilian leaders are often uncomfortable and which veterans capitalize on politically. As public confidence plummeted in most institutions of government and civic life in America, it held roughly constant for the military, leading the public to blame elected leaders and praise the military in ways that encourage broader military involvement in politics.[3]

But contemporary concerns about the military becoming a partisan political force are largely unfounded. Despite norm-shattering behavior by a small but influential coterie of politicians, military leaders, and veterans, the constitutional, legal, and normative boundaries of civil–military relations in America remain robust. And the central reason the US military abjures political involvement is that the leaders understand organically what survey research on civil–military has revealed: while partisan civilians encourage the military wading into our political and cultural disputes, they respect the military less when they do.[4] Needing to recruit a volunteer military, and reveling in the approbation of the public, the military consider it in their self-interest to restrain their own involvement. Such discipline doesn't extend to veterans, whom the public do not separate from the military, and who have every right as citizens not in active military service to engage in politics.

There are basically only two essential tests of the health of civil–military relations in the US:

- can the president fire military leaders with impunity? and
- will the military carry out policies they don't agree with?

The American military easily meets both of those standards. For all of the discomfort of our febrile political moment, the American military remains dedicated to not being a threat to democracy. That professionalism could conceivably prove problematic with the election of what Pauline Shanks-Kaurin terms an "unprincipled principal" as president, were Congress to cede even more of its constitutional authorities to the executive for partisan purposes or politicians prove able to circumvent or discredit the military leadership, or should governors be eager to utilize them to advance partisan policies offering National Guard units to other states or the federal government.[5]

What emerges from litigating the historical cases is a deep and abiding gratitude that this country had George Washington at its inception to establish the standard to which our military continues to aspire. Even other Founders lacked his starchy and often weary integrity on civil–military issues. In a system of government designed to distribute power and check abuse by building in contending forces, generations of American military leaders have navigated the inherent frictions by Washington's example. Washington wasn't always right, but he was exemplary often enough to validate Bismarck's observation that God has a special providence for drunks, babies, and the United States of America.[6]

Preview

The book begins with Washington. Chapter 2 recounts General Washington's career as soldier and statesman, highlighting the extent to which his political experience informed his behavior in uniform. In particular, his devotion to the American experiment in republican governance and unwavering example of subordination to civilian supremacy over the military. Washington never demanded of Congress, he implored. He didn't insist Congress resource his preferred strategy, he adapted his strategy to the political constraints. When Alexander Hamilton urged him to lead an effort to frighten the Continental Congress into voting itself revenue powers, Washington refused, cautioning that the military was "a dangerous instrument to play with."[7] Washington did use the stature of his military office for the political purpose of strengthening the fledgling institutions of government, but he proved that a professional military is not incompatible with civil liberty. The care he exercised in the examples he set fashioned the culture of the American military that persists to this day. But not everybody is George Washington . . .

Chapter 3 reviews the bad examples that follow Washington's sterling performance. In contravention of President Adams's policies, Colonel Alexander Hamilton raised an army with designs on threatening Thomas Jefferson's political partisans and conquering foreign lands. General James Wilkinson helped foment Aaron Burr's plot to overthrow the US government. General Andrew Jackson exceeded his orders and invaded Florida, risking war with Spain and embroiling President Monroe in constitutional trouble with Congress. General Zachary Taylor and Major John Fremont took military actions of grave political consequence without political direction in the Mexican War. General John Fremont emancipated slaves in Missouri while President Lincoln was insisting the Civil War wasn't about slavery, and might have provoked the border states' secession. General Robert E. Lee and other officers from southern states violated their commissions by choosing state association over the federal government, something that had been resolved during the Constitutional Convention by having military oaths sworn to the Constitution. And General George Armstrong Custer politicked his way out of trouble numerous times despite active involvement in partisan activity, eventually collapsing the president's policy of bringing Native Americans into citizenship.

That such a variety of experiences of military ambition or over-reach of authority exist in the first century of the US demonstrates the inherent tensions between civilian authorities and military initiative. The secessionists provide the only instance of organized military opposition, and, in that case, they didn't lead the stampede to violence, they joined it.

Chapter 4 begins with the military choosing to obey the commander in chief rather than carry out the law when President Lincoln's suspension of habeas corpus was judged unconstitutional. It recounts the development of a standing military in the US, first retained after the Civil War to occupy states of the defeated Confederacy. No American military officer has ever been in as difficult a position as was General Ulysses Grant after the Civil War. Because of the vituperative disagreements over the post-Civil War settlement, Congress impeached and was threatening to arrest the president, and the president was threatening to disband Congress. Forced to choose which of the two constitutionally prescribed sources of civilian oversight to obey, Grant determined Congress had the superior claim. He obeyed the law rather than the commander in chief, reversing the polarity from the start of the war.

Violent political and cultural irredentism was a problem immediately in the seceded states after the surrender of the Confederate armies. The insurgency was directed not at the Union military forces but at Black Americans and their advocates. After a decade of occupation, the US government conceded, electing to withdraw forces from the southern states. The legislation that codified that political agreement, Posse Comitatus, strictly constrains domestic utilization of the American military.

While trust and comity between the military and civilian leaders make the American system work best, General Ranald Mackenzie's raid into Mexico in 1873 demonstrates that too much trust can also unbalance the system, removing oversight.

Chapter 5 spans the time from the 1898 Spanish–American War to Truman's firing of General Douglas MacArthur in 1951. In a time of enormous geopolitical and technological upheaval, as the United States ascends to become the dominant state in the international order, it's quite striking how few instances occur of the military attempting to supersede the authority of civilian officials. Admiral William Sims subordinated US forces to British command in contravention of President Woodrow Wilson's direction, and Wilson effectively submerged Sims under another commander. General MacArthur refused orders limiting military operations and public pronouncements, and the military leadership supported President Truman firing him. In both instances, the rebels considered their judgment superior to the civilian leadership and viewed themselves as canny political actors, only to find themselves outplayed by actual politicians.

The great leaps forward in military professionalism and innovation during the early 1900s and the inter-war years of the 1920s and 1930s were largely the result of intellectual ferment generated within the military itself. Far from resisting change, military leaders sought to capitalize on it with educational, technological, operational, and doctrinal adaptation. And in World War II, the largest and most consequential war the US has ever fought, the civil–military system worked incredibly smoothly – so smoothly that the father of American civil–military study, Samuel Huntington, derides the military leaders of that war for giving too much ground to their political masters.

What gets characterized as military usurpation is legitimate debate over the size, cost, and strategy for US forces. Military leaders argue within government policy councils, and that failing, those leaders and veterans take the case public to influence congressional action. But that, too, is how the American system is designed to function: it is Congress that really controls United States defense policy. Serving military officers are enjoined by the Constitution and by commitment upon promotion to give their advice not only to the commander in chief but also to Congress. It does not constitute a revolt for them to do so; they are exercising what President Eisenhower exasperatedly described as "legalized insubordination."[8]

Chapter 6 covers the modern American military, the one that emerges from World War II and is given form by the 1947 National Security Act. The transformation commences with the struggle over racial integration, something three of the four services bitterly resisted as deleterious to unit cohesion and unfair to impose on the military when society hadn't desegregated. The crucible of combat changed attitudes, which perked up from commanders and ended opposition. In both the Cuban missile crisis and the Vietnam War, military leaders' advice was vastly beyond civilian leaders' practical political boundaries, leading to military exclusion from policy counsels and leaving them with the choice of compliance or denouncing a president's strategy and resourcing. In both cases, the military properly deferred to their civilian superiors, and the public learned, perhaps too well, to blame the civilian leadership for outcomes in war.[9]

The US ended conscription in 1973, and the American military rebuilt itself into a professionalized force, a transformation that consumed a decade but of which it is justifiably proud. The military it produced triumphed in the 1991 Gulf War and catapulted a legislatively empowered chairman of the joint chiefs of staff into the limelight. The assertiveness with which General Colin Powell worked civilian leaders and sought to affect public attitudes was novel and uncomfortable for a civilian leadership in whom the public ceased to repose confidence.

America's twenty-first-century wars saw the rise of veteran activism accusatory of civilian misjudgments but, given the wars' extended duration and inconclusive outcomes, surprisingly little antagonism between civilian and military leaders. The arguments seldom had a clear civil versus military dynamic, the mistakes were predominantly civilian in nature, and the military accepted firings and made do with strategies and resources poorly aligned to political objectives. What does come through clearly is that the disparity in public standing between politicians and the military is both incentivizing suits to hide behind uniforms in making the case for policies before Congress and with the public and leading to suspicion by many politicians that military judgments are designed not solely as professional expertise but also for political effect: Presidents Obama, Trump, and Biden all believed the military was trying to limit their ability to enact preferred policies.

Chapter 7 explores the domestic challenges to the American military remaining outside of politics. There are three: politicization in the broader body politic, mistakes by military leaders widening the aperture of vulnerability to political manipulation, and ambition by a political demagogue to break the good order and discipline of the military to recruit insurrectionists. The combination has produced a dramatic decline in public trust in the military – it is now at the lowest level in more than twenty years, roughly equivalent to attitudes in 1975.[10] Fortunes of war do not appear to negatively affect attitudes about the military: confidence dives only in 2018. Research by Peter Feaver demonstrates that the American public begins to view our military comparable to the Supreme Court: brimming with integrity when agreeing with respondents' political views and disgracefully politicized when not.[11] The public is actively pulling the military into the fray, and the only impediment to politicization is the professional restraint of the military itself.

General Mark Milley isn't the only military leader who stumbled into political thickets, but his choices exacerbate public perceptions of a military leadership actively engaging in political and cultural fractures. A main driver of perceptions about military politicization has resulted from veterans endorsing political candidates, speaking at political conventions, and claiming to speak for the active-duty force. And norms are eroding across the political spectrum of excluding military images from political advertisements and appearances.

But the arsonist of politicization is Donald Trump and the political movement he represents. In striking contrast to the deference generally shown the American military, Trump denigrated war hero John McCain, insulted a Gold Star family, reportedly referred to the military as "suckers and losers," accused "the generals" of corruption, used meetings with troops as campaign events, and pardoned servicemen convicted of war crimes at courts-martial. These actions are putting political pressure on military leaders not seen since at least Thomas Jefferson was president, and probably not ever in American history.

It is requiring heroic discipline on the part of military leaders to navigate these political developments. At the time of this writing, they appear to be lowering their profile, interpreting their roles more narrowly, emphasizing regulations for behavior, and trying to discourage veteran political activism. However, it is both unfair and likely to be insufficient to rely solely on the military to police the civil–military relationship. Civilians have responsibilities they are shirking to respect the apolitical space our system is designed to provide the military.

An epilogue concludes this study surveying the two foundational books in the field of civil–military relations. It was famously said that all Russian literature emerges from Gogol's *The Overcoat*, and all of us who work on American civil–military relations emerge from Huntington or Janowitz's overcoats. The field of study in the US really begins with Samuel Huntington's *The Soldier and the State*. Huntington creates the lexicon of objective civilian control (separate spheres of civilian and military decision, wide latitude for military autonomy) and argues that the liberality of American society is incompatible with an effective military.

Huntington pairs with Morris Janowitz's *The Professional Soldier*, a book that introduces academically rigorous interdisciplinary research but also advocacy for subjective civilian control of the military. Janowitz would term Huntington's professionals to be absolutists, believers that victory is the sole purpose of utilizing military force, when what Janowitz considers more appropriate for the nuclear age is a mix of heroic leaders, military managers, and technologists.[12] Both Huntington and Janowitz smuggle political views into scholarship, Huntington advocating conservatism and Janowitz advocating for a military more receptive to liberal political involvement.

Successor generations of experts have contributed enormously to understanding the military itself and the civil–military nexus. Risa Brooks, Rosa Brooks, Jessica Blankshain, David Burbach, Eliot Cohen, Lindsay Cohn, Jason Dempsey, Charles Dunlap, Peter Feaver, Lawrence Freedman, Alice Hunt Friend, Doyle Hodges, Ole Holsti, Mara Karlin, Richard Kohn, Carrie A. Lee, Jason Lyall, Max Margulies, Suzanne

Nielsen, Michael Robinson, Avishay Ben Sasson-Gordis, Naunihal Singh, Don Snider, Heidi Urben, and Russell Weigley have all made seminal contributions and are referenced throughout the book. What emerges from the fulgency of their work is a consensus in two areas, both summarized here by Eliot Cohen:

- The traditional conception of military professionalism assumed that it is possible to separate an autonomous area of military science from political purpose. But this sharp separation breaks down in practice.[13]
- The imperatives of politics and of military professionalism invariably, and appropriately, tug in opposite directions; inevitably too, professional judgments require scrutiny rather than unthinking acceptance.[14]

In addition to works by scholars of civil–military relations, we are living through a renaissance of veterans' literature from our contemporary wars, writers contributing to understanding of the experiences of war and reintegration to civilian society through policy analysis, memoir, and fiction. A selected bibliography of both scholarship and literature is at the end of the book.

While Frank Gavin would consider engaging the literature of civil–military relations a dispiriting conclusion to this book, it provides an opportunity to wrestle with the most important ideas that this history unearths: how to sustain a military strong enough to protect the country yet that does not become a threat to democracy and what the appropriate means of dissent might be when military leaders disagree with the judgments of their elected superiors.

Conclusion

Friction among competing power centers such as this history reveals between civilian leaders and their military advisors and commanders is endemic by design in the American system. It is no less important in civil–military relations than in other checks and balances of the disputatious model – perhaps more so, since military forces could bring violence to bear. That a military so proficient and so respected and sometimes even adored by the public as ours has never posed a threat to democracy is a legacy to treasure.

INTRODUCTION

The American military has so internalized Washington's example that the "unequal dialogue" between civilians and the military that positions them structurally inferior to elected or appointed civilians is unquestioned.[15] They also fundamentally accept that elected or appointed civilians have "a right to be wrong."[16] Americans are so accustomed to our system of civil–military relations that we often fail to appreciate how uncommon in other free societies is the wide latitude the US military gets in policy formation, and how vanishingly rare it is for so powerful a military not to become a power broker in the country's politics.

In the American experience, the key to military subservience has been the deep and principled commitment of our military itself to civilian supremacy. It begins with Washington, strengthens as the country develops the need for a standing military, and becomes a subject of veneration within the military itself as the military professionalizes in the era of the volunteer force. The current ferocity of partisan politics is testing that military's ability to remain outside fulminating political and cultural debates. And while military leaders fumble their way through these challenges, a free society should probably prefer the problems of a military inexpert at politics than a military leadership of adroit politicians, for, while the former draw criticism for their clumsiness, the latter are likely to produce the praetorian sense of superiority that has destroyed so many democracies.

There is no easy prescription for ensuring that a military strong enough to protect the nation remains subservient to its political leadership. No silver bullet. Just as the circumstances that produce the unlikely outcome Americans have come to take for granted of a powerful and admired military that restricts itself from becoming either a threat to elected leaders or capturing the state through political influence, so the means of preserving it are vague and unsatisfying: prudence, restraint, trusting and being trustworthy by both the civilian and military leaders. Politics, like warfare, remains a frustratingly human and interpersonal undertaking.

After fifty years of a professional, all-volunteer force, small compared to the population, the American military gets the political leadership it deserves, and vice versa. If the military can't find ways to foster the "intimate, easy relationship born of friendship and mutual regard between the president and the Chiefs" that General Maxwell Taylor advocated (but was mostly an impediment to), they will be excluded from crucial policy deliberations and their military advice will often not reflect the political parameters within which civilian leaders are operating.[17] And if the civilian leaders don't give some deference to military experience, they are not only less likely to wield military force effectively, they are less likely to be shielded by the military leadership and veterans when difficulties arise and Congress demands accountability.

Chapter 2

Origin Story

The Founding Fathers weren't romantics – except for sybaritic Thomas Jefferson, of course, who was an outlier on virtually every scale. What Jefferson said of his religion holds true of him more broadly: he is a sect by himself.[1] The rest were practical men, learned enough to shun the quicksilver cosmopolitanism of Athens for the sturdy civic-mindedness of Rome. They modeled themselves after Marcus Aurelius' stoic responsibility rather than Themistocles' clever turning of the oracle's meaning about the wooden wall of Athens.

George Washington is rightly remembered as the founding-est of Founding Fathers, the one indispensable man. Historian and biographer Joseph Ellis best contextualizes him:

> Benjamin Franklin was wiser than Washington; Alexander Hamilton was more brilliant; John Adams was better read; Thomas Jefferson was more intellectually sophisticated; James Madison was more politically astute. Yet each and all of these prominent figures acknowledged that Washington was their unquestioned superior.[2]

Garry Wills writes, "Washington already stood for an entire people, before some observers even suspected there *was* a people ... he was the embodiment of stability within a revolution."[3] Washington had a majesty about him. He was, as poet Christopher Logue describes Hector from *The Iliad*, "historic in his own time."[4] Benjamin Franklin's biographer contrasts the two men, describing Washington as "a remote figure, a legend, a monument while he lived."[5] As early as 1790 his birthday was celebrated as a national holiday.

Nowhere is Washington's indispensability more resonant than in the story of American civil–military relations. Absent Washington, the role and relationships of the American military to its government and its citizenry would have a very different trajectory. Much as political scientists look for systemic drivers, so much of the early history of America as a country depends on the person and character of George Washington as to all by itself validate the great man theory of history.

No other commander could have held the starving army together during the Revolutionary War. Perhaps no other man would have declined the offer of becoming emperor. None would have been so sensitive to political concern about standing armies or so trusted to establish policy for it. He defined the boundary between military and civilian by resigning his commission after the war and taking off his uniform to stand for elected office. No other would have had the stature to brush Congress back from using the military as a threat against consolidated federal power. No other could have enforced federal authority against rebellious citizens without discrediting the federal government. George Washington's choices set standards that continue to shape the professional comportment of the American military even now.

Washington was the most experienced soldier in the American colonies, having served in the British Army during the French and Indian War (and published an account of his service to justify his lack of success!). Elected to the Continental Congress meeting in Philadelphia in 1774, George Washington bought a new sash and epaulettes for his military uniform and ordered a copy of Thomas Webb's *A Military Treatise on the Appointments of the Army*.[6] A year later, as war loomed, Washington received 106 of the 108 votes cast for Virginia delegates to the Second Continental Congress, and (as John Adams snidely reported to Abigail) not only took his uniform with him but alone among the delegates wore it to legislative sessions. He also ordered more books on warfare, a touching fingerprint of his modesty to better prepare for command.

Barbara Tuchman describes Washington as having "a kind of nobility . . . making him the only and obvious choice for Commander in Chief."[7] His being a Virginian helped cement allegiance among the colonies; his physical stature and taciturn manner reinforced his suitability. His selection by the Congress was unanimous. Joseph Ellis assesses that "more delegates could agree that Washington should lead the American army than that there should be an American army at all."[8]

The Founders were deeply distrustful of military forces. Many of the original causes of colonial discontent centered on taxes required of Americans to support the British military, which, after its victory on the Plains of Abraham ending the Seven Years' War, seemed unneeded. Prominent among the "history of repeated injuries and usurpations, all having in direct object the establishment of an absolute Tyranny over these states," outlined in the Declaration of Independence are that:

> He has kept among us, in times of peace, Standing Armies without the Consent of our legislatures.
> He has affected to render the Military independent of and superior to the Civil power.
> For Quartering large bodies of armed troops among us:
> For protecting them, by a mock Trial, from punishment for any Murders which they should commit on the Inhabitants of these States.

John Adams was reviled for his legal defense of British soldiers' conduct, even as he demonstrated that the rule of law prevailed in the colonies and trials by jury could produce fair verdicts.[9]

The Founding Fathers weren't just suspicious of British soldiers, considering their care burdensome on the public. They were also suspicious of American soldiery's potential for corrosion or overthrow of democracy. Samuel Adams observed that:

> A standing Army, however necessary it may be at some times, is always dangerous to the Liberties of the People. Soldiers are apt to consider themselves as a Body distinct from the rest of the Citizens. They have their Arms always in their hands. Their Rules and their Discipline is severe. They soon become attachd to their officers and disposd to yield implicit Obedience to their Commands. Such a Power should be watched with a jealous Eye.[10]

Washington's starchy integrity soothed these concerns, and, while he spoke little, when he did speak it was in the language of a revolutionary tribune: he responded to the British challenge about the legitimacy of his rank with "I cannot conceive any more honourable, than that which flows from that uncorrupted Choice of a brave and free People – the purest Source and original Fountain of all Power."[11]

Civilian Primacy

Perhaps the most powerful and precious of all the legacies left by George Washington to the republic he grew gray and nearly blind in defense of was his foundational subordination of the military to elected leaders.[12] Washington does not demand of the Congress, even in the worst of the winter of 1779–80, with "discouragement close to despair"; he pleads and entreats.[13] Joseph Ellis writes:

> Washington did not use the term "civilian control," but he was scrupulous about acknowledging that his own authority derived from the elected representatives in the Congress. If there were two institutions that embodied the emerging nation to be called the United States – the Continental army and the Continental Congress – he insisted that the former was subordinate to the latter.[14]

Washington wrote to Samuel Huntington, the president of the Congress in that dire winter of 1779–80: "I find our prospects are infinitely worse than they have been at any period of the war, and that unless some expedient can be instantly adopted, a dissolution of the army for want of subsistence is unavoidable. A part of it has been again several days without bread."[15] Nor was Washington exaggerating the danger: he'd had to hang two leaders of an uprising among troops encamped at Morristown for demanding full rations.[16]

It wasn't a passing moment of anguish for the commander of the revolutionary army; the deprivations experienced by his forces were enduring and endemic throughout the conflict. Washington wrote a long and agonized letter in similar vein to Henry Laurens from Valley Forge two full years earlier: "I am now convinced beyond a doubt, that unless some great and capital change suddenly takes place in that line this Army must inevitably be reduced to one or other of these three things. Starve – dissolve – or disperse, in order to obtain subsistence in the best manner they can."[17] Washington describes having "ordered the Troops to be in readiness, that I might give every Opposition in my power; when behold! to my great mortification, I was not only informed, but convinced, that the Men were unable to stir on account of provision, and that a dangerous mutiny, begun the night before and which with difficulty was suppressed by the spirited exertions of some Officers, was still much to be apprehended." Reflecting on the demands of commanding this mutinous deserting army, General von Steuben concluded: "Caesar and Hannibal would have lost their reputations."[18]

Congress never provided what the revolutionary army needed. It fell to the nobility of the cause, the lethal consequences for rebels of British victory, and Washington's majestic leadership to hold the Army together and, as far as possible, compensate for deficiencies in food and ammunition.

Washington was not a brilliant general; he was barely a competent one. In 1754, during the French and Indian War, he'd overseen a massacre at Jumonville Glen, surrendered Fort Necessity to the French, and then led his force into destruction at Monongahela. But what Washington lacked as a military thinker he more than compensated for as a leader: he wrote operational plans his army was incapable of carrying out and that would have resulted in disaster, but he was routinely saved by having cultivated junior commanders of intrepidity, such as Nathanael Greene and Alexander Hamilton and the Marquis de Lafayette, who ignored his plan and improvised to produce success.[19] Empowering subordinates to think for themselves and take initiative as opportunities afforded – what the military terms "mission command" – so often associated with the Wehrmacht, exists also in the American army from its beginnings.

Washington did not get to fight the war the way he wanted. He didn't get the recruits, weapons, or provisions he needed. Although he was himself a slaveholder and initially opposed to the practice, want of recruits caused his recourse to enlisting free Blacks in the Continental Army.[20] To the Congress he provided his best military advice, explained his plans, initiated a civilian–military Board of War and Ordinance to facilitate coordination, showed the committee of the Continental Congress the needs to carry out those plans, and remonstrated in public circulars and private correspondence for more support.[21] Still he could not adequately resource his plans. The plain fact was that the colonies lacked the means to fight the war in the way Washington wanted. He wanted to fight in the way that the British would fight, the way he'd been taught by the British Army before they considered him too unpromising to provide a regular commission.

He attempted in three unsuccessful battles in late 1775 and early 1776 direct attacks on British defenses. His objective was that "a Stroke, well aim'd at this critical juncture, might put a final end to the War."[22] It was a European conception of warfare, concentrating forces for a decisive battle that defeated the enemy. He struck at British forces in Quebec, anticipating "the consequent possession of all Canada," and failed ruinously.

After narrowly escaping the capture of his entire army in the battle of Long Island, Washington adapted his strategy to shift his objective from winning to not losing. He could not win fighting like the British because he lacked the advantages available to Britain. But, as long as he kept an army in the field, Americans had a revolution. And so in August of 1777 he grudgingly adopted the "war of posts" strategy, urged on him by his officers, that he considered "a more diluted form of cowardice," of fleeting engagements after imposing casualties on Britain without risking his own army in major battles.[23] George Washington adapted his strategy to the resources made available by the Continental Congress rather than demanding Congress provide the resources necessary to execute his preferred strategy. In doing so, he established the precedent that elected leadership determines the military strategy in the United States.

The high point of Washington's restraint – the most glittering of his many shining moments – came during a threatened mutiny at Newburgh, New York, in 1783. Restless during encampment for the two years of "phony peace" that existed while a political settlement was being negotiated, exasperated with the paucity of supplies, and goaded on by civilian politicians desperate to find a way to pay the nation's bills or angling to use soldiers as sympathetic pawns in a larger issue of establishing federal power, officers mooted insurrection against the Continental Congress. They drew up a list of demands and threatened to lead troops to abandon the war effort and march on Philadelphia to usurp political power.[24]

After their victory at Yorktown, the Continental Army was encamped at Newburgh to monitor British occupation of New York City during the peace negotiations. While the Congress had committed to pensions of half pay for life to the soldiers who'd won American independence, they hadn't been paid. Not only did Congress not have authority under the Articles of Confederation to raise revenue, but some states had explicitly outlawed lifetime pensions. Mounting exasperation is evident in the official remonstration from the Army to the Congress, which included the ominous warning that "any further experiments on their [the Army's] patience may have fatal effects."[25] As Richard Kohn describes it, "During those long, boring months of 1782, a growing feeling of martyrdom, an uncertainty, and a realization that long years of service might go unrewarded – perhaps even hamper their future careers – made the situation increasingly explosive."[26]

Alexander Hamilton (then in Congress) was central to the plotting, believing the virtuous cause of army pensions could break congressional opposition to revenue bills.[27] That is to say, from the very foundation of the republic, politicians were using the military for political purposes. Hamilton supported sending an ultimatum to Congress that the Army would not disband unless paid, admitting the purpose was to force the revenue measure.[28] The officers demands warned that they would, "If war continues, remove into the unsettled country; there establish [themselves] and leave an ungrateful country to defend itself."[29] Hamilton encouraged Washington to lead the effort, which Washington declined, strenuously cautioning that an army was "a dangerous instrument to play with."[30]

In the sentimental recounting of the Newburgh conspiracy, Washington learns of their plans, appears unexpectedly at a gathering of the plotting officers, and asks to see their list of demands. Taking it, he fumbles with his glasses, embarrassedly explaining, "I have grown not only gray but almost blind in the service of my country," which serves to shame the officers. Washington did evidently adopt that pose and say those words, but ascribing to them the effect of snuffing out the mutiny overlooks two other crucial elements of Washington's comportment.

The first is that he didn't just wander into the insurrectionists' meeting. Washington learned of their plotting and called them together to explain themselves, denounced their plans as treason, and asserted his authority over them. He arrived with Major General Henry Knox, 6 foot 6 and 240 pounds, who'd supported numerous protests to Congress but was there to strong-arm the mutinous officers into signing a pledge of allegiance to the Continental Congress or take them into custody for court-martialing.[31] Washington wasn't relying on sentimentality to defuse the insurrection; he came prepared to enforce discipline. The sentimentality was a grace note, a political ploy to soften resistance.

The second, and the important lesson for contemporary civil–military relations, is that Washington agreed with the insurrectionists' criticisms of Congress. He didn't just acknowledge their concern; he endorsed their complaints. He had encouraged them to put their grievances in writing and deliver them to the Congress, and he wrote privately to congressional leaders with deep concern. But Washington insisted that Congress did not have to be good at its job to merit political primacy and the unquestioning subordination of the American military. Washington told the assembled discontented officers that

> This dreadful alternative of either deserting our country in the extremest hour of her distress, or turning our arms against it, which is the apparent object, unless Congress can be compelled into instant compliance, has something so shocking in it, that humanity revolts at the idea. My God! . . . sowing the seeds of discord and separation between the civil and military powers.

He cautions them not to "adopt measures which may cast a shade over that glory which has been so justly acquired, and tarnish the reputation of an army which is celebrated through all Europe for its fortitude and patriotism." He assures them they will have his utmost exertions in attaining their aims from the legislature. And he concludes:

> in the name of our common Country – as you value your own sacred honor – as you respect the rights of humanity, and as you regard the Military and national character of America, to express your utmost horror and detestation of the Man who wishes, under any specious pretences, to overturn the liberties of our Country, and who wickedly attempts to open the flood Gates of Civil discord, and deluge our rising Empire in Blood.
>
> By thus determining – and thus acting, you will pursue the plain and direct Road to the attainment of your wishes. You will defeat the insidious designs of our Enemies, who are compelled to resort from open force to secret Artifice. You will give one more distinguished proof of unexampled patriotism and patient virtue, rising superior to the pressure of the most complicated sufferings; and you will, by the dignity of your conduct, afford occasion for posterity to say, when speaking of the glorious example you have exhibited to mankind – "had this day been wanting, the world had never seen the last stage of perfection to which human nature is capable of attaining."[32]

It was a barn burner, quickly sent to the Congress and rushed into print.[33] And it succeeded in defanging a threat by the Army to the nascent civilian institutions of governance, the first genuine democracy in over a thousand years. As steady a hand as James Madison had considered the situation alarming, and Congress awarded the Army government bonds amounting to five years' full pay in lieu of lifetime pensions.[34] Whether or not the discontent was genuinely building to an actual coup d'état, Washington's comportment established both an enduring standard of military acceptance of civilian superiority in the American system of government and that Congress is not required to be good at its job to merit that structural superiority. Washington's adroit handling of the conspiracy cemented the principle that subjugation to elected civilian leaders was about who the military were as an institution.

Swords into Ploughshares

Political though it was, Washington's retirement from the Army is his second greatest contribution to civil–military relations in America.

As Washington disbanded the Army, he described them as "little short of a standing miracle."[35] His last official act was a public letter to the state governments extolling the advantages won by the revolution and envisioning the future peace and prosperity of the republic. Washington wrote elegiacally and at length about all that had been achieved, assessing that "At this Auspicious period the United States came into existence as a Nation, and if their Citizens should not be completely free & happy, the fault will be entirely their own." But he also warned: "This is the time of their political probation: this is the moment when the eyes of the whole World are turned upon them – This is the moment to establish or ruin their National Character for ever – This is the favorable moment to give such a tone to our fœderal Government, as will enable it to answer the ends of its institution."

It was a call to common purpose, a sentiment widespread among the military leaders of the revolution. As Alexander Hamilton similarly wrote to John Laurens (then still fighting the British in the Carolinas), "We have fought side by side to make America free, let us hand in hand struggle to make her happy."[36]

Washington's circular to the states was also unabashedly a political act by a serving soldier. It opens with this fulgency:

> The great object, for which I had the honor to hold an Appointment in the service of my Country being accomplished, I am now preparing to resign it into the hands of Congress, and to return to that domestic retirement; which it is well known I left with the greatest reluctance, a retirement for which I have never ceased to sigh through a long and painfull absence, and in which (remote from the noise and trouble of the World) I meditate to pass the remainder of life, in a state of undisturbed repose: But before I carry this resolution into effect, I think is a duty incumbent on me, to make this my last official communication, to congratulate you on the glorious events which Heaven has been pleased to produce in our favor, to offer my sentiments respecting some important subjects which appear to me to be intimately connected with the tranquility of the United States, to take my leave of your Excellency as a public Character, and to give my final blessing to that Country, in whose service I have spent the prime of my life, for whose sake I have consumed so many anxious days and watchful nights, and whose happiness, being extremely dear to me, will always constitute no inconsiderable part of my own.

Washington surrendered his military station with a direct eye to his political future. He acknowledged, "I am stepping out of the proper line of my duty," or at least that his actions could be perceived that way. But he cast the political future of what he termed the American empire as both fragile and historically important: "the States shall adopt at this moment, they will stand or fall, and by their confirmation or lapse, it is yet to be decided whether the Revolution must ultimately be considered as a blessing or a curse: a blessing or a curse, not to the present Age alone, for with our fate will the destiny of unborn Millions be involved."

He proceeded to outline four characteristics a successful political future for the country required:

> 1st An indissoluble Union of the States under one federal Head.
> 2ndly A sacred regard to public Justice.
> 3dly The adoption of a proper Peace Establishment – and
> 4thly The prevalence of that pacific and friendly disposition among the people of the United States, which will induce them to forget their local prejudices

and policies, to make those mutual concessions which are requisite to the general prosperity, and, in some instances, to sacrifice their individual advantages to the interest of the community.

Not only did he list them, he proceeded at great length to expound upon them (the circular clocks in at more than four thousand words).

Washington does toward the end provide his counsel on military issues: confidence in the Congress negotiating a just peace, the importance of states retaining militia for defense, and the moral responsibility of care for wounded veterans. He also attached his correspondence concerning army pay and pensions, justifying the soldiers' demands

> that provision should be viewed as it really was, a reasonable compensation offerd by Congress at a Time when they had nothing else to give to the Officers of the Army for services then to be performed. It was the only means to prevent a total dereliction of the Service – it was a part of their hire, I may be allowed to say, it was the price of their blood and of your Independancy – it is therefore more than a common debt, it is a debt of honor – it can never be considered as a pension or gratuity nor be cancelled untill it is fairly discharged.

But, in doing so, he was overtly lobbying elected officials using his rank and public admiration of the military and positioning himself to be the federal executor of those policies.

It is nonetheless consequential that he resigned his commission before standing for elected office, separating those spheres of military service and political office. Washington presented himself to the Confederation Congress in Annapolis on December 23, 1783, and said: "The great events on which my resignation depended having at length taken place; I have now the honor of offering my sincere Congratulations to Congress and of presenting myself before them to surrender into their hands the trust committed to me, and to claim the indulgence of retiring from the Service of my Country."[37]

It was one more important example of subordination to elected governance, and it also set the precedent that military officers set down their arms before entering the sphere of electoral politics. Washington resigning command was the act of greatest significance to his fellow citizens during his lifetime – of all his contributions to the republic, it was the most eulogized when he died.[38] Yet it was not untainted with politics.

Restraining the Dogs of War

George Washington's unique stature and revolutionary virtue made him the obvious choice for the role of chief executive, but, as the debates over the Constitution reveal, military dominance of governance remained a deep-seated concern. He alone was capable of allaying them, and served to do so.

Concerns about a standing army, always an element of Republican politics, were fanned into flame with the presence and quartering of British soldiers, so it is not surprising that the issue figured prominently in the debates over the Constitution. Richard Kohn writes that "no principle of government was more widely understood or more completely accepted by the generation of Americans that established the United States than the danger of a standing army in peacetime."[39] When Boston was under British siege in 1775 and appealed to the Continental Congress for reinforcement, the Provincial Congress of the Bay Colony nonetheless declared: "we tremble at having an Army (although consisting of our countrymen) established here, without a civil power to provide for and control them."[40]

While still in active military service, Washington became a founding member of the Society of the Cincinnati, created in 1783 "as a watchdog for officer interests."[41] Lucius Quinctius Cincinnatus was a farmer who took up arms in defense of Rome and, having legally achieved complete power over the state – twice – resigned, retired, and beat his sword into a ploughshare to symbolize he had no aspiration to reassert power.[42] The society's hereditary membership caused public concern, predictably from Thomas Jefferson but also from Benjamin Franklin, that it was attempting to establish an American aristocracy from the revolution's military leadership.[43]

As Samuel Adams had worried, the Continental Army came to see itself as more virtuous than the public it had defended. They were "the chosen few who preserved and protected the original ethos of 1775–76 after it had died out among the bulk of the American citizenry."[44] And, after the war, opposition to retaining a standing force was strongest in the areas where the Continental Army had been stationed or operating.[45] So hesitant were the newly independent American colonies to retain a military force that, under the Articles of Confederation, the assent of nine states was required in addition to a congressional request to raise an army.

Federalists believed a stronger central government than had been provided under the Articles of Confederation was essential to preserve the goals of the revolution, and flexibility was required, especially in matters of defense, to respond to emergent threats and evolving circumstances. Anti-Federalists feared consolidated power and sought to preserve the states' authority. Neither side rejected the need of the federal government to raise forces quickly in the case of enemy attack; the question was how expansive the authority should be and what checks were required to be put into place to prevent the federal government becoming a tyranny. These political differences had military roots: Federalists were veterans of Washington's army, and Anti-Federalists were militia men.[46]

Article I of the Constitution, which delineates the powers of the legislative branch, reserves to the Congress, in Section 8,

> To declare War, grant Letters of Marque and Reprisal, and make Rules concerning Captures on Land and Water;
> To raise and support Armies, but no Appropriation of Money to that Use shall be for a longer Term than two Years;
> To provide and maintain a Navy;
> To make Rules for the Government and Regulation of the land and naval Forces;
> To provide for calling forth the Militia to execute the Laws of the Union, suppress Insurrections and repel Invasions;
> To provide for organizing, arming, and disciplining, the Militia, and for governing such Part of them as may be employed in the Service of the United States, reserving to the States respectively, the Appointment of the Officers, and the Authority of training the Militia according to the discipline prescribed by Congress[.]

The very language "to raise and support Armies" in the Constitution demonstrates a preference for calling up militia rather than sustaining a professional military force. Naval forces were considered much less a threat, both because their operations at sea were less a burden on the populace and because historically it had been armies, not navies, that undertook to overthrow governments.[47]

Debates over how to ensure those charged with the use of violence on behalf of the state did not become a threat to liberty were a central concern in debates over the Constitution: thirteen of the eighty-five *Federalist Papers* directly address the issue.[48] The constitutional provisions on raising armies and maintaining a navy were countered by the Anti-Federalist Brutus, who recounted in sixteen published letters the historical destruction of liberty in Rome and in England under Cromwell and argued for more explicit restrictions on calling an army into being, including approval by two-thirds of both houses of Congress.[49]

Also writing under the pseudonym Publius, Alexander Hamilton, James Madison, and John Jay collectively argued in eighty-five salvos of what we now call the *Federalist Papers*. Three of this magnificent trove are concerned at length with the Army question.

Federalist no. 41, written by Madison, begins with the issue of whether the Constitution vests too much power in the federal government. Madison argues: "in all cases where power is to be conferred, the point first to be decided is, whether such a power be necessary to the public good; as the next will be, in case of an affirmative decision, to guard as effectually as possible against a perversion of the power to the public detriment." He then takes several specific provisions for consideration. The first is security against foreign danger, and he makes the case for flexibility: "How could a readiness for war in time of peace be safely prohibited, unless we could prohibit, in like manner, the preparations and establishments of every hostile nation? The means of security can only be regulated by the means and the danger of attack. They will, in fact, be ever determined by these rules, and by no others."[50]

Madison acknowledged the Anti-Federalist point that "A standing force, therefore, is a dangerous, at the same time that it may be a necessary, provision. On the smallest scale it has its inconveniences. On an extensive scale its consequences may be fatal. On any scale it is an object of laudable circumspection and precaution." And then he elegantly turns the Anti-Federalist concern about a standing army endangering the republic by arguing that a strong central government reduces the need for a standing army: "The Union itself, which it cements and secures, destroys every pretext for a military establishment which could be dangerous. America united, with a handful of troops, or without a single soldier, exhibits a more forbidding posture to foreign ambition than America disunited, with a hundred thousand veterans ready for combat." And he darkly intimated that a weak central government would tempt American states to warring with each other.

Hamilton took up his cudgels in defense of the Army clause in *Federalist* nos. 24 and 25. In *Federalist* no. 24, he argues that the Constitution isn't requiring a standing army and that Congress, not the executive, has authority to check its power. Hamilton's derision takes the form of incredulity at the arguments against an obviously sensible protection both on the frontier and to deter European encroachment, but he settles in to seriousness:

> Previous to the Revolution, and ever since the peace, there has been a constant necessity for keeping small garrisons on our Western frontier. No person can doubt that these will continue to be indispensable, if it should only be against the ravages and depredations of the Indians. These garrisons must either be furnished by occasional detachments from the militia, or by permanent corps in the pay of the government. The first is impracticable; and if practicable, would be pernicious. The militia would not long, if at all, submit to be dragged from their occupations and families to perform that most disagreeable duty in times of profound peace. And if they could be prevailed upon or compelled to do it, the increased expense of a frequent rotation of service, and the loss of labor and disconcertion of the industrious pursuits of individuals, would form conclusive objections.

The naval case was easier to make and quickly dispensed with in the closing paragraph: "If we mean to be a commercial people, or even to be secure on our Atlantic side, we must endeavor, as soon as possible, to have a navy."

In *Federalist* no. 25, Hamilton addresses why the national rather than state governments should have the authority for defense: "The territories of Britain, Spain, and of the Indian nations in our neighborhood do not border on particular States, but encircle the Union from Maine to Georgia. The danger, though in different degrees, is therefore common. And the means of guarding against it ought, in like manner, to be the objects of common councils and of a common treasury."[51]

Hamilton takes further Madison's case about division among states, highlighting that the Articles of Confederation prohibit states from having "either ships or troops, unless with the consent of Congress." In characterizing the Anti-Federalist concern, he says that

> All that kind of policy by which nations anticipate distant danger, and meet the gathering storm, must be abstained from, as contrary to the genuine maxims of a free government. We must expose our property and liberty to the mercy of foreign invaders, and invite them by our weakness to seize the naked and defenseless prey, because we are afraid that rulers, created by our choice, dependent on our will, might endanger that liberty, by an abuse of the means necessary to its preservation.

And he concludes *Federalist* no. 25 with a stem-winder of caution that the Anti-Federalist proposals, being impractical, encourage disrespect for governance:

> nations pay little regard to rules and maxims calculated in their very nature to run counter to the necessities of society. Wise politicians will be cautious about fettering the government with restrictions that cannot be observed, because they know that every breach of the fundamental laws, though dictated by necessity, impairs that sacred reverence which ought to be maintained in the breast of rulers towards the constitution of a country, and forms a precedent for other breaches where the same plea of necessity does not exist at all, or is less urgent and palpable.

Brutus responded to the Federalists in his ninth letter, arguing that they were preying on public fear and essentially maintaining that the government should have unlimited power: "It is admitted then, that a standing army in time of peace, is an evil. I ask then, why should this government be authorised to do evil? If the principles and habits of the people of this country are opposed to standing armies in time of peace, if they do not contribute to the public good, but would endanger the public liberty and happiness, why should the government be vested with the power?"[52] He also takes apart Hamilton's argument that no distinction exists between the people and the government.

Acknowledging that ratification of the Constitution would inevitably result in Washington's election as president, Brutus asserts: "It is a well known fact, that a number of those who had an agency in producing this system, and many of those who it is probable will have a principal share in the administration of the government under it, if it is adopted, are avowedly in favour of standing armies."

Standing against the assembled intellect and expression of Hamilton, Madison, and Jay was no small feat. The most politically prominent Anti-Federalist was Patrick Henry, whose ringing speeches in the Virginia House carried enormous weight, especially as he was a dedicated Unionist, the first revolutionary to declare himself an American rather than a Virginian.[53] Henry objected to the "centralizing tendency" of the Constitution, and he craftily used the example of Washington as Cincinnatus to make his case against it:

> In great dangers this power has been given. – Rome had furnished us with an illustrious example. – America found a person worthy of that trust: She looked to Virginia for him. We gave a dictatorial power to hands that used it gloriously; and which were rendered more glorious by surrendering it up. Where is there a breed of such Dictators? Shall we find a set of American Presidents of such a breed? Will the American President come and lay prostrate at the feet of Congress his laurels? I fear there are few men who can be trusted on that head."[54]

Anti-Federalists were persuasive enough to necessitate amendments to the Constitution as a requirement for ratification. Both the second and third amendments modified the Army clause of the Constitution:

> Amendment II: A well regulated Militia, being necessary to the security of a free State, the right of the people to keep and bear Arms, shall not be infringed.
> Amendment III: No Soldier shall, in time of peace be quartered in any house, without the consent of the Owner, nor in time of war, but in a manner to be prescribed by law.

The second amendment was designed to give states the ability to provide for security on the frontier or during foreign attack if the chief executive declined to act or could not act with the promptness necessary – and to give states some recourse against the possibility of a standing army being turned against the people. The third amendment was to prevent any recurrence of impositions laid down by the British Army and prevent the federal government from exporting onto the public the cost of raising and maintaining an army. It is surprisingly little alteration to the Constitution's endowment of authority to the federal government on the question of standing armed forces.

During the Constitutional Convention, Elbridge Gerry, representing Massachusetts, opposed popular election of the president on the grounds that it would result in the public's admiration producing leadership by the military "in every instance."[55] Gerry's concern would not be borne out in every instance, although Americans have tended to elect victorious military commanders to the presidency. But it was certainly borne out in the person of George Washington. Washington was the unanimous choice of all sixty-nine presidential electors in 1788–9. And, because his cabinet contained the leaders of the emergent political factions Washington worried would destroy the republic, one presidential term did not suffice. It was Jefferson who persuaded Washington to stand for a second term, arguing, "North and South will only hang together if they have you to hang on."[56] And, once again, George Washington was the unanimous choice of the electors.

Commander in Chief

George Washington is the only American president to have led troops on a military campaign while in office. In 1794 a populist uprising over imposition of the first federal tax precipitated President Washington to call up thirteen thousand militia and march west to confront his fellow Americans in Pennsylvania. Termed the Whiskey Rebellion, what began as harassment of federal tax collectors burgeoned over two years into a secessionist movement seeking to liberate territory west of the Allegheny Mountains from federal control.[57]

There was precedent, both of taxation and violent opposition, in the American republic. In 1787, four thousand citizens of Massachusetts attempted to raid the Springfield armory to take up arms against the Massachusetts government. While both state and private militia sufficed to prevent the overthrow of the state government, Shays's Rebellion figured prominently in debates over the creation of a federal government more capable than that provided for by the Articles of Confederation. Both Shays's and the Whiskey Rebellions mined the seam of economic difference between the barter economies of rural areas lacking capital and currency and the more lucrative market commerce of urban areas and coastal ports.[58]

Without taxing authority before 1789, the Confederation Congress borrowed to fund federal operations, including the war effort. The federal tax objected to on the frontier had been imposed by Congress as a necessity for paying off Revolutionary War bonds that consolidated federal and state debts. Which brings Treasury Secretary Alexander Hamilton into the picture. The tax fell most heavily along the frontier, aggravating complaints about federal failure both to protect settlers against Native attacks and to acquire from Spain American access to the Mississippi River, so important economically in the west.[59]

The rebels were predominantly Revolutionary War veterans, hard and capable frontiersmen accustomed to making their way with little assistance or even governance beyond local authority. They tarred and feathered the tax collector and whipped the officer delivering judicial warrants. By 1794 violent harassment had become an organized military insurgency of several thousand people.[60]

President Washington was too capable a politician to start with force. When the violent opposition began, he sent federal peace commissioners (all Pennsylvanians of political or judicial stature) to negotiate with the rebels and also pressed governors in the affected states to use their authority, including militia, to enforce compliance with the federal mandate.

Washington further issued a presidential proclamation published in newspapers across the country declaring the insurrectionists' acts "subversive of good order, contrary to the duty that every Citizen owes to his Country and to the laws, and of a nature dangerous to the very being of Government: And whereas such proceedings are the more unwarrantable, by reason of the moderation which has been heretofore shewn on the part of the Government, and of the disposition which has been manifested by the Legislature (who alone have authority to suspend the operation of laws)."[61] Washington exhorted the insurrectionists to desist, directly stating that, "all lawful ways and means will be strictly put in execution, for bringing to justice the infractors thereof and securing obedience thereto."

Hamilton took flamboyantly to the broadsheets under a pseudonym, accusing opponents of considering every exercise of federal authority an attempt to overthrow democratic governance. "It is a position too untenable and disgustful to be directly advocated – that the government ought not be supported in exertions to establish the authority of the laws against a resistance so incapable of justification or excuse ... ye cannot but remember that the government is your own work – that those who administer it are but your temporary agents; that you are called upon not to support their power, but your own power."[62]

Washington strictly complied with the Militia Act of 1792, which required certification by a Supreme Court justice that a state of rebellion existed before the chief executive could call militia into federal service. He received that certification on August 4, 1794. Washington issued another proclamation extolling the forbearance of federal authorities, condemning "many persons in the said western parts of Pennsylvania [who] have at length been hardy enough to perpetrate acts which I am advised amount to treason, being overt acts of levying war against the United States," and, outlining the legal basis for his actions, called up militia, "feeling the deepest regret for the occasion, but withal the most solemn conviction that the essential interests of the Union demand it."[63]

Washington's army consisted solely of militia (an irony, given his lifelong derision for their battlefield contributions and indiscipline) provided by governors from Pennsylvania, Virginia, Maryland, and New Jersey.[64] Governors had to resort to compulsory service to provide the militia and experienced not just protests but riots and armed resistance – the governor of Maryland had to dispatch eight hundred troops to quell one draft riot.[65] The Whiskey Rebellion wasn't an isolated tax uprising on the frontier; it had the potential to discredit the federal government much more broadly and to position the military as the enforcers of unpopular domestic law against an American public unconvinced of the legitimacy of either the law or the federal government.

The 12,950 militia mustered into federal service presented a force larger than Washington had commanded at Yorktown during the Revolutionary War. But Washington, who as commander of the Continental Army during the revolution had reluctantly adopted a Jacobin strategy, now found himself in the circumstance he'd imposed on Britain's army: he led the organized military fighting a guerrilla war at great distance from its supply base. Insurrectionists numbering in the several thousand left anonymous threats, endangered tax collectors, burned the property of neighbors complying with the tax, robbed the mail, and had their identities protected by local citizenry.

Washington and Hamilton rode with the militia, reviewing troops (and the progress of canals), but Washington rested operational command of the force in the Virginia governor, Light-Horse Harry Lee. While seeing no combat, the force proved sufficient to the task of intimidating compliance.[66] Insurrectionists didn't confront Washington's army, local citizens signed loyalty oaths, arrests were made without incident, troops were stationed in recalcitrant counties to ensure compliance, and rebels were marched into Philadelphia for trial, although most were acquitted and Washington, having reasserted federal authority, pardoned the rest.[67]

Washington would write in his Address to Congress that year (what we now term the State of the Union address), "for though I shall always think it a sacred duty to exercise with firmness and energy the constitutional powers with which I am vested, yet it appears to me no less consistent with the public good than it is with my personal feelings to mingle in the operations of Government every degree of moderation and tenderness which the national justice, dignity, and safety may permit."[68] The equanimity of his policy met with widespread approval, proving that a democratic government could compel compliance with its laws and retain public support. His actions also set the precedent, consequential fifty-seven years later, that sections of the country had recourse through political channels but no option of secession.

During Shays's Rebellion in 1787, Washington argued: "You talk, my good sir, of employing influence to appease the present tumults in Massachusetts. I know not where that influence is to be found, or, if attainable, that it would be a proper remedy for the disorders. Influence is not government. Let us have a government by which our lives, liberties, and properties will be secured, or let us know the worst at once."[69] Federal authority must be upheld, by force if necessary. The United States might very well have known the worst at once in 1794 had George Washington not been in office to bring his unique influence to bear on the first secessionist crisis in American history.

Probably no other politician in America at the time could have forcibly quelled a rebellion using military force without creating serious and widespread concern among the public about tyranny.[70] Thomas Jefferson would have excused the insurrection, as he had Shays's Rebellion, writing indulgently from Paris in its support that "the tree of liberty must be refreshed from time to time with the blood of patriots and tyrants."[71] And, in fact, Jefferson's faction repealed the whiskey tax after gaining power in 1800. Without Washington's restraining hand, Alexander Hamilton might well have done what his detractors believed he was conspiring to do: "exercise absolute power over the American people and punish political enemies in government."[72] Hamilton had advocated early resort to force in North Carolina in 1792 and was publicly accused during the Whiskey Rebellion of "a refinement of cruelty," in having fomented the rebellion in order to expand federal authority and suppress it.[73] John Adams's long-standing concern about mob violence would likely have inclined him to use force, but his reputation for monarchial tendencies would probably have complicated governors remanding militia to federal use for the purpose. Washington alone possessed both the commitment to demand federal authority and the equanimity to exercise it with restraint in order to signify that the shared authority of states and the federal government serve to legitimate domestic uses of military force and that a law-abiding American public need not fear their military.

Conclusion

Washington was not apolitical. He was deeply, profoundly a politician. He received his original commission through political connections, used his veteran status for political ends, published an exculpatory account of his service in the British Army, wore his uniform in sessions of the Continental Congress, was selected as commander of the Continental Army for political reasons, adopted intimations of physical frailty to shame officers into compliance with civilian control, made his last act as General Washington a political appeal, and as president personally led troops to enforce federal authority against insurrectionists. His posterity project after the Revolutionary War was to have Congress pay for the transcription of his military correspondence.[74]

His every act was imbued with politics, and the consciousness of their consequence caused that great man to weigh those acts in light of strengthening the nascent republic. As his resignation address makes clear, he gave his views on national matters while in uniform. But he deferred to the institution of Congress as inherently superior to the military in power, in responsibility, and in judgment. His conduct not only set crucial precedents, but also bought time for the institutions and norms of the nascent nation to gel.

Moreover, American politicians have been using for political purposes the civic virtue accorded to our military since the inception of our country. Not only wholly civilian politicians but also veterans have been willing to utilize public admiration for military service in service of other purposes. George Washington was uniquely positioned as a bulwark against politicization of the military and set boundaries that still today govern military conduct in political circumstances.

His politicking was institution-strengthening, within the American military, in cementing its role subordinate to civilian authority, clarifying the responsibility of compliance with the Constitution and federal law and in calling his fellow citizens to the higher purpose of holding together the nation. He did not give in to the temptation of political activism, even when it advanced his own preferred policies. Even fearing a potential mutiny, he did not use it to advantage with Congress; instead, he sternly cautioned against using the military for political advantage and warned of the dangers of fanning insurrection for political purposes – even political purposes he strongly supported, which were strengthening federal power and providing pay and pensions.

Washington was political but he was not partisan. Not only because his foundational civil–military acts occurred before political parties were properly formed – his subsequent presidential administration was rent asunder by the twin political parties thrashing their way out of the amniotic sac of early American politics – but also because he supported federal and state authorities in furtherance of their constitutional and statutory authorities.

George Washington understood that his every action as a leader in military service and in his subsequent political career would cast bright beams of precedential light into the future of the republic. And his political skills were essential to his service, both in uniform and out.[75] A lesser politician would have been less able to hold the Army together through the long, depressing slog of retreats and lack of provisions. A lesser politician would have been less able to hold the republic together as the Constitution sunk roots in American governance, less able to withstand the tectonic plate movements as political parties emerged, less able to utilize the talents and constrain the foibles of so many exceptional men. George Washington "proved that a professional army was not incompatible with civil liberty."[76] And so the Marvel Comics origin story of civil–military relations is the story of George Washington as both general and politician.

As Britain's King George remarked upon hearing Washington had declined the crown offered him by the Newburgh conspirators, "if He did He would be the greatest man in the world."[77] As, indeed, for all his faults and failings, he was.

Chapter 3
Bad Examples

After the Revolution, the Continental Army dissolved and was furloughed piecemeal; soldiers returned to their communities as the militia model that was both more responsive to local concerns and more comfortable culturally for Americans was reasserted.[1] The subsequent hundred years encompass some genuinely dangerous examples of military activity contrary to elected direction. The norms Washington established were slow to sink roots, and it is generally the case that military coups are most likely in newly formed states.[2] America's political and military leaders struggled to apply Washington's precepts to prevent the military becoming a threat to its democracy from the founding through the four years of quasi-war with France. For nearly three decades, the US was hemmed in by superior European powers' possession of territory to the north, west, and south. Civilian leaders wrestled with how to discipline popular but insubordinate field commanders. The great conflagration of civil war forced capitulation of seceded southern states and attempted to create a new socio-political order after the abolition of enslavement. And the government was called on to meet settler demands for protection as they relentlessly expanded through Native American territories.

President John Adams had the leader of his political faction raise and lead an army and threaten to use it against domestic political opponents, while fending off a congressional inquiry from those political opponents and averting a war the US would have lost against a far stronger foreign power. Thomas Jefferson's senior military officer was a Spanish spy who plotted with Aaron Burr to foment secession and mount a military coup to overthrow the United States government. President James Monroe experienced a popular military leader invade and occupy a foreign country, risking another war the US would have been likely to lose and putting the president in constitutional jeopardy with Congress. President Polk suffered soldiers exceeding their orders in two theaters of the Mexican War, precipitating congressional investigation of him. President

Abraham Lincoln endured both a military governor of a politically critical border state enacting policies contravening his administration on the central issue tearing the country apart and military officers violating their oath and taking up arms against the federal government, but he also experienced the closest and most supportive civil–military relationship in American history. Custer's politicking destroyed trust with his political leadership and led to his last stand, collapsing President Grant's Indian peace policy under public outrage.

In every case, the bad examples are individual officers, prominent officers, challenging elected political authority. Also, the individual officers had a history of usurping behavior, but their excellence in combat shielded them from weighty consequences. Senior officers excused their behavior on the argument that their proficiency in battle or their public celebrity merited special treatment.

It should not be a surprise that it was incredibly challenging to navigate the white-water rapids of a new nation congealing, breaking apart, struggling to come back together on different terms than those on which it was founded and expand control across a populated continent. Nor that the normative boundaries set by George Washington's foundational examples were sometimes traduced. Civil–military relations in democratic societies are difficult in the best of times, a question of equipoise and balancing of competing interests. The marvel is not that there were tensions and excesses across these momentous decades for the United States, but that the political system and the political culture of the society were so easily able to contain them.

Has Anyone Ever Had a Worse Job Than President John Adams?

John Adams, suspected by his fellow Bostonians for defending British soldiers in court, wizened yet exasperating, and largely ignored by the Continental Congress, the spare to Washington's heir as vice president yet excluded from cabinet and counsels, standing in Washington's shadow as his successor, exiled to the new capitol where he was socially uncomfortable to do a job (negotiating with Congress) for which he was profoundly unsuited, his cabinet clandestinely controlled by Alexander Hamilton scheming against him, his main political opponent Thomas Jefferson installed as his vice president, wrenched by the emergence of political parties neither of which he led, the country teetering on the brink of war with France that would have been disastrous for the young republic, unquestionably had an unenviable job. And then there is the New Army.

Spectators of contemporary American politics justifiably worry about democratic corrosion, partisanship, and domestic extremism. Yet they often overlook the frequency with which those fevers emerge from within the American body politic and are magnified by a political system designed to be lashed tightly to public attitudes. Perhaps the most accurate description of Americans comes from historian Bertha Ann Reuter in 1924: "people too radical either in religion or politics or both to live peaceably in their original home."[3] In fact, the era of American history in which democracy was most dangerously tested was the 1790s and early 1800s. Institutions were still being constructed, norms had not yet gelled. As Joseph Ellis emphasizes, Americans lacked even the vocabulary, short of declaring political opponents traitors.[4] Every single one of the Founding Fathers feared democracy was foundering.[5] And it was.

In return for France's financial and military assistance – overt and essential participation, really – during the American revolution, the US government committed by treaty to the defense of French interests in the Caribbean. Those commercial and geopolitical interests were under blockade by Britain and the Netherlands from 1792, a circumstance from which US businesses were handsomely profiting across the five years of war among those European powers. The next year, Congress claimed any US fiduciary obligations to France were severed with the head of Louis XVI.

The great diplomatic and political success of George Washington's presidency was keeping the fledgling American republic out of Europe's wars, which had stretched geographically to the Caribbean. The achievement had four elements: Washington's 1793 declaration of neutrality, the 1794 Neutrality Act, the Jay Treaty with Great Britain, and Washington's executive order preventing militarization of merchant shipping.[6]

Although the Neutrality Act restricted the president's ability to go to war, President Washington supported it, welcoming legislative endorsement of his policy of neutrality. As a demonstration of the popularity in America of supporting France in its belligerence against several European states, the bill's passage was sufficiently contested that Vice President Adams had to cast a tie-breaking vote in the Senate.

The Jay Treaty resolved issues outstanding from the American revolution, in particular settlement of claims to Loyalist property. Absent a settlement, Britain had been refusing commerce, something badly needed for American prosperity. Senate consent to ratification of the Jay Treaty was a close-run thing, the Senate demanding negotiating transcripts, which Washington refused and set the precedent of executive privilege in separating the powers of American government.

The French government objected to the Jay Treaty and American shirking of obligations and set to privateering in American waters, claiming the right of access to US ports and the ability to auction captured ships in the US, rights denied to the US in French ports and courts.

The American navy had largely been disbanded after the Revolutionary War; in fact, the only ships the US government commanded after 1785 had been purchased by Treasury Secretary Alexander Hamilton for the Revenue Service. Consequently, French privateers captured more than three hundred American merchant vessels, roughly 6 percent of the total commercial fleet.[7] By the end of this quasi-war, France had purloined more than two thousand American ships.[8]

In their scramble to reassemble defenses, in 1794 Congress authorized the construction of six frigates. American civil society contributed, nearly doubling the frigate fleet by "subscription ships," whose purchase was sponsored by cities. Britain also assisted the US side, contributing to the naval construction, reducing the French threat by trapping fleets in port, sharing intelligence, and allowing US merchants to operate from British bases and join Royal Navy convoys (of which there were more than four times as many as the US could flag) that freed US Navy ships up for offensives.[9]

The US electoral structure originally apportioned the vice presidency to the runner-up for the presidency. In 1796, that placed John Adams's fiercest rival and ideological opponent, Thomas Jefferson, as his potential successor. While Jefferson led the faction opposed to expanding federal power and supportive of revolutionary France, Adams led nothing; leadership of the Federalists resided in Alexander Hamilton. European powers, and France in particular, agitated within the United States for support in their war with Britain; French Ambassador Genet was actively recruiting privateers, and French agents were infiltrating Spanish territories in North America with ambitions to establish them as a French colony and restrict westward American expansion to east of the Mississippi River.[10]

President Adams attempted negotiations with France, which were insultingly spurned.[11] All President Adams had authority to do without congressional action was lift Washington's executive order prohibiting merchant ships arming to defend themselves. Jefferson and Madison's ploy to get the release of the negotiating record (believing it would shame Adams and build support for France) backfired by revealing France's outrageous demands – but, in keeping with the febrile attitudes of the times, started incitement for war against France. "Millions for defense but not one cent for tribute," was the rallying cry.

In the craze for war with France, Congress repudiated the defense treaty, cut off trade, passed the Alien and Sedition Acts restricting speech and allowing the imprisonment and deportation of foreign agitators, appropriated funding for both maritime and land forces, established the Department of the Navy and created the Marine Corps, and authorized the use of military force to resist France capturing vessels or invading, but not to attack French territory. This first authorization for the use of limited military force was sanctioned by Congress without a formal declaration of war.[12]

France and the United States skirmished at sea in the Caribbean for over two years, Hamilton's revenue cutters operating alongside the reconstituted American Navy. When Captain Stephen Decatur captured a French privateer who protested the US was not at war with France, Decateur summed up the aggrieved sensibility of the US in his reply: "No, but your country is with mine."[13] France's setbacks in combat against European powers, its domestic political upheavals, and Napoleon's clandestine acquisition of the Louisiana Territory from Spain drove an end to conflict with the US; the quasi-war concluded with the Franco-American Convention of 1800.[14]

The quasi-war is remembered mostly for its maritime confrontations, as Congress had limited the means to maritime reprisals. But justifying premonitions from the debates over the Constitution, it was the raising of an army that created the prospect of a civil–military crisis.

Fearing that the weakness of American sea power and coastal defenses could result in an eventual invasion by France during the quasi-war,

Congress authorized President Adams to raise a Provisional Army. Adams stalled, preferring to build fortifications. He did not, however, have control of his administration. Alexander Hamilton, who'd resigned in fury from the Adams administration, was fighting Jefferson's Democratic-Republicans in domestic politics and accusing Adams of failing to defend against French influence west of the Mississippi.

Worries about war with Britain and the inadequacy of militia forces had encouraged consideration of a standing army in 1794, but the legislative proposal for even 10,000 soldiers failed; James Madison jubilantly reported that it "was strangled more easily ... than I had expected."[15] Despite French successes at sea, Congress rejected several provisional army proposals as threats to the internal well-being of the country, eventually consenting only in 1798 to raising a New Army – separate from the dilatory Provisional Army – of up to 30,000 soldiers.

That New Army had been politicked into being by Alexander Hamilton, and Federalists advocated for his command of it. Adams's only play to prevent Hamilton assuming head of an army (he'd considered reactivating the entire general officer ranks of the Revolutionary War to prevent Hamilton commanding it, since Hamilton had been only a colonel) was to appoint George Washington, who agreed to command so long as it was a ceremonial appointment unless France invaded.[16] President Adams's wife shrewdly noted: "those who expected to have filled the place, dare not publickly avow this disappointment."[17]

But the president was not in control, and Hamilton ascended to operational control of the force. Adams suspected Hamilton of setting up to declare martial law, but (despite Abigail Adams's castigation) that actually underestimated Hamilton's ambition, which was to break Republicans in Virginia by force, then march down "through the Louisiana Territory and into Mexico and Peru, liberating all the inhabitants from French and Spanish domination and offering membership in the expanded American republic."[18]

Adams stalled every element of Hamilton's plans for the New Army's formation; training began in parallel to congressional debates over its demobilization.[19] Adams's revenge against Hamilton came by negotiating peace with France; even though it came too late to assist his own re-election, it negated the need for a standing army. The expense and irrelevancy of the New Army, coupled with the bitter split between

Adams and Hamilton over it, impeded Adams standing and, in the most contentious election of our nation's history, assisted Thomas Jefferson's success on the thirty-sixth ballot in the House of Representatives over Aaron Burr to become our nation's third president.

But it is nonetheless striking that a political actor outside the commander in chief's authority was given command of a large standing army. And it was a genuine threat to democracy that Hamilton intended its use to intimidate and even incarcerate or attack political rivals. Moreover, he had no executive or legislative authority to use that army in conquest of Spanish or French territories. Quite the opposite: the Congress had been explicit that its authorization for the use of force was limited to preventing capture of US maritime assets or responding to a French invasion. The republic was saved from those exigencies by smart diplomacy from the man with the worst job in the country.

Cry Treason!

James Wilkinson was distinguished in war: aide to Nathanael Greene during the siege of Boston, to Benedict Arnold during the siege of Quebec, and to Horatio Gates during the battle of Saratoga. Politically brevetted to brigadier general at the age of twenty, he was part of the Conway plot to sideline George Washington; perhaps looking to divert suspicion from himself, General Gates forced Wilkinson's resignation from the Army in 1778. Wilkinson's political connections allowed him to re-establish himself by 1782 as a brigadier general in the Pennsylvania militia and be elected the following year to the state assembly.

Before accepting those commissions and taking those oaths of office, however, Wilkinson swore allegiance to the king of Spain.[20] His commercial aim was to deliver the political loyalty of American settlers in Kentucky and further west to Spain; to that end, he got himself elected chairman of the convention at which the counties of Virginia debated separating off into the Kentucky territory. In return for his efforts to prevent Kentucky's statehood in the Union, he was paid by Spain $7,000 and a grant of 60,000 acres of land in the Spanish territories west of the Mississippi River.

Wilkinson returned to active military service during the 1791 war against Native American tribes in the Northwest Territory and was subsequently a finalist for commanding general of the Army (then called the Legion). But the superior professionalism of General Anthony Wayne and suspicions about Wilkinson's relationship with the Spanish government prevented it.[21] Subordinate to Wayne in the field, Wilkinson wrote anonymous letters to newspapers and undercut Wayne to politicians, even to President Washington, and even after Wayne's crushing defeat of the Native Americans at the battle of Fallen Timbers.[22] In retaliation, General Wayne investigated Wilkinson's Spanish relationships and revealed the financial connection. However, fortunately for Wilkinson, Wayne's sudden death prevented a court-martial and Wilkinson was elevated to senior officer of the Army.

During the quasi-war with France, Wilkinson was subordinated, titularly, to George Washington, who had been recalled to service, and practically to Alexander Hamilton. He was assigned to take hold of the Mississippi River and the city of New Orleans with a reserve corps of troops should war break out with either France or Spain. When President Adams deftly defused the crisis over war with France, Wilkinson was again elevated to senior officer of the Army; he served nearly twelve years in the role, an agent of Spain throughout.

Espionage against the United States for a foreign power is treasonous, but it is not a civil–military crime. James Wilkinson's infamy in civil–military relations comes from his role in the 1805 conspiracy to overthrow the US government by former Vice President Aaron Burr. He stars as both villain and hero, an active plotter who also revealed the crime to President Jefferson. Burr was arrested and tried, but ultimately acquitted.[23]

The plot they cultivated was to break off western states into an independent nation. Wilkinson, who had harbored that ambition since his Kentucky days of the 1780s, was influential both because of his military role and because President Jefferson had, at Vice President Burr's urging, made him concurrently the governor of Louisiana. Moreover, Wilkinson was personally invested in land that would have given him political standing, even leadership, of the newly independent country.

After President Jefferson's re-election in 1804 and Burr's expulsion from the ticket, Burr contrived with the British to sever Louisiana in return for a half million dollars and a naval fleet.[24] The British minister to the US reported to London:

In regard to military aid, he said, two or three frigates and the same number of smaller vessels to be stationed at the mouth of the Mississippi to prevent its being blockaded by such force as the United States could send, and to keep open the communications with the sea would be the whole that would be wanted; and in respect to money the loan of about one hundred thousand pounds would, he conceived, be sufficient for the immediate purposes of the enterprise.[25]

Burr also conspired with the Spanish to disjoin the western territories from the United States and capture the US capitol.[26] Daniel Morgan, a formidable fighter from the revolution, reported to President Jefferson from Pennsylvania that Burr had told him "with two hundred men he could drive congress, with the president at its head, into the river Potomac, or that it might be done; and he said with five hundred men he could take possession of New York."[27]

Wilkinson, of whom it was said "he never won a battle or lost a court martial," switched sides and alerted President Jefferson that Burr's plans were "demonstrative of a deep, dark and wicked conspiracy."[28] Wilkinson claimed "nought but an immediate peace in Europe can prevent an explosion which may desolate these settlements, inflict a deep wound on our republican policies, involve us in a foreign conflict, and shake the Government to its very foundation." In order to exculpate himself, he explained, "By masking my purposes and flattering his hopes, I expect to discover the extent and leading characters of the combination in that city; and, till this is effected, I shall carry an equivocal exterior to every person who may see me, excepting my confidential officers." Jefferson had his former vice president arrested and charged with treason for attempting to seize New Orleans and establish it with assistance from Britain and Spain as the capitol of an independent state including American territories and Mexico.

The prosecutors described General Wilkinson as "the *alpha* and *omega* of the present prosecution." Encoded letters between Burr and Wilkinson evidenced the plot, and Wilkinson testified against Burr at his treason trial, implicating himself in the process. The "ciphered letter" revealed that the

> plan of operations is to move rapidly from the falls on the 15th of November, with the first five hundred or one thousand men, in light boats now

constructing for that purpose – to be at Natchez between the 5th and 15th of December – then to meet Wilkinson – then to determine whether it will be expedient in the first instance to seize on or pass by Baton Rouge. On receipt of this send Burr an answer – draw on Burr for all expenses.[29]

While Wilkinson had clearly altered the correspondence, it nonetheless clearly had Burr claiming "protection of England is secured" and seeking commissioned officers under Wilkinson's command to participate. Wilkinson also used his governance power to summarily arrest people who could connect him to Burr and their attorneys, preventing their trial testimony.[30]

Supreme Court Chief Justice John Marshall presiding dismissed the treason charge against Burr, precedentially defining treason narrowly to an overt act during wartime, and brought him to trial for "high misdemeanors." Of those Burr was also acquitted. President Jefferson fumed, writing to General Wilkinson that Marshall's verdict was "equivalent to a proclamation of impunity to every traitorous combination which may be formed to destroy the Union." Thirty years later, when Texas declared its independence from Mexico, a self-satisfied Aaron Burr proclaimed, "what was treason in me thirty years ago, is patriotism now."[31]

The jury were more aggrieved at General Wilkinson than they were at Aaron Burr: although he was not on trial, they considered indicting him. The jury foreman concluded Wilkinson was "the only man I ever saw who was from the bark to the very core a villain."[32] Wilkinson would remain on active duty as the senior officer in the Army, although he was investigated by Congress and again court-martialed during the presidency of James Madison, "prompted by his continuing private ventures and intrigues."[33] He submitted receipts to Spain's governor in North America for $8,640 in recompense for information provided while the general in chief of the United States Army.[34] Writing decades later, Theodore Roosevelt condemned Wilkinson, concluding that, "in all our history, there is no more despicable character."[35]

Given how widespread suspicion about Wilkinson's loyalties had long been, his ejection from the Army in 1778, the miasma of corruption that surrounded him, his involvement in the Burr conspiracy, and two courts-martial, it is astonishing he remained for so long at the head of the American Army. Washington's example was fresh, and Washington himself still lived, yet even George Washington recommended him for a civilian post provisioning the Army after Wilkinson was forced out in 1778. Part of the explanation is that James Wilkinson was unctuously persuasive, a genius at insinuating himself with powerful men.

The second explanation, especially important after 1800, was partisanship. Wilkinson was not only political but overtly partisan in his politics to a much greater degree than any of his contemporaries. The election of 1800 remains the bitterest contest in American history: after Thomas Jefferson and the Democratic-Republicans surmounted Federalist control of the US government, they worked industriously to expunge the instruments of strong federal power that Washington, Hamilton, and Adams had put in place. Wilkinson pledged himself a Democratic-Federalist, which was uncommon among the cadre of officers from the Revolutionary War, and secured his elevation for the second time to the senior rank of the Army. So Thomas Jefferson was the first American president to vet senior military officers on a partisan basis.

One example of just how partisan Wilkinson's tenure was, enacted just as soon as he returned to command, was changing the grooming standards to prohibit the queue hairstyle (a sort of ponytail). The queue was the tactical gear of its day, a symbol the soldier was a warrior, and was especially favored by soldiers with Federalist politics. Wilkinson banned it by regulation after Jefferson's election. The move was deeply unpopular, one prominent colonel writing in his will instructions to "bore a hole through the bottom of my coffin, right under my head, and let my queue hang through it, that the damned old rascal will see that, even when dead, I refuse to obey his orders."[36]

Jackson's Invasion

You wouldn't know it to read American accounts, but the United States lost the war of 1812. Britain repelled assaults on Canada, strangled commerce, and burned the capitol city – all that even before defeating Napoleon so that Britain could turn its undivided attention to the operational backwater that was the New World. The US was caught in the web of Britain and France's reciprocal maritime embargos, ruinous to American trade: between 1804 and 1807, 731 American ships were captured by one or the other.[37] An America still too weak to assert itself internationally chafed at the impressment of American sailors and Britain's easy mastery of maritime commerce.[38] In thrashing to free itself, those Americans ambitious for continental expansion saw collateral benefits in prospects to wrest control of Canada from Britain and Florida from Spain.[39]

The US, too, was fighting a more consequential war in 1812, on its western frontier, called the Northwest Territory, against a powerful Confederacy of Native American tribes supported by Britain.[40] Shawnee leader Tecumseh had stitched together thirty Native American tribes whose land stretched from Lake Erie to the Gulf of Mexico, pulling together a larger fighting force than any other native chief in history, and designing a barrier to limit westward expansion of the United States' frontier.[41] The Shawnee repudiation of land cession and battlefield success against US forces precipitated doubling the size and dramatically improving the professionalism of the Legion (which was renamed the United States Army in 1796).

The ground campaign had four distinct theaters of operations: the Northwest Territory, eastern Canada, the Chesapeake (including Washington, DC), and the south. In the eastern theater, instead of forming a professional force, Congress called up 450,000 state militia to fight the British, ostensibly an overwhelming numerical advantage – but they came with all the typical deficiencies of militia in recruitment, training, and equipment. Chased from the White House by the advancing British Army in 1814, President Madison exclaimed: "I could never have believed so great a difference existed between regular troops and a militia force, if I had not witnessed the scenes of this day."[42]

Fighting in the south began with raids by both settlers and Native Americans, escalating in 1813 to engagements involving more than five thousand militia, the US Army, and Creek warriors under Major General Andrew Jackson's command. British forces operating in Spanish Florida fought Jackson's army along the Gulf Coast, culminating in 1815 in a two-front joint force attack from Florida's Atlantic coast and Louisiana to cut off US access to the major commercial artery of the Mississippi River. Jackson's repulse of this British effort in the battle of New Orleans made him a national hero, even though it occurred after the peace treaty between Britain and the United States had been signed.

Although the war with Britain concluded with a return to the prewar status quo, the southern border between the US and Spanish West

Florida remained violent, with Native American Seminole harboring escaped slaves and contesting land encroachment. US forces were authorized to pursue Seminole into Spanish Florida in 1817, violence escalating into atrocity. In 1818, President Monroe placed Major General Jackson in command of what would become the First Seminole War. Monroe authorized Jackson's deployment of forces to defend the border with Spanish West Florida against Seminole raids; Jackson instead invaded and occupied Pensacola, where his forces remained for nine months in occupation of territory of a country with which the US was not at war.

Jackson defended his actions as a preemptive strike, necessary to disperse gathering Seminole forces and deter future attacks against Americans in the border lands – but he had at the start of the campaign written President Monroe recommending the seizure of Florida from the Spanish.[43] Moreover, he continued into Florida beyond the border lands to garrison several hundred troops at St Marks and continued to the Gulf of Mexico, despite encountering almost no Native Americans for two weeks and two hundred miles on the march or at the destination.[44] Jackson fought the Spanish garrison at Pensacola and ordered his force on to complete the conquest of Florida by taking St Augustine. President Monroe overrode Jackson's instruction to the force, bringing the invasion to a halt.[45]

Jackson unquestionably exceeded his orders; the administration informed Congress that Jackson had been explicitly instructed not to initiate engagement with Spanish forces.[46] His justification for the campaign against Spain was explicitly insubordinate. Presuming Secretary of War John C. Calhoun to be an ally, Jackson suggested continuing the invasion all the way to Cuba to "embarrass" the administration.[47]

Jackson's actions not only risked war with Spain but were also unconstitutional. Secretary of State John Quincy Adams confided to his diary: "the question is embarrassing and complicated, not only as involving that of an actual war with Spain, but that of the Executive power to authorize hostilities without a declaration of war by Congress." Jackson clearly understood that, in undertaking the campaign as he did, he would be acting unconstitutionally, because he wrote President Monroe:

> The executive government have ordered, and, as I conceive, very properly, Amelia Island to be taken possession of. This order ought to be carried

into execution at all hazards, and simultaneously the whole of East Florida seized, and held as an indemnity for the outrages of Spain upon the property of our citizens. This done, it puts all opposition down, secures our citizens a complete indemnity, and saves us from a war with Great Britain, or some of the continental powers combined with Spain. This can be done without implicating the government. Let it be signified to me through any channel (says Mr. J. Rhea) that the possession of the Floridas would be desirable to the United States, and in sixty days it will be accomplished.[48]

Monroe denied ever having done so. When confronted by President Monroe for exceeding his orders, Jackson retorted that Gaines's previous orders were only instructive, not binding on him as Gaines's successor in command and superior officer.[49] That is, he was unbound by the president's instruction to his predecessor.

The president and his cabinet were unanimous in the conclusion that, for both domestic and international reasons, placatory actions needed to be taken to avert war with Spain and its European allies and to restore constitutional order. However, they worried about the domestic consequences of repudiating so popular a military leader. Adams cautioned that, "If they disavow him [Jackson], they must give offence to all his friends, encounter the shock of his popularity, and have the appearance of truckling to Spain."[50]

Public reaction was apprehensive about the prospect of war and Jackson's "constitutional nonchalance" but supportive of the acquisition of Florida.[51] In defense of his actions, Jackson insisted Spain was providing assistance to violent Seminole at war with the United States. President Monroe declined to support Jackson's claim, although he could easily have asserted that Spain was in violation of its treaty obligation to prevent Native American attacks into US territory.

Monroe formally returned control of Florida to Spain and, while not endorsing Jackson's invasion, described it as "justified by military necessity as he [Jackson] saw it." Both houses of Congress conducted investigations that concluded strongly critical of Jackson's actions.[52] Henry Clay publicly accused Jackson of being a threat to civilian government, resurrecting the Founders' fears of Athens's and Rome's collapse and comparing him to Caesar. Jackson's campaign had, however, demonstrated to Spain their inability to prevent the US taking Florida, and they ceded it to the US by treaty in 1819.

As Russell Weigley concludes, Jackson was "acting less in any distinctively military interest than on behalf of his political convictions about American expansionism."[53] From the distance of fifty years later (and a subsequent pattern of norm-violating behavior by President Andrew Jackson), a biographer of Jackson concluded of the latter's invasion of Florida:

> General Jackson, in the conduct of this campaign, had exercised imperial functions. He had raised troops by a method unknown to the laws. He had invaded the dominions of a king who was at peace with the United States. He had seized a fortress of that province, expelled its garrison, and garrisoned it with his own troops. He had assumed the dread prerogative of dooming men to death without trial. All this may have been right. But if he had been Andrew I, by the Grace of God, Emperor of the United States, could he have done more? Could the autocrat of all the Russias, leading an expedition into Circassia, do more?[54]

Andrew Jackson's ambition to deliver Florida into US possession was his recommendation to the president at the inception of the campaign. It was not authorized and, when enacted, was reversed. He had arrogated unto himself judgments that were properly either presidential or congressional, or both. His actions incurred the risk of war with a major European power and violated the constitutional proscription on the president engaging in acts of war without congressional authorization. He utilized funds appropriated by Congress for domestic insurrection (war against Native Americans) for the purpose of international war. In addition, Jackson's public popularity constrained the president's policy choices for dealing with the risks of war – that is, a military officer's insubordination imposed a steep political price on the president because of public deference to that officer's prior battlefield success.

Hot Pursuit

To give a sense of how cliquish and politicized the US Army became as a result of Jefferson's presidency, Zachary Taylor was commissioned in 1808 by Jefferson into James Wilkinson's New Orleans command; Taylor would later testify as a character witness for Wilkinson in one of his many courts-martial proceedings.[55] Taylor owned extensive cotton fields and two hundred slaves and dined with Andrew Jackson. His daughter married Jefferson Davis.

But Taylor was a serious soldier who fought with distinction in the War of 1812 against Tecumseh's Shawnee and in the Blackhawk War before coming to national attention as "Old Rough and Ready," commanding in the Second Seminole War. Brigadier General Taylor was President Polk's choice to command the force poised for war with Mexico in 1845 over the location of the border after the annexation of Texas. He was selected over more senior officers, including Winfield Scott, because Scott's politics were known to be Whig, while President Polk was a Democrat.[56]

Taylor's army proceeded as ordered into the disputed territory between the Nueces and Rio Grande rivers. Ulysses Grant, a captain fighting under Taylor, would later write in his memoirs: "we were sent to provoke a fight, but it was essential that Mexico should commence it."[57] Taylor blockaded the Mexican city of Matamoros, which removed President Polk's deniability for starting the war.[58] Polk nonetheless reported to Congress that Mexico had invaded the US, a claim that precipitated congressional investigation (spearheaded by Representative Abraham Lincoln), while Taylor received congressional commendation and was feted as the heir to military heroes George Washington and Andrew Jackson.[59]

President Polk so resented Taylor after he let the Mexican forces slip away during the battle at Monterrey that he put in play a second invasion force under Winfield Scott, moving by sea, to land at Veracruz and march on Mexico City. Polk even stripped much of Taylor's force, transferring it to Scott's command (Polk would later also fall out with Scott and relieve him of command). Ordered to remain in Monterrey, Taylor sought engagement with a superior force under Mexican General Santa Ana at Buena Vista. While the action was reported as a great victory, Taylor came very close to losing his army, which would have likely terminated the campaign that, when successful in 1848, would net for the United States territory that would become California, Nevada, Utah, and parts of Colorado, New Mexico, Arizona, and Wyoming. Taylor fumed that "the battle of Buena Vista opened the road to the city of Mexico and the halls of Montezuma, that others might revel in them."[60] General Taylor saw no further action during the war.

Having committed himself to serve only a single term as president, Polk did not run for re-election in 1848. Both Taylor and Scott were drafted to compete for the Whig nomination. In a three-way presidential race, and never having held political office, Taylor was elected, with little known of his politics beyond a commitment to allow acceding states to determine for themselves whether to permit slaveholding. He died of a stomach ailment sixteen months later. Winfield Scott, Taylor's rival for accolades in the Mexican War, remained on active duty another thirteen years and led the Army into the Civil War.

While Scott and Taylor's expeditions to the south garner most of the attention, Brigadier General Stephen Kearney's expeditions in the west secured what would become New Mexico, Arizona, Nevada, Utah, and California. The New Mexico territory he achieved without firing a single shot (although there were subsequently several significant insurgencies), and he proceeded to promulgate a legal code of conduct and appoint a civilian government.[61]

The United States Navy acted as midwife to the independence of California on the mistaken belief that Army Major John Fremont was acting under orders rather than on his own initiative in bolstering the settlers occupying what would become San Francisco.[62] Commodore John Sloat had been ordered to wrest San Francisco from Mexican control if war should break out; however, hearing of Fremont's involvement, he landed Marines and sailors at San Francisco and took possession for the United States. Fremont marched his army south, Kearney marched his army west, Commodore Robert Stockton landed at Los Angeles, and their combined forces established dominion, although control was contested for six months before Mexican residents in California fully conceded in January of 1847. It was an elegant joint operation between the Navy, Marines, and Army, organized under the political authority of the civilian consul, touched off by Fremont's unsanctioned initiative.

Zachary Taylor's disobedience and Fremont's support of civil action in San Francisco show mid-nineteenth-century military officers taking initiatives of great political consequence without political approval. Taylor blockading Matamoros exposed the president's false statements to Congress, and he put his army and the war effort more broadly in jeopardy at Buena Vista though ordered to remain in garrison.

Fremont's initiation of action in California is a far lesser infraction than Taylor's. It wasn't really his fault that Sloat misapprehended his actions; communications were difficult in the uproar of raising the Bear Flag; they were in different parts of the state and in different military services. But it's indicative of just how unusual Fremont's actions were that Sloat assumed he would not have been doing so unless under orders.

President Polk didn't trust any of the three leading commanders in the Mexican War. He suspected all three were angling to be his successor – and he was right in that suspicion. While there is no evidence Taylor had political motives in disobeying Polk's restrictions, he was operating in a politicized milieu from well before the war and moved quickly into elected politics. He returned from Mexico in December of 1847, was on the presidential ballot in 1848 while still on active duty, and only resigned his commission in January of 1849, shortly before taking office as president.[63] General Winfield Scott, too, harbored political ambitions and was Taylor's competition for the Democratic nomination in 1848. Major John Fremont resigned from the Army, was elected to the Senate in 1850, and was the Republican nominee for president in 1856. The fluid ease of political action by officers from the Jefferson administration through to the Civil War raises doubts about the durability of Washington's example.

Fremont's Proclamation

Surprisingly, for a drawn-out civil war, and one in which the commander in chief involved himself directly in military strategy and relieved the overall military commander three times, there was remarkably little friction between civilian and military leaders in the Union Army. Which is not to say the president wasn't frequently exasperated with his military commanders. President Lincoln wrote sternly and often to them about their reticence and fired (brevet) Lieutenant General Winfield Scott, Major General George McClellan, and Major General Henry Halleck without challenge before finding a commander in Ulysses Grant, whom he felt understood his political perspective and had designed a military campaign consistent with it.

The two key tests of American civil–military relations are (1) whether the president can fire senior officers with impunity and (2) whether the military will carry out policies they disagree with. Union officers easily pass the first test. There are also no overt instances of military leaders refusing to carry out the president's policies. McClellan could be accused of what Peter Feaver characterizes as "shirking" – that is, stalling and finding excuses for not carrying out known policies – but he was all that stood between Lee's army and the US Capitol, so caution was not without basis, and he made a plausible case for his reluctance to commit to battle in terms of inadequacy of his forces or the necessary time for preparations.[64]

The only borderline instance of a senior officer in the Union Army disobeying political instruction from the civilian leadership during the Civil War was by Major General John C. Fremont, who commanded the Western Department that included the border states of Missouri and Kansas. Fremont declared martial law over Missouri in August of 1861, established execution as the penalty for captured secessionists, and announced the emancipation of slaves, both the latter two in contravention of federal policy.[65]

Pitched combat was occurring between Union forces and the Missouri State Guard, which is what precipitated Fremont declaring martial law.[66] But the war in 1861 was not yet officially a war about slavery, President Lincoln choosing to center the political argument on secession and desperate to keep the slaveholding states of Maryland, Missouri, and Kansas in the Union.[67] Fremont hadn't consulted either his civilian or military superiors about the proclamation; the president learned of it when reading the newspaper. President Lincoln considered emancipation "not within the range of military law or necessity" and traducing civilian federal authority.[68]

Fremont was a national celebrity for mapping the Oregon Trail and reports of his expeditions in the West (it was he who named the opening to San Francisco Bay the Golden Gate).[69] He is suspect because of his history of politicking: he had galloped into Sonoma with a brace of Pawnee bodyguards to proclaim the Republic of California under the protection of the United States, had founded the Republican Party in California, had been the state's first senator, and had been the Republican nominee for president in 1856. In addition to his political history was a track record of insubordination: in pre-statehood California his superior officer had him arrested and court-martialed for mutiny.[70] Rather reinforcing Fremont's reputation for politicking, President Polk had commuted the court-martial sentence and reinstated him to military service.

President Lincoln asked Fremont to rescind the proclamation, which he refused to do unless directly ordered – that is, forcing the president to pay a consequential political price with abolitionists and positioning Fremont himself as the "true" abolition advocate. The president then ordered Fremont to bring the proclamation into compliance with federal policy, which he did.[71] While General Fremont had not refused to comply with a direct order, his proclamation establishing policy inconsistent with federal guidance and his endeavor to increase the political price to the president for bringing his actions into compliance with policy badly damaged trust between him and both his civilian and military superiors.

Lincoln relieved Fremont of command five weeks later. However, he minimized the cost by making the case for administrative incompetence by Fremont rather than insubordination or his abolitionist views, thus demonstrating his political genius. The president's accomplices in determining Fremont unfit to remain in command were Quartermaster General Montgomery Meigs and Adjutant General Lorenzo Thomas, showing the institutional army's support for the civilian leadership rather than backing Fremont's insubordination.

Technically, Fremont was coloring inside the lines, since the president had supported his declaration of martial law; he'd justified the death penalty for secession and the abolition of slavery as military necessities, and he'd reversed those policies when ordered by the commander in chief to do so. But Fremont clearly knew his martial law measures were contravened by federal policy and was positioning himself politically as an alternative pole around which abolitionists could gather rather than continuing to support a president cagey on the cause of slavery. His choices were the opposite of McClellan's ostensible shirking, because Fremont intended to use military authority to advance political causes beyond the civilian leadership's direction and thereby change those policies.

All Enemies Foreign and Domestic

The major civil–military violation of the American Civil War was on the southern side: the repudiation by officers of the Union Army who defected to the Confederacy. Those officers had individually sworn an oath to

> bear true allegiance to the United States of America, and that I will serve them honestly and faithfully against all their enemies or opposers whatsoever, and observe and obey the orders of the President of the United States, and the orders of the officers appointed over me, according to the rules and articles for the government of the Armies of the United States.[72]

In choosing to resign their commissions and take up arms against the federal government, those officers justified their decision on the basis that they could not take up arms against their state. Robert E. Lee, offered command of the Union Army, resigned his commission instead, saying, "If Virginia stands by the old Union, so will I. But if she secedes (though I do not believe in secession as a constitutional right, nor that there is sufficient cause for revolution), then I will follow my native State with my sword, and, if need be, with my life."[73] The other eight colonels from Virginia continued their service in the Union Army, as did the senior officer from Virginia, Major General Winfield Scott, who was also the senior officer in the Union Army. Lee accepted command of Virginia's Provisional Army three days after declining Scott's offer to command the Union Army.

In resigning their commissions to fight for their states instead of the federal government – to fight for their states *against* the federal government – the officers of the Union Army who resigned their federal military commissions violated their oath. They also violated the standard President Washington had established during the Whiskey Rebellion, that states would have federal support in redress of grievances provided they used the political framework of the Constitution, but had no option of secession from the Union.

The oath originated as a pledge of loyalty and began to be administered in 1775, in George Washington's army, when officers renounced their allegiance to King George III, naming and pledging to help sustain the colonies as "free, independent, and sovereign states." Confederacy defenders then and now parallel the southern states' secession to the thirteen colonies' declaration of independence, and there is some justification in the language of the original Continental Army oath – except that the issue was raised and resolved during the debates over the Constitution. America's Founders had envisioned precisely this problem of whether loyalty to an individual state or the federal government should take precedence for the military. The oath was updated after independence for officers to affirm their loyalty "true to the United States of America, and to serve them honestly and faithfully against all their enemies opposers whatsoever; and to observe and obey the orders of the Continental Congress and the orders of the Generals and officers set over me by them."

Prior to ratification of the Constitution, an American's primary loyalty was to their state, because the Articles of Confederation merely aggregated the states' powers and did not create a federal superstructure over them. But debates over the Constitution were primarily debates over the distribution of authorities between the federal government and states. Opponents of the Constitution argued that a federal army would splinter if ever called upon to put down a domestic insurrection, because soldiers would place loyalty to their state above that to the United States.[74] The concern was remedied by having military officers swear their loyalty oath to the Constitution, explicitly placing loyalty to the United States in a superior position to state loyalty.

The oath requirement is contained in the same section of the Constitution as the supremacy clause, Article VI, the passage that clearly states that the Constitution and federal law take precedence over state constitutions and laws – the Constitution is "the supreme law of the land."[75] Alexander Hamilton explicitly connects them in *Federalist* no. 27:

> It merits particular attention in this place, that the laws of the Confederacy, as to the *enumerated and legitimate* objects of its jurisdiction, will become the Supreme Law of the land; to the observance of which, all officers legislative, executive and judicial in each State, will be bound by the sanctity of an oath.

Officers of the National Guard take their oath to both the Constitution and the governors of their states, since their call-up into federal service requires the assent of the state's governor. But Lee and the other officers who resigned their commission were neither guardsmen nor militia; they were federal officers. Treason is a federal crime; there is no state equivalent. As no less a source than George Washington said, "the Constitution which at any time exists till changed by an explicit and authentic act of the whole people is sacredly obligatory upon all."[76]

After the cascade of resignations by officers defecting to the Confederacy, Congress in 1862 made an "ironclad" version of the oath that required affirming candidates had "never voluntarily borne arms against the United States."[77]

The debates over federal government supremacy were not arcane or undiscoverable in 1860. Debates over states' rights and constitutional supremacy were central to American politics for the three decades leading up to the Civil War. Numerous other Union soldiers from southern states understood and acknowledged the constitutional design of the oath and remained in Union service, which makes ludicrous Lee's statement to Grant after the surrender at Appomattox that "I have always been a Union man."[78] While many leading Confederate officers were eventually pardoned by the federal government, Robert E. Lee never was.

Last Stand

George Armstrong Custer was named for a minister and worked as a school teacher before entering West Point in 1957, where he amassed a staggering 726 demerits.[79] Custer himself recounted that "Only thirty-four graduated, and of these thirty-three graduated above me."[80] As a soldier, he was courageous, dashing, ambitious, and a publicity hound. He designed his own uniforms and in 1862 was promoted to captain and demoted to second lieutenant in the space of twelve days. But by June of 1863 he was a brigadier general of volunteers (so not the regular army) with no previous command experience, heading up a cavalry brigade. In his first action, he led a charge that left half his soldiers casualties and from which he had to be rescued.[81]

Custer redeemed himself gloriously during the Gettysburg campaign by interdicting J. E. B. Stuart's 6,000 cavalrymen and forestalling their arrival at Cemetery Ridge that was essential to the Confederate battle plan. With characteristic flair, Custer's report of the battle attests: "I challenge the annals of warfare to produce a more brilliant or successful charge of cavalry."[82] Assigned subsequently to General Philip Sheridan's command for the Shenandoah campaign, Custer continued to distinguish himself in battle.

After the war, Custer unsuccessfully attempted to make his fortune in banking, considered running for Congress, and campaigned with President Johnson in 1866. In part because of his political activities, Custer was assigned to command the 7th Cavalry at Fort Riley, Kansas, far from the corridors of power. He was neither a popular nor a particularly proficient commander: his unit experienced frequent desertions, and he ordered deserters shot, the wounded denied medical treatment.[83] He was arrested for desertion in 1868 and convicted at court-martial for "absence without leave, conduct to the prejudice of good order and military discipline, and the unmerciful treatment of deserters," but General Sheridan got Custer's sentence reduced so that he could campaign against the Cheyenne. Custer succeeded in driving the Cheyenne onto reservations only after the massacre of non-combatants at Washita, in which he took native women and children as hostages. In 1874, while scouting in the Dakota territory, Custer flamboyantly declared the discovery of gold, triggering a rush to the territory of the Lakota Sioux.

Even while Custer was campaigning, he was politicking. He wrote a glamorizing serialized autobiography, *My Life on the Plains, or Personal Experiences with Indians*, to keep his name circulating and to vehemently criticize President Grant's Indian peace policy.[84] In the spring of 1876 he testified before Congress, alleging numerous instances of corruption by Secretary of War William Belknap and by President Grant's brother Orville.[85] He also wrote anonymous accounts of corruption for the *New York Herald* as part of a campaign to get himself the Democratic nomination for president in 1876.[86] After the congressional testimony, Grant had Custer arrested for desertion and stripped him of command for the Sioux campaign; however, he relented when General Sheridan appealed for Custer's reinstatement.

Custer returned to the Dakota Territory determined to restore his political prospects and charged with bringing onto reservations Lakota, Arapahoe, and Cheyenne. Elements of those tribes numbering in the thousands, gathered on the Little Big Horn River under Sioux chief Sitting Bull, were attacked by 584 soldiers of Custer's 7th Cavalry.

Native warriors under Crazy Horse overwhelmed Custer and his men, counting coup and killing them all.[87] The bodies were stripped, scalped, and mutilated.[88]

Custer's last stand became the most culturally significant event of the American Indian Wars. Longfellow wrote an elegiac poem about it, Anhauser Busch advertised it, Custer's widow campaigned relentlessly to gild his reputation, and it created a groundswell of public antagonism toward Native Americans and Grant's Indian peace policy. A path to citizenship for Native Americans would not be reopened for another fifty years.[89]

Custer was responsible for the most consequential policy impact of any civil–military violation: by fumbling into combat with the Sioux at Little Big Horn he collapsed President Grant's policy of Native American "naturalization" into citizenship. The destruction of the 7th Cavalry so shocked the American public that the policy became unsustainable. Grant bitterly resented Custer for it, saying, "I regard Custer's Massacre as a sacrifice of troops, brought on by Custer himself, that was wholly unnecessary – wholly unnecessary."[90] Even General Sheridan, Custer's longtime protector, criticized Custer's recklessness.[91]

The fault is not Custer's alone: he was clearly following orders in pursuing and fighting the tribes of the Dakota Territory. His superiors, Generals Sherman and Sheridan, unquestionably believed an extermination campaign necessary for those Native Americans who would not consent to being removed to reservations. But Custer's intramural politicking and vaunting ambition were indulged by his military superiors in ways that encouraged further recklessness. That recklessness had fatal consequences, not only for Native Americans and the 7th Cavalry but also for the president's policy. Custer's involvement in the impeachment and resignation of Belknap collapsed trust with his commander in chief, and his subsequent conduct of the campaign produced a political disaster for Grant and a civilizational disaster for the Native Americans of the plains.

Conclusion

The first century of American politics has several notable examples of civil–military failings: Hamilton planning to use the New Army to attack

Jeffersonians and invade Central America, Wilkinson plotting a coup, Jackson invading Spanish Florida, Taylor and Fremont taking military actions of great political consequence exceeding their orders, Fremont abolishing slavery under martial law in Missouri, Lee and others resigning their commissions to fight against the US government, and Custer politicking his way to disaster at Little Big Horn.

It is not enough to excuse these violations by saying it was an earlier time, because Washington had already established the norms that governed military subordination to civilian leaders. George Washington set a demandingly high standard – so high, in fact, that even he on occasion failed to meet it. The falterings of Alexander Hamilton, James Wilkinson, Andrew Jackson, Zachary Taylor, John Fremont, Robert E. Lee, and George Custer in their time shook the foundations of America's civil–military compact. They showed how difficult it is to maintain normative prescriptions but also how enduring norms can be, because the infractions did not recalibrate the standards of civil–military relations. Instead, self-correction within the military and supervision by elected political leaders reinforced Washington's standards of subordination by the military to civilian control and separation of the military from elected politics.

Another conclusion to draw from the history of bad examples is how frequently their perpetrators excelled at the profession of arms. Exceptions would not have been made for them were they not brilliant at the military's core tradecraft of combat.

Chapter 4

A Standing Army

The Union Army didn't demobilize after the Civil War because it was called on to occupy the states that had seceded and to supervise their governments until they had met the conditions for readmission to federal governance structures. Military officers had pervasive political as well as military authority in the occupied states, enforcing emancipation and civil rights, even relieving elected officials they judged politically irredentist. Moreover, the military's wartime leadership had grown accustomed to a freedom of action uncomfortable after the war to civilian leaders, even in the north, that became circumscribed with reasserted civil authority.

No military officer has ever had to make decisions as difficult for American civil–military relations as did Ulysses Grant after the Civil War. George Washington set the standards for military comportment in a political context, but Ulysses Grant had the most challenging application of the rules, namely choosing between the two constitutionally mandated sources of civilian authority over the military when they were in conflict with each other. It was a terribly fevered moment in American history, the first impeachment of a president. Grant's grim determination that served the national cause so well during the war proved a crucial stabilizing force at a time that Congress was threatening the arrest of the president, and the president was threatening to disband Congress.

As Americans abandoned Reconstruction, that reassertion produced legislation incredibly important for the relationship between America's military and its civilian society, namely, Posse Comitatus, which restricts the use of the military for domestic law enforcement. The 1878 law repudiating occupation of former secessionist states had horrific consequences for the civil rights and very lives of Black Americans. It also in the longer run gave the American public a different relationship with its military, because the Posse Comitatus Act prevents the military from suppressing civilian activity unless the president declares an insurrection or invasion is occurring. National Guard troops under the authority of state governors are the military force with which most Americans interact, and then mostly as relief workers in natural disasters. The Act builds into the system a political price elected officials have to pay for repressive use of the military domestically. It requires the president to win the political argument about the nature of civil unrest and to be accountable both to the Congress for funding and political support and to state governors for use of guard troops. Much of the foundationally positive attitudes of Americans toward their military comes from not fearing them as a repressive civic force.

The Indian wars that burgeoned as settlers moved into native territory produced a different kind of civil–military danger: the avoidance of accountability. Because the president, the secretary of war, and the military chain of command had forged deep bonds as military confreres during the Civil War, field commanders such as Ranald Mackenzie were given handshake instructions – "orders" that were informal and therefore unaccountable to congressional oversight. The Remolino raid into Mexico exemplifies that there can be too much trust in civil–military relations.

Produce the Body

The right of habeas corpus is an American inheritance from our British past, requiring the state to produce a person in the state's custody for judicial proceedings. The right is enshrined in Article 1, Section 9, of the US Constitution: "the Privilege of the Writ of Habeas Corpus shall not be suspended, unless when in Cases of Rebellion or Invasion the public Safety may require it." It serves to ensure the government can prove detentions and arrests are lawful, and that the government does not substitute military courts for civil proceedings.[1] It "prohibited the government from detaining persons who could claim the protection of domestic law outside the criminal process, *even in wartime*, except under the auspices of a valid suspension."[2]

The national capitol being below the Mason–Dixon line, it was in 1861 abutted by the Confederacy, putting the federal government in desperate physical jeopardy. Almost as soon as the Civil War broke out, troops marching to Washington, DC, were attacked by mobs in Baltimore, Maryland. The first casualties of the war were the sixteen dead and eighty-five wounded in the riot as soldiers returned fire.[3] Rebels operating in Maryland destroyed telegraph and rail lines, attacked military patrols, and attempted to poison military provisions and kidnap public officials.

President Lincoln invoked the Insurrection Act and authorized the military to suspend habeas corpus, first in the geographic area between Washington and Philadelphia; later the domain was extended to New York City and eventually encompassed the entire country. The suspension permitted military arrests and, for both civilians and law enforcement officers charged with aiding the rebellion, allowed demonstrations to be broken up by military forces and civilians to be tried by military tribunals.

Supreme Court Chief Justice Roger Taney (deciding a circuit court case) ruled in June of 1861 that only Congress, not the president, had authority to suspend habeas corpus – that Lincoln's actions were unconstitutional. President Lincoln declared the ruling invalid, and continued the policy, but defended his actions to the Congress as both necessary and constitutional due to the insurrection.[4] Congress, however, could not muster the votes to legislate an extension of suspension authority to the president.

The military also continued to carry out a policy judged unconstitutional – choosing to obey the commander in chief rather than the law – arresting Maryland Congressman Henry May and a full third of the Maryland General Assembly to prevent them voting to secede from the Union.[5] Prominent journalists and political commentators were also arrested. When challenged to produce the accused in Baltimore, the Army responded, "at the date of issuing your writ, and for two weeks previous, the city in which you live, and where your court has been held, was entirely under the control of revolutionary authorities."[6]

As concern about the vulnerability of the capitol receded, in February of 1862 President Lincoln ordered all political prisoners released and offered amnesty for treason committed, provided that no further aid was provided to the Confederacy. But six months later, faced with rioting as conscription was extended, Lincoln again suspended habeas corpus throughout the entire country, giving the military the authority to arrest civilians discouraging enlistments, interfering with conscription, or aiding the Confederacy.

It took until 1863 for Congress to legislate for itself and the president the ability to both suspend habeas corpus for the duration of the Civil War and retroactively indemnify the president against legal challenge for suspending the writ. But President Lincoln had persisted for nearly two full years in a policy judged unconstitutional, and the military had tried American civilians in courts-martial subsequently also declared unconstitutional.

The focus of this book is predominantly on the behavior of leading American military figures. The country was consumed in the fire of civil war, and Abraham Lincoln is the closest we come to a secular saint in American history. But the precedent is ominous of the president accruing to himself a right restricted to the Congress by the Constitution and, when the chief justice of the Supreme Court determines it unconstitutional, continuing the action in violation of the ruling by a co-equal branch of government. The political, constitutional, and legal thrashing gives a sense of just how novel, dangerous, and consequential the circumstances of the Civil War and its aftermath were for America.

Adjusting to Peace

In the Union, the strongest friction between civilian and military leaders occurred in the years after President Lincoln's assassination. Lincoln and Grant had a remarkable mutual understanding and respect. Lincoln greatly appreciated Grant's determination not to yield on the battlefield and his strategic acumen for orchestrating the Union armies across the theaters of war, and Grant was deeply admiring of the president's unwavering commitment to reunifying the country, his political skill in sustaining the war effort, and his deference on military matters. Grant's biographer Ron Chernow concludes: "Lincoln had been betrayed by so many generals, he was endlessly grateful for the loyalty of Grant and Sherman."[7]

Upon selecting Grant as commanding general of the Union armies, Lincoln wrote to him:

> The particulars of your plans I neither know, nor seek to know. You are vigilant and self-reliant; and, pleased with this, I wish not to obtrude any constraints or restraints upon you. While I am very anxious that any great

disaster, or the capture of our men in great numbers, shall be avoided, I know these points are less likely to escape your attention than they would be mine – If there is anything wanting which is within my power to give, do not fail to let me know it. And now with a brave Army, and a just cause, may God sustain you.[8]

Grant replied he was "astonished at the readiness with which everything asked for has been yielded without even an explanation being asked. Should my success be less than I desire . . . the least I can say is, the fault is not with you."[9]

Illustrative of their mutual respect is an instance of Grant's exasperation with the poor combat performance of "political generals" – although he himself received his commissions to colonel, brigadier general, and major general by grace of Illinois politicians. When elevated to command of the Union armies, Grant sent Lincoln a list of a hundred general officers appointed for political reasons that he considered a hindrance to the war effort and wanted relieved of command. President Lincoln agreed to only a sparse few of them.[10] Grant didn't even protest, understanding that the movements of the armies were not the only front of the war, and that Lincoln needed political generals such as Benjamin Butler and Carl Schurz to keep support from crucial communities and interests for the war effort.

President Lincoln's support for Grant never wavered – not early in the war when the Women's Christian Temperance Union alleged he'd been drunk during the battle of Shiloh (occasioning Lincoln's famous retort "well, I wish some of you would tell me the brand of whiskey that Grant drinks. I would like to send a barrel of it to my other generals"), and not even after Grant's costly gamble to shatter the Army of Northern Virginia in a culminating battle at Cold Harbor, which resulted in seven thousand Union casualties in a single day, more than four times what the Confederacy suffered in the engagement.[11] Grant self-critically wrote, "at Cold Harbor no advantage whatever was gained to compensate for the heavy loss we sustained."[12] It was the only battle of the war he regretted. Lincoln declined to criticize Grant even though the death toll and perceived failure of the overland campaign sparked further politically perilous anti-war sentiment during the 1864 election.

Generals Grant and Sherman and Admiral David Porter had met with the president shortly before he was killed, and Lincoln had outlined his post-war policies at length:

> Let them once surrender and reach their homes, they won't take up arms again. Let them go, officers and all. I want submission and no more bloodshed ... I want no one punished, treat them liberally all around. We want those people to return to their allegiance to the Union and submit to the laws.[13]

Lincoln also urged an end to the war before radical Republicans took Congress in the election, presaging a punitive policy the president did not support and that he feared would spark a guerrilla war. And it was post-war policy that occasioned the jarring civil–military confrontations after Lincoln's assassination.

No military leader has ever had to navigate the political difficulties that Ulysses Grant did. A vice president from a southern state selected for commitment to the Union but floundering when thrust into the presidency veered wildly from demanding a blatantly punitive policy to overtly defending the pre-war southern social, economic, and racial order. President Andrew Johnson's feuds with Secretary of War Stanton and Republicans who controlled Congress after 1864 threatened the country's constitutional order and left General Grant uncertainly navigating between the two constitutionally derived branches of civilian control of the American military, the president and the Congress.

By Johnson's account, Grant supported his policies for the first two years.[14] In that time frame, though, two civil–military infractions were committed by the leadership of the victorious Union armies, one by Sherman and the other by Grant. Both represent a pretty natural transition from wartime commanders with expansive spans of authority having their latitude constricted as peacetime conditions allowed civilian leaders to reassert their control. In Sherman's case, sharp resentment notwithstanding, there was no real threat to civilian control; in Grant's case, he clearly circumvented political authority, but events resolved the circumstance before it required civilian assertion. Grant's real test would come later.

Confederate armies continued to fight in the deep south even after Lee's surrender of the Army of Northern Virginia, the fall of the Confederate capitol at Richmond, and the abscondment of Confederate president Jefferson Davis. When General Sherman finally achieved the capitulation of the last major Confederate army, he offered terms he believed consistent with former President Lincoln's direction to him, Grant, and Porter at City Point. But attitudes had changed with Lincoln's assassination, and the generous terms Sherman offered were not only inconsistent with the policy of the current commander in chief, Andrew Johnson, but extended well into political territory, offering citizenship to Confederate soldiers, the re-establishment of courts, and the restoration of property.[15]

The entire Johnson cabinet – including Grant – refused Sherman's terms, Secretary of War Stanton most vociferously for Sherman having traduced political authority. Grant delivered the repudiation in person to Sherman to soften the blow, but Sherman was embittered by Stanton's public campaign besmirching his honor and became overtly insubordinate. While marching his army toward Washington, he denied the secretary of war could issue him orders, insisting only the president had command authority.[16] Once in Washington, though, Sherman demobilized his army without objection, and the crisis passed with no greater destabilization than Sherman snubbing Stanton at the parading of the armies.[17]

Grant's violation of civil–military practice, like Sherman's, involved denying the authority of civilian leaders on whose areas of responsibility they intruded. General Grant had protested the transfer of his wartime powers back into Secretary Stanton's civilian hands, which proceeded over his objection, but they had no unusual or significant frictions. While Grant didn't much like Secretary of War Stanton (in his memoirs he wrote disparagingly of Stanton's lack of strategic acumen: "he could see our weakness, but he could not see that the enemy was in danger"), they had common cause both during and after the war.[18]

Grant's civil–military infraction of the immediate post-war period comes in purposely counteracting the secretary of state on a matter of international policy. While a lesser violation in magnitude, it bears resemblance in type to Andrew Jackson's justification for invading Florida, which is denying the enemy sanctuary from which to launch attacks on US territory. And, like Jackson's actions, it was designed to skirt civilian supervision and make elastic the constraints of civilian orders.

France conquered Mexico in 1864, Emperor Maximilian allowing the settlement of Confederates fleeing US federal armies and political control. Several thousand Confederate settlers established themselves south of the Rio Grande River to be out of the reach of US federal law and military action. During and after the Civil War, Secretary of State Seward advocated a placatory policy toward Mexico to prevent war with France or assistance to the Confederacy.

Grant wanted aid to liberal forces in Mexico, considering it a continuation of stamping out the last vestiges of Confederate political and military insurrection. He put his case in writing to President Johnson: "I regard the act of attempting to establish a Monarchical Government on this continent, in Mexico, by foreign [bayonets] as an act of hostility against the Government of the United States. If allowed to go on until such a government is established, I see nothing before us but a long, expensive and bloody war."[19] Without receiving presidential approval, Grant covertly sent arms and ammunition to Mexican liberal forces and dispatched General Philip Sheridan, the commander of the military district encompassing Texas, with 50,000 troops to the border.[20]

For a wartime general who had commanded a million soldiers, and whose responsibilities for the destruction of secessionist war efforts continued, Grant's independent actions may have seemed well within wartime boundaries. But Grant would not have undertaken actions during the war that could have precipitated a foreign country recognizing the Confederacy without President Lincoln's express approval. He disrespected President Johnson in a way he would never have disrespected President Lincoln, because he believed he was carrying out the superior intent of the previous president.

Sheridan understood, even acknowledged, that Grant was acting without government approval, writing that Grant had cautioned him "to act with circumspection, since the Secretary of State, Mr Seward, was much opposed to the use of our troops along the border in any active way that would be likely to involve us in a war with European powers."[21] The military assistance actually reinforced Seward's diplomacy, however, and Emperor Maximilian was defeated and executed by Liberal forces, ending the potential for confrontation between Seward and Grant. The issue does not appear to have damaged Grant's relationship with either Johnson or Seward, but perhaps the looming confrontations over Reconstruction overshadow historical commentary on this lesser incident.

Both Sherman's and Grant's extensions beyond their military authority into political issues are understandable adjustments from the expansion of independent action granted to commanders in wartime, and encouraged by the wartime president, to the more restrictive and intrusive civilian authority commonly exercised in peacetime. The political climate had also changed with Lincoln's assassination in ways toward which both the civilian leaders and their military counterparts were recalibrating.

Constitutional Crisis

The major civil–military confrontations of the 1860s occurred in the final years of the Johnson administration. The subject that occasioned the constitutional crisis in which civil–military relations had a prominent role was the Reconstruction of the Confederate south: under what terms to allow readmission of Confederate states to the Union, what civic and economic role Black Americans would have, and the physical protection of Blacks, Republicans, and northern businessmen terrorized by a burgeoning insurgency in the conquered southern states.

General Grant, seldom a comfortable politician, was pinioned between an erratic president denying the legitimacy of congressional legislation and a Congress determined to set Reconstruction policy and constrain the powers of the executive branch. Grant was the most popular man in the country, and he allowed President Johnson to capitalize on his popularity, appearing at partisan White House events, and even taking a three-week political barnstorming tour with Johnson.[22] Grant just once in the early years of Johnson's presidency used his standing to affect policy, threatening to resign if Johnson (in his initial punitive phase) revoked the terms of Robert E. Lee's surrender and prosecuted Confederate soldiers for treason. Johnson acceded to Grant's preferred policy.[23]

While Grant participated in cabinet meetings on Reconstruction, he spoke only to specific military issues. But he did provide political cover for a failed president's failing policy – an example of debate that continues today about whether serving military leaders have a responsibility to publicly support an administration's policy. After damning reports of rising violence in the vacuum left by the president's Reconstruction policy, Johnson sent General Grant to tour the southern states. Grant produced an exculpatory report that he subsequently repudiated as commanders raised alarm about insurgent lawlessness intended to restore the antebellum southern political, economic, and social order. But his report gave the president valuable political cover at a time when support for his policy was waning. It is unclear whether the report represented a serving officer loyally supporting the elected leadership's policy, Grant's political naiveté, given that violence was already terrorizing Blacks and supporters of their rights, or the dawning of his political ambitions, given the public desire for the burdens of war to be over.

The bitterest direct confrontation between the military and civilian leaders was overtly political. It occurred in February of 1866, as tensions between the president and Congress boiled. President Johnson, believing Grant and the military would side with the Congress in any executive-legislative confrontation precipitated by Reconstruction, attempted to send Grant out of the country, to Mexico, for extended negotiations. Grant declined, offering General Sheridan, who was already in the region, or General Sherman if Sheridan wasn't sufficiently senior.[24] Grant privately told Sherman he would disobey the order because it was patently political, "a plot to get rid of him" during the constitutional crisis.[25] The president instructed Sherman to take command of the Army in Grant's absence; Sherman declined to do so, informing the president, as Grant had not, that General Grant would not be going to Mexico.

President Johnson castigated Grant for insubordination in a cabinet meeting, asking the attorney general whether it was legal for Grant to refuse an order to participate in the Mexico negotiations. Grant flatly refused on the argument that, as a serving officer, he had a responsibility to carry out the commander in chief's military orders, but the president had no authority to order him beyond the military realm.[26] And the attorney general allowed Grant's justification and action to stand.

As the president became more erratic and confrontation with Congress more severe, Grant wrote Sheridan he feared President Johnson would attempt to disband Congress by declaring it "illegal, unconstitutional, and revolutionary." Fearing a political confrontation that restive southern states might use to reignite the Civil War, Grant had weapons removed from southern arsenals and instructed Sheridan that "Commanders in Southern states will have to take great care to see, if a crisis does come, that no armed headway can be made against the Union."[27] Nor was Grant's concern an exaggeration: from our safe historical distance it's easy to lose sight of how tenuous was control of the southern states in this period, and how much the nation was felt to be careening into another violent disaster.

Republicans' strong showing in the 1866 congressional election exacerbated tensions with the president, culminating in Johnson's impeachment. Congress passed the First Reconstruction Act, lumping the southern states into five military districts, requiring passage of the Fourteenth Amendment and Black male suffrage as a condition of political organization of a state. President Johnson vetoed the Reconstruction Act, but Congress overrode the veto.

Congress also passed a Tenure of Office Act, denying the president authority to dismiss congressionally confirmed cabinet officers. The legislation was designed to protect Secretary of War Stanton and his role enforcing Reconstruction as legislated by Congress over the president's objections. Congress extended the protection against removal to General Grant and also legislated a restriction on the president issuing orders directly to the five military governors instead of through Grant. President Johnson argued these legislative gambits impinged on presidential authority, a violation of the constitutional separation of powers.

Congress's Second Reconstruction Act in 1867 extended military authority further in the southern states to supervise elections and register voters. Grant wrote Sheridan, commander of the military district including Texas and Louisiana, who stridently enforced Reconstruction, "there is a decided hostility to the whole Congressional plan for Reconstruction at the 'White House,' and a disposition to remove you from the command you now hold. Both the Secretary of War and myself will oppose any such move, as will the mass of the people."[28]

General Sheridan removed the governor of Louisiana for refusing compliance with Reconstruction, required mayors to hire Union soldiers for 50 percent of the police force, and integrated public transport. But Attorney General Henry Stanbery determined that military officers did not have the authority to suspend elected officials. When Johnson ordered Grant to circulate the attorney general's opinion to military commanders, Grant undercut the policy by telling commanders they could interpret the ruling any way they liked.[29] In the Third Reconstruction Act (also legislated in 1867), Congress explicitly authorized military governors to suspend elected officials. President Johnson vetoed the bill; Congress again overrode the veto.

President Johnson relieved General Sheridan over Grant's objections but, acknowledging the president's authority, Grant made no attempt to keep Sheridan in place. Instead, he responded by instructing military commanders not to reinstate elected politicians Sheridan had removed – another clear instance of overtly working to undermine the commander in chief's direction. President Johnson considered replacing General Grant with General Sherman, but Sherman again refused. Johnson confronted Grant on October 12, 1867, asking whether he would support Congress having Johnson arrested or deposed from office; Grant cryptically answered that "he should expect to follow orders."[30]

When President Johnson considered firing Secretary Stanton despite the Tenure of Office Act restriction, Grant argued against it – in writing – but nonetheless agreed to become the temporary secretary of war when Johnson only suspended rather than fired Stanton. That is, the senior military officer consented to the removal of the civilian secretary of war and to replace him while remaining on active duty as commander of the Union Army.

In December of 1867, Grant was called to testify before the House Judiciary Committee considering impeaching the president and was questioned on his policy differences with the president over charging Confederate officers with treason, Reconstruction, and firing Stanton. While it is common for Congress to press military leaders about policy differences with the president, Congress compelling Grant's testimony was the most trying moment in American civil–military history because, in the heat of an unprecedented conflict over constitutional powers, the country's senior military officer was being required by one constitutional authority over the military to be used as the means to indict the other constitutional authority over the military. General Grant testified that he considered Congress to be the controlling authority, not the president.[31]

President Johnson's suspicion proved well founded that the military would side with a Congress bent on enacting the previous president's policy over the direction of the current president, but that neither that political suspicion nor the policy difference constituted a constitutional basis. The issue of whether Congress has the constitutional authority to prohibit the president dismissing a cabinet official was not resolved until

1926, when the Supreme Court ruled that the Congress does not have that authority.[32]

The Senate Committee on Military Affairs reinstated Stanton as secretary of war in January of 1868, putting Grant in legal jeopardy: the penalty for his continuing as secretary was five years in prison and a $10,000 fine. President Johnson offered to pay the fine and even serve the prison time in his stead if Grant were convicted, in order to keep Stanton from reclaiming the position.[33] Grant complied with the congressional mandate instead.

Grant committed to writing his version of events surrounding the dispute and surreptitiously provided it to the press, which, biographer Ron Chernow concluded, "virtually guaranteed he would be the Republican nominee for president."[34] It was not uncommon for prominent military leaders in the eighteenth and nineteenth centuries to run for the nation's highest federal office. The roster includes George Washington, Aaron Burr, Andrew Jackson, William Henry Harrison, Zachary Taylor, Franklin Pierce, Winfield Scott, John C. Fremont, and George McClellan. Generals Taylor, McClellan, and Scott had even been on active duty while campaigning for the presidency – Scott contesting for the Whig Party's nomination in 1840, 1844, 1848, and 1852, the latter three instances while he was the commanding general of the Army.[35] McClellan only resigned his commission on election day in 1864; like Taylor, Grant resigned his commission only after being elected. In fact, Grant did not resign from military service until the morning he took the oath of office to become president of the United States.

Without the sage and emollient leadership of President Lincoln, both of the Union Army's wartime heroes somewhat lose their civil–military moorings: Sherman disavowing secretary of war authority to issue orders; Grant arming Mexican insurgents and sending troops to the border without presidential authority and over the explicit objections of the secretary of state, participating in partisan political events while on active duty, shirking presidential orders and overtly working against the commander in chief's known policies, undercutting rulings by the attorney general, being complicit in the removal and also reinstatement of his civilian superior, allowing himself to become a candidate for the presidency while on active duty, and remaining on active duty after being elected.

Grant justified his decision on the basis that Reconstruction was so important that the president could not be allowed to fill the position with an opponent of the policy.[36] Not only was the senior military officer actively impeding the president's policy, he accepted a civilian position he was offered anticipating that his popularity would sway Congress, tamping down the political wildfire.

Grant's logic prevented the president appointing someone who opposed Congress's policy, even though Congress would have had to confirm that appointment and would not have done so were the nominee opposed to its policy. It also removed from the Congress its responsibility of carrying out the civilian political processes constitutionally established for adjudicating separation of powers disputes. A stand-off between the president and Congress might have resulted in an extended abeyance of effective policy, but it's a very expansive view of the military's role in politics to supersede the political remedies embodied in the Constitution. And, while he didn't choose to be the arbiter of the Constitution, Grant did insert himself into the politics of the dispute by accepting the job of secretary of war. But, in the end, he complied with the law and took himself out of the political process.

What might Grant have done instead? If he had refused to step into Stanton's job, the president would surely have filled it with someone willing to carry out Johnson's policies. But that is the president's prerogative. Stanton would have had the standing to sue the president, testing the constitutionality of the Tenure of Office Act. It is unlikely the Senate would have consented to the ratification of any appointee virulently opposed to Reconstruction, but there were many more emollient figures than Stanton who might have threaded the needle of supporting the president's policies without alienating congressional supporters of Reconstruction.

Perhaps the outraged Senate would have convicted the president in the impeachment and sought to remove him from office, further straining the sinews of American democracy. Johnson didn't have a vice president, leaving Speaker of the House of Representatives Schuyler Colfax next in the line of succession. Colfax was an Indiana Republican, more in line with the policies Stanton and Grant advocated. Keeping the military out of the wrangling between the president and Congress would have forced civilians to utilize the constitutional processes designed to adjudicate political disputes.

Grant and some of the military governors would likely have been relieved of their commands. That again is the president's prerogative – all senior military officers serve at the pleasure of the president. And if Grant's firing were an accomplished fact, Sherman, who was much less supportive by then of Reconstruction, might well have accepted the position. The outcome would have been unquestionably worse for civil rights and supporters of Reconstruction, especially in the southern states. One way to evaluate Grant's choices is to consider that he bought three years' time for Reconstruction, perhaps more, since, while he was likely to be elected president in 1868 anyway, he would have had to reverse much of what Johnson would have done in the meantime.

Grant's comportment in the Johnson administration represents the gravest series of evasion and outright insubordination by a military commander to the commander in chief in American history. And yet, his failures need to be weighted by the degree of difficulty of his circumstances, which were also unprecedented: a president refusing the legislative authority of Congress, operating in the colossal maelstrom of America coming to terms with its failure to live up to the truths it holds to be self-evident, a rising fire of violent insurgency as Black Americans attempted to take their rightful place as citizens, and Congress impeaching the president for the first time in American history and asserting powers beyond the constitutional boundary of its authority.

No American military leader in history has been forced to choose so starkly between the two constitutional sources of civilian oversight of the military. Grant was forced into arbitrating the Constitution, a politicized position in which he never ought to have been put by either the president or the Congress. When forced, he made the most democratic choice on the most fundamental issue, which is that, in peacetime, it is the Congress's authority that is supreme in matters of military policy. And, for that, he should be commended.

Insurrection

The Civil War was fought to preserve the Union and vanquish slavery, both of which were achieved at the terrible cost of 1,500,000 American casualties. When southern armies surrendered, the fourteen Confederate states came under military occupation. How to reconstitute the Union

– how the states' civilian governments would be re-established, what rights Black Americans would have, and under what terms states would be readmitted to representation in Congress – was the consuming political issue of the years 1865 to 1876.[37] The United States government won the war against the Confederacy in 1865, but across the following nine years it fought and lost against a vicious insurgency that stripped Black Americans of their rights as citizens in most of the states that had comprised the Confederacy.

In the fear that transmuting Blacks from their constitutionally inferior status as three-fifths of a person would substantially increase southern states' congressional ranks (it added forty new seats) that would then reverse Reconstruction, or that the courts would overturn the 1866 civil rights legislation, the great political questions were framed as amendments to the Constitution. Between 1865 and 1870, the three Reconstruction Amendments (13, 14, 15) were passed by Congress and ratified by the Union states. Adherence to them was made one condition of re-establishing state governmental authority and readmission to the whole for those states that had seceded.

The Thirteenth Amendment in just two sentences abolished slavery in 1865, making general the limited emancipation President Lincoln had proclaimed in 1863 as a measure applicable to states at war with the Union.

The Fourteenth Amendment is the longest, most consequential, and most litigated amendment to the Constitution. It set to establish political rights for Black Americans, defining citizenship by birthright and naturalization. Section 1 incorporates the fundamental thrust: "No State shall make or enforce any law which shall abridge the privileges or immunities of citizens of the United States; nor shall any State deprive any person of life, liberty, or property, without due process of law; nor deny to any person within its jurisdiction the equal protection of the laws." The Fourteenth Amendment also gave grounds for excluding members of Congress elected or appointed by states if those persons had taken and violated an oath to support the Constitution or participated in insurrection or rebellion. Unless explicitly pardoned, it prohibited former Confederate soldiers from office and allowed Congress to refuse to seat unreconstructed Confederates elected by readmitted southern states.

As with the brevity of the Thirteenth Amendment, in only two sentences the Fifteenth Amendment explicitly enfranchised Black men: "The right of citizens of the United States to vote shall not be denied or abridged by the United States or by any state on account of race, color, or previous condition of servitude."

The Fourteenth and Fifteenth Amendments established the federal right to overturn state constitutions or legislation that prevented Black Americans from exercising their political and civil rights. Their passage and ratification were not the battleground; their enforcement was the proving ground for political strife, and terrifying violence was the means by which white Americans brutally resisted the political and social order imposed by federal troops after the Confederacy's defeat.

The physical battlegrounds were the southern states, in particular Louisiana, South Carolina, Georgia, and Florida, where Ku Klux Klan organizations terrorized Blacks attempting to vote, hold office, or partake of the rights of citizens, and white Republican office holders were also targeted and frequently assassinated. White supremacists contested by intimidation and violence the exercise of Black rights and Republican office holders as early as 1866 and with increasing blatancy and impunity.

The US Army supervised elections in every southern state except Tennessee, permitting freed slaves to vote but denying the franchise or the ability to run for office to leading white Confederates. This practice produced Republican governments in ten states and numerous Black legislators. Insurrection was rapidly organized and widespread: during the 1868 election over two thousand politically motivated murders were committed in Alabama alone.[38]

The terrorization of both Blacks and Republicans by the Klan and like-minded organizations precipitated more stringent congressional legislation in the Enforcement Acts and the Ku Klux Klan Act. Violence had reached such magnitude by 1871 that President Grant declared martial law in South Carolina and empowered the Justice Department to intervene and prosecute cases where southern localities and states would not bring charges or witnesses and juries were either so complicit or so endangered that justice could not be served.

Biographer Ron Chernow extolls Grant's enforcement of Reconstruction, writing that Lincoln was the emancipator but Grant the liberator of Blacks. President Grant repeatedly sent federal troops to protect legislatures and polling places; General Philip Sheridan, military governor of Louisiana and Texas, replaced the governor of Louisiana, to great outcry in both north and south about the military superseding elected officials. During the contested 1876 presidential election, when white supremacists produced alternative governors and alternative presidential electors, Grant had federal troops supervising the counting of ballots in Louisiana, South Carolina, and Florida.

While Rutherford B. Hayes is derided by historians for trading an end of Reconstruction to secure the electoral votes of southern states and gain the presidency in 1876, which he evidently did, solely blaming Hayes wrongly exonerates the rest of American society. Because, in fact, by 1876 the Supreme Court had overturned major legislative elements of Reconstruction, and northern publics' support had waned despite the well-known and -documented reign of terror being conducted to prevent Black voting, office holding, or the exercise of civil rights. By 1874, in his second term, even President Grant had raised the standard for sending federal troops, requiring governors to demonstrate they had exhausted state resources for maintaining law and order and, in important instances, allowing widespread violence to occur before sending troops to reinforce governors. He also put Blacks at risk of violence in Ohio in order to preserve Republican Party prospects for electability. Even that most stalwart defender of Black civil rights wavered as public support dissipated. The United States lost the war to confer civil rights on Black Americans for the reason most governments fail to defeat insurgencies: Americans lost the will to persevere against them.

The tragedy of Reconstruction's collapse is not particularly a civil–military story, although General Sheridan sending federal troops to remove the Louisiana governor shocked even northern sensibilities. But the sorrowful failure of Reconstruction is directly relevant to American civil–military relations because, as part of its erasure, Congress passed legislation that continues to restrict the use of US military forces for domestic law enforcement.

The Posse Comitatus Act of 1878 prohibits the use of federal armed forces for law enforcement purposes unless authorized by Congress, requested by a state legislature, the president proclaiming that the country is under invasion, or there exists an insurrection requiring force to put it down.[39] In Latin, *posse comitatus* means the power of the community;

the Act served to protect communities in the former Confederate states from federal troops enforcing the Reconstruction Acts. For nearly ninety years the Posse Comitatus Act protected white communities from their Black fellow citizens having the liberty to practice their civil rights.

The Act came after twelve years of military occupation and electoral supervision by the Army of the former Confederate states of Alabama, Arkansas, Florida, Georgia, Louisiana, Mississippi, North Carolina, South Carolina, Tennessee, Texas, and Virginia. The Constitution places authority for law enforcement predominantly with the states, so to the states it returned in 1878, and to the Congress returned elected officials from the southern states.

Domestic use of federal troops predates the occupation of the Confederate states. Presidents Washington, Adams, Jefferson, and Jackson used troops domestically to enforce federal authority, all mainly over objections to paying taxes.[40] Presidents Taylor and Grant used federal troops to prevent Americans from fomenting rebellion in Cuba and Canada. Presidents Jackson and Hayes used federal troops to quell labor unrest. President Buchanan dispatched federal troops to compel Mormons in Utah to comply with federal law. Presidents Van Buren and Taylor declined state officials' requests to call up federal troops to tamp down election riots. President Buchanan and the Congress allowed federal troops to be called on to enforce the Fugitive Slave Act.

The Constitution proscribes the use of US military forces domestically in all cases except insurrection or invasion. In order to mobilize the US military for such uses, the president must either have congressional authorization, invoke the 1807 Insurrection Act, or request National Guard troops from state legislatures for law enforcement purposes.[41]

The Insurrection Act allows the president to use federal military forces and the National Guard to suppress rebellion, insurrection, and civil disorder. It can be invoked by the president at the request of a state legislature or governor, or if an insurrection prevents enforcement of the law, or when a state fails to enforce the Constitution. Invoking the Insurrection Act relieves the president of needing the consent of state legislatures or governors for the domestic use of military forces.[42]

National Guard troops are what the Constitution meant by a "well-regulated militia." Legislatures and governors (if the legislature cannot convene) can request invocation of the Insurrection Act to bring federal forces into their states, and have done so, but state governors legally can also refuse the use of their state National Guard troops by the federal government for domestic missions.[43] As a counterweight, the 1903 Militia Act allows the Pentagon to withhold funding to states should they refuse, and 1916 legislation allows the federalization of National Guard troops for deployments outside the US; thus, even when withholding is threatened, it is seldom enacted.

Title 10 of the US Code affixes on the secretary of defense the responsibility for ensuring military personnel, equipment, or facilities are not utilized for law enforcement.[44] The reach of the law now extends to Department of Defense civilians and contractors. Although the Insurrection Act was invoked with some frequency during the nineteenth century, Posse Comitatus has been predominantly a restrictive law, seldom invoked to provide federal assistance. The first time a governor requested federal aid was in Nebraska in 1879 for the protection of the courthouse during the trial of a prominent outlaw; the secretary of war denied the request.

Across the initial sixty years of Posse Comitatus, presidential authority to employ military forces domestically was principally utilized to break strikes: President Cleveland sent troops to break a railroad strike, President McKinley sent troops to break a miners' strike in Idaho, President Theodore Roosevelt sent troops to intimidate miners in Nevada, President Wilson sent troops to break a miners' strike in Colorado, President Harding sent troops to break a miners' strike in West Virginia, and President Hoover sent troops to clear out "Bonus Army" World War I veterans encamped on the Anacosta Flats protesting lack of pay.[45]

In the 1940s, presidents began using federal troops called in by governors to quell race riots, especially after the assassination of Martin Luther King, Jr., in 1968 and the Los Angeles riots in 1992 following the Rodney King verdict exonerating police conduct. The most controversial uses of the military for law enforcement have not been under federal authority, but by state governors employing National Guard troops during Vietnam War and draft protests, in the cases of Ohio and New Mexico to tragic effect when in 1970 Guard forces killed or wounded protesters on college campuses.[46]

But the most resonant use of American military forces for law enforcement in living memory has been to carry out the Fourteenth Amendment.

The Enforcement Acts of 1870–1 provide an exception to the restrictions on the use of military forces for law enforcement when state officials fail to protect constitutional rights, but the authorities were dormant from 1877 through 1954, when President Eisenhower resurrected the provisions to force desegregation of public schools in Arkansas, because the governor refused to comply with the Supreme Court ruling in *Brown vs. Board of Education* that "separate but equal" schools for different races were unconstitutional. Governor Orval Faubus deployed Arkansas National Guard troops to prevent Black students entering the premises of schoolhouses. Eisenhower federalized the entire Arkansas National Guard to take them out of the governor's authority and sent in the 101st Airborne to protect Black children from crowds of white protesters as they went to school. Presidents Kennedy and Johnson continued to use Title 10 provisions to advance civil rights enforcement in Mississippi and Alabama, respectively.

Growing out of twenty-first-century concern about terrorism, the attorney general was given authority to request of the secretary of defense emergency military assistance for the specific, narrow purpose of dealing with threats involving nuclear materials. Posse Comitatus was modified in 2006 to permit the use of military forces during major public emergencies to "restore public order and enforce the laws of the United States . . . as a result of a natural disaster, epidemic, or other serious public health emergency, terrorist attack or incident."[47] That expansion of authority was repealed by Congress the following year.

Consistent with Title 10 provision of assistance to law enforcement, military forces have been deployed along the US–Mexican border under Presidents Obama, Trump, and Biden to assist Customs and Border Patrol agents, but they are prohibited from search, seizure, or arrest.

Posse Comitatus constraints reside in Chapter 13, Title 10, of the US Code and continue for practical purposes in their original form, restricting federal military forces from domestic law enforcement unless authorized by Congress, requested by a state legislature or governor, or upon declaration of the Insurrection Act by the president. And, by twentieth-century resurrection, the president retains authority to use military forces domestically to enforce citizens' constitutional rights.

Restricting the domestic use of the military freed it up to focus on its own profession. Beginning in the 1870s and accelerating, the US military focused on warfare. Posse Comitatus is also a major reason for the strong bond between the American public and its military – because the public doesn't fear its domestic use. And, as the Congressional Research Service concludes, "as a practical matter compliance is ordinarily the result of military self-restraint."[48] Just about the only experience the American public has of its military consists of their contributions in natural disasters such as fires or floods or the advancement of civil rights.

Border Wars

Ulysses Grant in his memoirs described Ranald Slidell Mackenzie as "the most promising young officer in the Army."[49] Mackenzie graduated at the top of his US military academy class in 1862 despite clocking 350 demerits for things such as laughing in the ranks and absconding from the police. Within two years he was a brigade-commanding colonel of artillery; within three, he was commanding a division of cavalry and then an infantry corps. By the age of twenty-five, he'd been wounded six times and received seven brevetted promotions, ending the war as a major general.

After the war, Mackenzie volunteered to command a regiment comprised of white, Black, and Native American soldiers and spent the rest of his career on America's western frontier, commanding relatively small and dispersed detachments, so was less observed than staff officers or those commanding in larger formations closer to government supervision. But inspection reports rate his 4th Cavalry as the finest in the Army. He successfully fought the Kiowa, Ute, Arapaho, Kickapoo, Apache, and Comanche.

It was in this context that Mackenzie led a punitive and officially unsanctioned raid into Mexican territory. Native Americans had pushed back the frontier of settlement as soldiers protecting homesteaders were pulled east into the great conflagration of the Civil War and with restrictions on militia in formerly Confederate states during Reconstruction. With Custer's defeat at Little Big Horn, President Grant abandoned his peace policy, subordinating Indian agencies under military control and issuing orders "to subdue all Indians who offered resistance."[50]

Mackenzie was responsible for west Texas, the great Llano Estacado, where the most ferocious of remaining Indian tribes, the Comanche and Kiowa, lived and operated. The Mexican government encouraged Kickapoo settlement south of the international boundary as a buffer against further encroachment into Mexican lands by American settlers and to keep the Comanche and Kiowa on the American side of the border. The Kickapoo were magnificent raiders of cattle and horses, and the stretch of territory between San Antonio and the Rio Grande River contained 90,000 livestock with fewer than 4,500 residents.[51] They also trafficked in torture and prisoners.

Mackenzie did not share the romanticized version of westward expansion exemplified by Custer with his buckskins and long blond curls; writing to the chief of staff of the Army, General Philip Sheridan, Mackenzie argued that Indian marauders "must be punished or they must be allowed to murder and rob at their own discretion."[52] Among the challenges of shielding settlers from Indian raids was that the Kickapoo would retreat across the US–Mexican border for sanctuary. The Mexican government refused to allow American incursions into the country, even in hot pursuit (given that Americans had already forced cession of more than a third of Mexico's territory).

American Secretary of State Hamilton Fish negotiated unsuccessfully both with the Kickapoo to bring raiding to an end and with the Mexican government to police them. In April of 1873, Secretary of War William Belknap and General Sheridan visited Mackenzie's command and instructed Mackenzie to conduct a cross-border raid into Mexico. They did not, however, formally order Mackenzie to conduct the operation, as that would violate the peace with Mexico, and the president would need a congressional declaration of war. Mackenzie explicitly asked, "General Sheridan, under whose orders and upon what authority am I to act?" Sheridan replied:

> Damn the orders! Damn the authority. You are to go ahead on your plan of action, and your authority and backing shall be Gen. Grant and myself. With us behind you in whatever you do to clean up this situation, you can rest assured of the fullest support. You must assume the risk. We will assume the final responsibility should any result.[53]

General Sheridan assured Mackenzie that the president wanted it done, General of the Army William Tecumseh Sherman wanted it done, and

Commander of the Missouri (which comprised all of the great plains) General Sheridan wanted it done. And Mackenzie himself wanted it done, to establish strategic depth of a buffer on the Mexican side of the border and to strike a punitive blow against both the Kickapoo and the Mexican government. The military logic of the argument is clear, echoing Jackson in Florida and Grant wanting to pursue renegade Confederates into Mexico.

Mackenzie's preparations spanned a month of scouting and training a strike force of 377 soldiers with Seminole scouts to invade Mexico at Rey Molino. On May 18, 1873, the 4th Cavalry struck Kickapoo, Lipan, and Mescalero villages 40 miles inside Mexican territory while those tribes' warriors were off raiding. The operations were regimented, with cavalry charging in organized platoons and rear detachments dismounted and setting fires, confiscating horses, and taking women and children prisoner. But they did not seek to occupy territory.

The 4th Cavalry traversed 140 miles in less than two days, returning to praise from the secretary of war and the Texas legislature for that violation of Mexican sovereignty. Mexico protested, but weakly and to no avail. To ransom their women and children, the Kickapoo agreed to reservation settlement in Oklahoma, and cross-border raiding largely ceased.

Formally, Mackenzie's conduct was unlawful, undertaken on trust that his chain of command would shield him from negative repercussions should either Congress domestically or the government of Mexico internationally exercise its authority to hold him accountable. He was actually asked by one of his soldiers during the return from the raid whether he'd had orders; when Mackenzie admitted he did not, there was a near mutiny. One soldier challenged: "then it was illegal to expose not only the lives of your officers and men, in action, but in event of their being wounded and compelled upon our withdrawal, through force of circumstances, to be left over there, probably to be hung or shot by a merciless horde of savage Indians and Mexicans." Another soldier said he wouldn't have gone had he known there were no orders. Mackenzie replied, "any officer or man who had refused to follow me across the river I would have shot."[54]

Sixty years earlier, when Andrew Jackson invaded and occupied Spanish Florida, the Monroe administration questioned the constitutionality of lacking congressional authorization; both the administration and General Jackson were subjected to congressional investigations, and the US ran the risk of war with a major European power. None of those troubles were visited on Ranald Mackenzie or the Grant administration. After Little Big Horn there was unity of view across the administration about the "Indian problem." In 1873 most of the political attention in Congress remained convulsed by the challenges of Reconstruction, and the military focused on the challenges of enforcing it. Mexico was consumed domestically with revolts against the restored republic, its military deposing governments rather than protecting its borders and its governments incapable of assertive international action.

Mackenzie's willingness to conduct military operations without orders is one of the last vestiges of army politicization before its professionalization. It demonstrates that it is possible to have too much trust in civil–military relations.[55] Born of the deep trust forged during the Civil War, both the civilian leadership and the military were veterans. They knew each other personally and understood they were being relied on for conduct that Americans living in settled safety opposed but that was necessary for protection of those Americans moving into the expanse of the west. Oversight and regulation were anyway loose in the "glittering misery" of the Indian fighting army.[56] What would no longer have been allowed in the east was celebrated in the conquest of the west.

It is also illustrative that Mackenzie's subordinates both suspected the lack of formal orders and objected to the extralegal action. The Indian fighting army was more egalitarian than the coastal army, and Mackenzie was a respected but unpopular commander (one of his lieutenants during the Civil War said of him then that the men hated him, but they "could not draw a bead on so brave a man as that").[57] But it still suggests a growing professionalization in the force, among both officers and enlisted men, even under the less restrictive conditions of the frontier and border in the 1870s, that Mackenzie was challenged about the legality of the Army's foray.

Conclusion

The American Civil War was the first war of the industrial age, featuring armies comprised of hundreds of thousands of soldiers operating in coordination across multiple theaters of war and utilizing railroads, telegraphs, iron-sided battleships, and accurate Minié ball bullets. The military leaders who fought that war became accustomed to broad authority, and, under President Lincoln's stewardship, a strong consensus on strategy for the conduct of the war and its aftermath. They accepted the commander in chief's authority even when his suspension of habeas corpus was determined to be unconstitutional. The tragic circumstances of Lincoln's assassination, and the political upheaval occasioned by his successor's efforts to redirect policy over congressional objections, led to the deepest constitutional crisis in American history other than that which had occasioned the war.

That there were so few friction points as the civilian leadership domesticated the victorious wartime commanders is a tribute to how deeply George Washington's example continued to condition the American military. General Sherman and General Grant had policy disputes with the civilian leadership about the span of their authority, but both conceded without coming anywhere near the threat of turning the military against the civilian leaders.

Questions of Grant's subordination during the constitutional crisis are the most difficult of any civil–military dispute to judge. His refusal to participate in the negotiations with Mexico, his intimation that he would appeal to the "mass of the people" to counteract the president's firing of Sheridan (which, in the event, Grant did not do), his undercutting the attorney general's ruling on the military removal of elected officials in Confederate states, his endorsement of Sheridan's successor's policies for which the president had fired Sheridan, his accepting the post of secretary of war while remaining on active duty, and his allowing himself to become a chess piece in the political confrontation between the president and Congress – all these are worrisome acts in the context of American civil–military relations. All, if they became precedents, could endanger civilian supremacy and embolden the military to take an abusive role in politics.

But that is to judge Grant's choices in a vacuum, leaching from his decisions the crucial and momentous times in which he was thrust, and for most of which there was no precedent to guide as Washington's choices guided subsequent generations. The nation was figuring out how to piece itself back together after a domestic rebellion that had consumed one million five hundred thousand military casualties. Despite the surrender of the Confederate armies and the occupation of seceded states by federal forces, the US actually did have a guerrilla war in the aftermath of the Civil War. It wasn't fought against the occupying military; its targets were the reformists and newly emancipated Black Americans. The president lurched from policies so punishing of Confederates that both the legislature and the military refused to enact them to supporting the re-establishment of the political, social, and economic structures of the antebellum south. A Congress without representation from the seceded states was struggling to determine how to repair the political union and attempting to force its authority on a recalcitrant chief executive. The dual threats of impeachment of the president by the Congress and the disbanding of Congress by the president were both novel and destabilizing. All of that risked reigniting secession by the occupied southern states.

That Grant made mistakes isn't surprising under those circumstances; what is amazing is how much he got right. And that he got the most important thing right: in peacetime disputes over military policy, he erred on the side of Congress as the most legitimate source of constitutional authority. No American military officer since Washington had ever made such important decisions, and Grant acquitted himself imperfectly but well.

Less difficult to judge is Grant's traducing of the Washingtonian precedent of resigning from military service before pursuing elected office. Likewise Mackenzie's willingness to commit military forces to combat in another country without formal orders.

Although the United States was founded in fear of a standing army, there are astonishingly few incidents of civil–military violations in the modern period. The coming of a standing army did not produce an increase in instances – quite the opposite. Even before the creation of the professional, all-recruited force in the 1970s, the twentieth century saw remarkably few bad examples. The Founding Fathers' fear of a standing army being a threat to civilian control has not only not been borne out, the experience of the world wars and the behemoth defense establishment during and after the Cold War have instead strengthened the strictures of military subordination, so much so that Samuel Huntington, in *The Soldier and the State*,[58] complains that the lack of friction between elected leaders and the military during World War II reflects poorly on the military as too docile.

Chapter 5

Dogs That Mostly Didn't Bark

With the emergence of the United States as an international force to be reckoned with at the turn of the twentieth century, the military became less a flow and ebb as campaigns demanded and more a permanent fixture in policymaking. With the end of Reconstruction, the Army bifurcated into a coastal army visible to civilian leaders and a grittier, less supervised "Indian fighting army." The coastal army, which comprised about a fifth of the total force, was stationed at established fortifications manning artillery to repel a seaborne invasion. But the majority of the 28,000 soldiers that constituted the US Army were stretched across the vast interior and border reaches of the country.[1] Their principal function was to protect settlers as westward expansion progressed ever further into Native American lands. But while settlers were often blamed by the military for provoking Native American violence, there were no significant frictions between US civilian leaders and the military other than Custer.

Small Wars

The Spanish–American War was neither a lurch for colonial possessions nor fomented by yellow journalism; American involvement in the Cuban independence struggle was reluctant and driven more by faith communities' horror at Spanish brutality than imperial aspirations.[2] President McKinley's policy was focused on arbitrating better conditions for Cubans, but domestic politics in Spain stalemated negotiations, and Congress authorized the use of force to assist Cuban independence, leading Spain to declare war on the US.

In February of 1898, more than 100,000 volunteers enlisted for military service on the night the USS *Maine* exploded and sank in Havana harbor – before the US had entered the war.[3] After Spain declared war on April 25, the Army scrambled to issue a call for an additional 50,000 troops for the conflict, tripling its size. Most did not arrive in either Cuba or the Philippines until after Spain conceded. General in Chief Nelson Miles (of Indian fighting fame) anticipated relying principally on Cuban forces and sending American soldiers only after the rainy season ended in October. The *American Military History* drily notes: "Secretary of War Russell M. Alger ignored General Miles' advice."[4] Army leaders complained publicly about the quality of rations (Miles took particular umbrage at "embalmed meat") and the toll of tropical diseases, but took in their stride the numerous political overrides of their plans. The history concludes: "Fortunately, it turned out that the really decisive fighting of the war fell to the much better prepared Navy."[5]

As in the Civil War, action in the eastern theater was the focus of public and media attention, but the most significant strategic action was in the west. In the Spanish–American War, the eastern theater was Cuba, where the Navy efficiently blockaded maritime traffic and sank the Spanish fleet, the Marines were the first ashore, and Teddy Roosevelt's Rough Riders garnered lavishly adoring press.

The western theater was the Philippines, where the US Navy destroyed Spain's fleet in the space of little more than an hour, Commodore Dewey reporting that, "though in the early part of the action our firing was not what I should have liked it to be, it soon steadied down ... To my gratification not a single life had been lost, and considering that we would rather measure the importance of an action by the scale of its conduct than by the number of casualties we were immensely happy."[6] The US occupation force encountered little opposition in Cuba, Puerto Rico, and Guam, but the Philippine independence movement fought ferociously until 1902. The Army's occupation force was ordered by President McKinley to "win the confidence, respect, and admiration of the inhabitants of the Philippines."[7] This, despite surging to 70,000 troops, it never did.

The Navy had been the first service to take professional education seriously, establishing a war college in 1884 and gathering a civilian and military faculty, including Alfred Thayer Mahan, to think seriously about maritime power (Mahan's lectures would become his book *Influence of Sea Power upon History, 1660–1783*). The Naval War College also was employed as a planning staff for the service, developing concepts of operations for potential conflicts.

While the US Navy moved smoothly to execute its blockade plans for Cuba and sink Spanish fleets in Havana harbor and Manila Bay, the Army was unprepared. By its own bitter admission it

> lacked a mobilization plan, a well-knit higher staff, and experience in carrying on joint operations with the Navy. The National Guard was equally ill prepared. Though the Guard counted over 100,000 members, most units were poorly trained and inadequately equipped ... The utility of the Guard was further compromised by question as to whether it was legal for Guard units to serve abroad.[8]

The Navy's proficiency and political enthusiasm from Theodore Roosevelt, former assistant secretary of the Navy and then president, drove policy toward naval expansion of both the fleet and bases and the adoption of revolutionary technology such as continuous-aim gunfire.[9] The Army's mixed record in the Spanish–American War occasioned a presidential commission to review its deficiencies.

Secretary of War Elihu Root fundamentally transformed the institutional structures of the Army; in 1901 he emulated the Navy in establishing a war college for the Army to "provide educational preparation for modern war." The Root reforms replaced the autonomy of the general in chief with a chief of staff more subordinate to civilian control and created a general staff on the Prussian model to provide better and longer-range planning.

Although Congress authorized an Army end-strength of 100,000 soldiers in 1902, it was only able to recruit 75,000 before 1914. To cover the deficiency, Secretary Root proposed greater control over militia forces, organizing them into a National Guard – an "organized militia" – and a reserve force patterned on the active-duty component. Those structures, adopted in law as the 1903 Dick Act and federally funded, persist to this day. Additional legislation in 1908 and 1914 extended federal authority further, allowing the president greater latitude to call up Guard forces and placing the reserve under federal authority.[10]

While the Monroe Doctrine was US policy from 1823, constabulary duties become routine for the American military only with occupation of Cuba and the Philippines after the Spanish–American War. Between 1898 and 1935, the United States intervened militarily in the Western hemisphere ten times, including extended occupations of Cuba, Honduras, Panama, Haiti, the Dominican Republic, and Nicaragua.[11] The Marine Corps was the force of choice for these "small wars" and developed formal doctrine beginning in 1921 that continues operational today.[12]

The Marine Corps' *Small Wars Manual* subordinates military operations to tactical political direction: "One of the principal obstacles with which the naval forces are confronted in small war situations is the one that has to do with the absence of a clean-cut line of demarcation between State Department authority and military authority." The doctrine makes clear that military forces are integrated with but subordinate to civilian directive, requiring "preparation of their war plans in close cooperation with the statesman. There is mutual dependence and responsibility which calls for the highest qualities of statesmanship and military leadership. The initiative devolves upon the statesmen."[13]

Throughout America's war with Spain and the Philippine–American war, there is virtually no instance of disagreement between civilian and military leaders over policy, strategy, resourcing, operations, or tactics. When the president deployed the USS *Maine* to Havana as a show of force, the military did not object. When the USS *Maine* exploded, the civilians offered no recriminations. Nor did the military stampede the politicians to war. The Navy's civilian and military leaders coolly anticipated opportunities for strategic gain and made the United States an imperial power. The Army expanded more than tenfold and undertook extended constabulary duties as occupation forces.[14] A civilian war secretary restructured the Army's force and established new responsibilities while the Marine Corps developed a concept of constabulary operations subordinate to political authority – all without significant civil–military friction.

The War to End All Wars

When war broke out in Europe in 1914, the United States endeavored to remain aloof from the conflagration. The war nonetheless evinced dramatic economic effects in the US, precipitating a three-month closure of the stock market and a short-lived bank run, but propelling the US out of recession by fostering a near tripling of exports by 1917.[15] American neutrality was profitable, trading with both sides until both the British blockade of goods going to continental Europe and German submarine warfare impeded trade. Reflecting broad public opposition to American involvement, in 1916 President Woodrow Wilson campaigned on continuing to keep the US out of the war. But buffeting by both Britain and Germany provoked a major American military buildup.

The 1916 Naval Act was designed to build on US Navy prowess exhibited in the Spanish–American War and produce a force second to none by 1923, a repudiation both to German submarine warfare and the British blockade of American goods. The Naval Act called for

- ten dreadnaught battleships, four of which had a displacement of 42,000 tons
- six battle cruisers (a less-armored version of battleships)
- fifty destroyers
- sixty-seven submarines

None were complete when the US entered World War I; most were never completed.

A parallel National Defense Act doubled the Army's standing force to 175,000, with latitude to expand in wartime to 285,000 "regular" (active duty) soldiers.[16] It also established the Reserve Officer Training Program (ROTC) to bring college-educated officers into the force, funded a fourfold increase in the National Guard to 450,000 soldiers and further expanded the president's authority to utilize them overseas, and created the basis for combining the active, guard, and reserve into a single force in wartime. From this point in 1916 forward, the United States would have a substantial standing military in peacetime.

Conscription was instituted in 1917, initially requiring registration for men aged eighteen to thirty; it would extend to age forty-five before the war ended. Twenty-four million men had registered by the end of hostilities. After arriving in France in the summer of 1917, General Pershing cabled back to Washington: "Plans contemplate sending over at least one million men by next May."[17] In fact, the American Expeditionary Force would burgeon to two million soldiers and suffer 255,000 casualties. So much changed as a result of both technology (airplanes, tanks, machine guns) and organization that "a soldier from today could go a century back in time and feel at home in the Army of 1917, while a soldier from the latter 1800s transported forward two decades would have been thoroughly disoriented by the vast change."[18]

For the Army, disputes during World War I were predominantly not between civilian and military leaders; they were principally interservice, as they remain. Secretary of War Henry Stimson was called on from 1910 to adjudicate a bitter disagreement between Chief of Staff Leonard Wood and Adjutant General Fred Ainsworth over their respective responsibilities that spilled into congressional involvement.[19] Within the Army, disputes raged over the role of Guard forces and how to incorporate reserves, but they were among civilians and the military, not between them. President Wilson's secretary of war, Lindley M. Garrison, resigned when the president declined to support the Army's proposal to replace the National Guard with a 400,000 soldier Continental Army.[20]

Women came into the naval force as nurses beginning in 1908; after Secretary of the Navy Josephus Daniels declared they could also become yeomen (ashore administrative duty rating), 11,000 women served in the Navy and the Marine Corps during World War I.[21] Nearly 22,000 women served in the Army's nursing and signal corps.[22] As so often in American military practice, policies with social significance were the result of manpower needs.

There was, however, a bitter political dispute over the end of the war into which the Army leadership was dragged. At issue was General Pershing's conduct on the day of the armistice. Pershing was known to have opposed the armistice, considering it "an acknowledgment of weakness and clearly means that the Allies are winning the war . . . Germany's desire is only to regain time to restore order among her forces, but she must be given no opportunity to recuperate and we must strike harder than ever."[23] American troops under his command continued offensive operations, including a major thrust, until the exact time that the armistice came into effect. More than 3,500 American casualties were suffered on November 11th.

Pershing's motivations were likely tinted by his ambitions for the US military to emerge from the war as the force that won it.[24] He argued strongly that the German terms should be rejected and only unconditional surrender accepted, and that if Britain and France sued for peace the US should fight on. But he was not alone in advocating for continued offensive operations until the armistice took effect. In fact, he was under orders to do so from General Foch, the allied military commander, as were British and French forces.

Pershing's conduct came under scrutiny only after the war, from families who'd lost soldiers and Marines on the final day and from Republicans in Congress. The Select Committee on Expenditures in the War Department created a subcommittee to investigate military decisions in the final hours of the war. The degree of hostility is reflected in an exchange between the committee counsel and a senior officer, General Fox Connor, who was testifying. Connor fulsomely expressed resentment at having his motives impugned, expecting deference to his military stature, but the counsel shot back: "I resent the fact that these lives were lost and the American people resent the fact that these lives were lost; and we have a right to question the motive, if necessary, of the men who have occasioned this loss of life."

The committee's initial report accusing the Army leadership of "needless slaughter" was vociferously contested by Democrats as unfairly discrediting the military as a means of damaging President Wilson. Criticism of the military conduct of the war was struck from the findings.[25] While Pershing was dishonest with the committee about his knowledge of the armistice, his conduct on the battlefield is defensible. The post-war criticism is a reminder of how ruthlessly politicians can and often do abuse the military for partisan gain.

Appealing to a Higher Purpose

With significant support from within the uniformed Navy, Admiral William Sims contested most of the major strategic decisions of the war, both privately and publicly. Sims blatantly disregarded President Wilson's policy on the US being an "associated" and independently operating force rather than an allied force operating integrally with French and British forces.[26] He instigated a campaign against his civilian superior, accusing Secretary Daniels and, by extension, President Wilson of prolonging the war and increasing casualties by 500,000 (practically double the number actually incurred in the war), resulting in a congressional investigation. Sims argued his judgment was superior to that of his civilian superiors and was justified by the urgency of learning the right lessons from the war.[27]

The dispute between Rear Admiral Sims and Navy Secretary Daniels was fundamentally an argument about how to modernize the Navy, but it included an egregious example of making an international agreement contravening the president's policy and several efforts by Sims and other senior officers to undercut and supplant the civilian leadership. They justified the insubordination as providing superior policies to those of civilian leaders, but Congress affirmed President Wilson and Navy Secretary Daniels's authority, squelching Sims's insurgent modernization efforts by concluding that the Navy's performance in the war had been "a great job greatly done."[28]

In 1902, Lieutenant William S. Sims had had a seminal role in the adoption of continuous-aim gunfire, which was opposed by the Navy's Bureau of Ordnance, by appealing outside his chain of command directly to President Theodore Roosevelt.[29] The innovation improved the accuracy of cannon fire at sea by 3,000 percent. Seen as a courageous reformist, Sims was promoted and named president of the Naval War College. But he was also a political partisan, critical in public of both President Taft and President Wilson's European policies, as well as the social policies of Secretary Daniels that included outlawing alcohol aboard ships and encouraging education for enlisted sailors.[30]

In 1915–16, Sims and other reformist naval officers advocated the creation of a general staff under a chief of naval operations, giving the uniformed Navy sole authority for the planning and conduct of war, and in 1916 they circumvented their civilian leadership to put the proposals directly before Congress. Congress upheld Secretary Daniels's opposition, the secretary cast a wary eye over promotions of most of the officers involved, and President Wilson directed an end to public commentary by serving officers.[31]

Despite his involvement, in 1917 Sims was elevated by Secretary Daniels to admiral and placed in command of US Naval Forces Operating in European Waters. While in command, Sims argued internally about anti-submarine warfare methods, materiel deficiencies, and personnel requirements. Where he clearly subverted civilian control was in allowing the assignment of US destroyers to British operational control – President Wilson's policy was that US forces were "associated" but not allied.

Instead of reversing the policy or relieving Sims, Wilson sent a senior officer, Vice Admiral Henry R. Mayo, to Sims's headquarters in London as the overall US Fleet Forces commander, providing an additional echelon of supervision.

Even while in command during the war, Sims was litigating policy. The substance of his accusations was that Congress had been diverted to shipbuilding away from essential internal restructuring of the Navy but that, with the emergence of submarine warfare, "our battleships can serve no useful purpose."[32] He accused both the Congress and the Navy Department of neglecting the changing nature of warfare. For his part, President Wilson considered that Sims's "judgment is warped," and that he "should be wearing a British uniform."[33] But Wilson discounted the relevance not just of Sims but of the military more generally:

> The experienced soldier, – experienced in previous wars, – is a back number so far as his experience is concerned; not so far as his intelligence is concerned. His experience does not count, because he never fought a war as this is being fought, and therefore he is an amateur along with the rest of us. Now, somebody has got to think this war out. Somebody has got to think out the way not only to fight the submarine, but to do something different from what we are doing . . . We have got to throw tradition to the winds.[34]

Sims, still in command in London, fomented a public relations campaign designed to rebut the president and get Secretary Daniels fired, or at least investigated by Congress. As the war concluded, President Wilson and Secretary Daniels returned him in rank to rear admiral (something that was not done to General Pershing or other commanders of the war) and in assignment to the War College; however, they approved his proposed book project provided that it should "contain nothing at all of a political nature and no criticism of the Department."[35] Sims's *Victory at Sea* was serialized for eleven months in 1919 and was awarded the Pulitzer Prize the following year.

Sims assiduously worked the referees (historians and journalists) to write stories about Daniels denying him and others of awards, prioritizing social reforms at the expense of military preparedness, and failing to understand modern warfare. He also wrote (and promptly leaked to newspapers) letters to Secretary Daniels criticizing his policy choices on submarine warfare, opposition to creating a general staff, and ostensible cronyism in awarding medals. He claimed civilian mismanagement extended the war by six months and cost a half million additional lives. President Wilson and Secretary Daniels considered court-martialing Sims, but declined in order not to "make him a martyr."[36]

In 1920 Republicans initiated a congressional investigation into Sims's allegations, which Sims relished as "a fight to the finish."[37] But, with adroit handling by the actual politicians, the investigation broadened and became a debate over civilian control, Secretary Daniels arguing that Sims and his uniformed supporters "fail to understand the genius of American [civilian] Administration."[38] Republicans accused both Secretary Daniels and Secretary of War Newton D. Baker of incompetence, hearings bogged down, and by July 1921, when the Senate issued its report (and a new administration was in office), Sims's advocacy for reforms in the Navy was portrayed as a "naval squabble."[39]

Sims's scheming against Secretary Daniels was perceived as vainglorious and political, and it discredited his legitimate criticisms of Navy practices. As Branden Little concludes, "the only naval 'lesson' the nation learned was that it had won the war."[40] Sims had considerable support among the uniformed Navy (other officers also published treatises highly critical of their civilian leadership), but he failed to engender a national movement for naval reform or the elevation of military over civilian judgment; what he did succeed at was discrediting the Navy's budget requests. He never repented of his insurrection, considering his behavior justified by the urgency of his policies being adopted and blaming his political campaign's failure on the politicians, writing that "it is to be greatly regretted that a committee of the Senate should make partisan reports of the evidence."[41] But Secretary Daniels got the last word, publishing relentlessly to recharacterize the record.[42] It is a reminder that even officers who consider themselves politically shrewd – and are seen by their military peers as politicians – are almost never as skilled as real politicians.

The Inter-War Years

The inter-war years were a time of fulgent experimentation in all the US military services and intense inter-service rivalry. Illustrative of the ferment and seriousness of disputes over the future of warfare within the military services, the commander of the Army's Air Service, Brigadier General Billy Mitchell, accused military leaders of "incompetency, criminal negligence, and almost treasonable administration by the War and Navy departments."[43]

In the years from 1919 to 1939, "military institutions had to come to grips with enormous technological and tactical innovation during a period of minimal funding."[44] Strong anti-war sentiment pervaded American society, leading to grandiose efforts to prevent future wars such as the 1928 General Treaty for Renunciation of War as an Instrument of National Policy, in which the US, Germany, Great Britain, France, Italy, Japan, and nine other states committed to "condemn recourse to war for the solution of international controversies, and renounce it, as an instrument of national policy in their relations with one another."[45] The treaty contained no enforcement provisions.

Another example of the ambition and naiveté of pacifistic arms control is the 1923 Washington Naval Conference, an effort to bring diplomacy out into the open, resolve potential conflict in Asia, and reduce the navies of the major powers. The Washington Naval Accords traded the expanded fleet envisioned by the 1916 program for agreed limits on the numbers and tonnage of the major navies. In return for foregoing the Big Navy and leaving its Pacific installations unprotected, the US attained parity with Britain's Royal Navy and limited Japan's navy to three-fifths and both France and Italy's navies to one-fifth of its own (Germany's navy had been severely restricted by the Versailles Treaty). A 1930 addition constrained cruisers and submarines. While the accords contained no enforcement provisions, they were honored by the signatories until Japan withdrew in 1936, with major effects on naval forces.[46]

The accords' restrictions drove thinking about how to deliver combat power when ships were stringently limited, leading to the development of the aircraft carrier.[47] The exclusion of submarines from restrictions fostered expansion of that force and its utilization in unrestricted operations against commerce.[48] Concurrently, the Marine Corps developed the concept of amphibious warfare.[49] The Army conducted large-scale exercises to understand mechanized warfare, including the Louisiana Maneuvers exploring how to utilize tanks.[50] Development of Plan ORANGE for conflict with Japan by the Joint Army–Navy Board influenced organizational development in both services. These experiments across the services would produce the leadership of the American military in World War II and the operational concepts they would employ.

But, as Williamson Murray concludes, "although small groups of officers in the armed services did much to transform the services, too much of the peacetime military was devoted to maintaining the status quo."[51] Still, all of the major innovations sprung forth from within the military services themselves rather than being imposed by civilian leaders: airplanes on carriers, amphibious assault troops, fast resupply at sea, Higgins boats, exploitation of the electronic spectrum to communicate, maneuver on the battlefield, and air warfare.[52] Nor did the military produce solutions rejected by the civilian leaders; while the military services grumbled at budget limits, the country's suffering during the Depression made the case difficult to prosecute.

Demobilization of the World War I force had been swift and stingy. In 1932, the worst year of the Great Depression, 25,000 destitute veterans and their families encamped in Washington, DC, to pressure Congress to accelerate the payment of bonuses promised during their military service; Congress declined. The Army chief of staff, General Douglas MacArthur, considered the movement a communist conspiracy and claimed that only 10 percent of the marchers were veterans.[53] With MacArthur personally leading the charge, 3,500 soldiers cleared the Bonus March encampments using bayonets, tanks, gas, and cavalry with drawn swords, chasing them out of the District of Columbia in contravention of President Hoover's repeated direction. When challenged, MacArthur declared himself "too busy and did not want either himself or his staff bothered by people coming down and pretending to bring orders."[54] Receiving news that the marchers had been forcibly dispersed in this way, Democratic presidential candidate Franklin Roosevelt privately declared it would win him the election.[55] It also announced the emergence of military veterans as a major political force.

The Curious Incident of the Dog in the Night-Time

The strangest and, if true, most dangerous threat to civilian governance was ostensibly revealed in 1932, when a highly respected retired general claimed to be planning a "military" coup of combat veterans that would arrest President Franklin Delano Roosevelt. Major General Smedley Butler said the plot was organized and funded by business tycoons. Despite congressional investigation, no evidence was ever found, and all the accused denied existence of a plot.

Smedley Butler was a two-time Medal of Honor recipient who had fought in the Philippine–American War and virtually every other American military engagement when he retired in 1931. He was frequently involved in enforcing US government policy in Latin America, military work he relished but found politically and ethically distasteful. He privately wrote in 1912: "What makes me mad is that the whole revolution is inspired and financed by Americans who have wild cat investments down here and want to make them good by putting in a Government which will declare a monopoly in their favor . . . The whole business is rotten to the core."[56] Butler tried to decline his first Medal of Honor, received for action in Veracruz, Mexico, in 1914, on the grounds that he'd done nothing to deserve it. He received his second Medal of Honor for combat in Haiti the following year. He agitated unsuccessfully for a combat command in Europe in 1917 but was instead assigned to run the largest debarkation post for US forces, serving with distinction.

Butler frequently trafficked in indiscreet public statements but existed in a state of grace because his father was chairman of the Naval Affairs Committee in the US House of Representatives. However, after his father's death he was court-martialed in 1931 at President Hoover's request for having drawn an Italian government demarche. Butler was the first American general officer arrested since Grant had Custer taken in 1873, though Butler wriggled out of the trial by apologizing.[57] He retired in 1931 and ran unsuccessfully for the Senate the following year.

Butler participated in the 1932 Bonus March on Washington, visiting the camp and giving speeches; when marchers were forcibly dispersed, he declared himself a "Hoover-for-Ex-President-Republican."[58] He organized veterans, "trying to educate the soldiers out of the sucker class," and agitated for "taking Wall St. by the throat and shaking it up."[59] He became spokesman for the American League against War and Fascism in 1935 and published a jeremiad titled *War is a Racket*, which argued "the only way to smash this racket is to conscript capital and industry and labour before the nation's manhood can be conscripted."[60] He recommended a referendum before going to war, with voting restricted to those who would serve on the front lines, and limiting military forces to the defense of US territory.

In 1933, Butler claimed that banking interests organized by Gerald P. MacGuire were conspiring to raise a force of 500,000 to arrest President Roosevelt and establish a fascist dictatorship under the former head of FDR's National Recovery Agency, retired General Hugh S. Johnson. Butler claimed MacGuire had attempted to recruit him to lead the force and told him the conspiracy had raised three million dollars to pay them. A House of Representatives investigation credited his claims but produced no evidence beyond Butler's testimony, and no criminal investigations were ever conducted. The *New York Times* dismissed Butler's allegations, saying, "the whole story sounds like a gigantic hoax."[61]

The Business Plot, as it was called, is consistent with Major General Butler's long-standing suspicion of business influence and resentment at being an instrument of US foreign policy driven by commercial interests. If such a conspiracy existed, Butler would indeed be the kind of leading veteran and smart tactician to plan it. But no such planning appears to have ever been conducted, no force recruited, no money advanced. Nor is it likely a Roosevelt confidant such as Johnson would have been part of a plan to arrest the president; more likely is that Butler was indignant at Johnson's ties to business and sought to implicate him. Butler's political activities and ambitions render plausible an explanation that he aimed to make a splash to assist future campaigns for high office.

It is important that Butler's political activism all took place after his retirement; he was a veteran, not in military service. And the other word for veteran is citizen. But, then and now, the American public treats veterans, and especially veterans who served in high ranks, as proxies for what the military thinks. They continue to carry the title of general, so their political behavior is taken as reflective of the military long after their service; in cases such as Butler's Business Plot, this proves problematic for the work of the military's leaders and their ability to forge bonds of trust with elected leaders.

Cry Havoc and Let Slip the Dogs of War

World War II necessitated the greatest military exertions in American history, and the military expanded from 200,000 personnel in 1939 to more than twelve million in 1945. America's military leaders had vast responsibilities and differed significantly and enduringly in their judgments from the commander in chief. And yet, there were virtually no civil–military infractions during the years 1939 to 1945. No policies were refused or shirked, no senior leaders were relieved of command for insubordination, and no disputes between them, individually or collectively with the civilian leadership, spilled into the public.

The system worked almost entirely on the personal relationships the president established with his military leadership, which Richard Kohn describes as "famously good."[62] Intermediate echelons of civilian control were largely excluded from the interaction between the president and the top military men, as was the other constitutionally prescribed source of civilian supremacy, the Congress. Policy influence migrated upward in the military from field commanders to the service chiefs and upward in civilian channels from the secretaries of state, war, and the navy to the president.[63]

The prominence of military staffs advocated by William Sims was made manifest, but the real emollient force was the active involvement and stupendous political skills of the chief executive. Franklin Roosevelt expanded service chief authorities and, beginning in 1937, initiated war plan reviews, personally selected service chiefs, shifted the Joint Board that developed war plans and made force structure recommendations from the military services to the White House, and began military staff talks with Britain. These decisions connected the president directly with military leaders. And because Roosevelt developed deeply trusting relationships with both the Army chief, General George Marshall, and the Navy chiefs, Admiral Harold Stark and his successor Admiral Ernest King, he could hide behind their uniforms to deliver congressional support.

Nor were those chiefs innocent of political and economic factors; Dean Acheson wrote of George Marshall, "when he thought about military problems, nonmilitary factors played a controlling part."[64] Marshall himself said: "I doubt there was any one thing, except the shortage of LSTs, that came to our minds more frequently than the political factors

... we were not in any way putting our neck out as to political factors, which were the business of the head of state – the President – who happened also to be the Commander-in-Chief."[65]

Another seminal factor in the smoothness of civil–military relations was that in 1942, on Marshall's advice, President Roosevelt appointed Admiral William Leahy as his chief of staff. The president had what was in effect both a chairman of the joint chiefs and a senior White House military advisor. Working from the White House, Leahy had a more ingrained sense of the president's political constraints and was a valuable intermediary explaining military judgments to the president.

The complexity and frustrations of running a global war offered no shortage of subjects for civil–military friction; what is exceptional is the good faith offered by both the president and his military leaders to resolve them internally and professionally. Kent Roberts Greenfield clocks twenty significant policy disagreements over grand strategy, rearmament legislation, the size of the armed forces, allied assistance, and post-war relations with the Soviet Union.[66] Chiefs offered their counsel, and the president took or rejected their advice.

There is just a single instance of Roosevelt snapping the military leadership to attention, and it resulted less from disagreement between himself and the chiefs than from frustration by the chiefs at Prime Minister Churchill's obduracy in advocating a Mediterranean focus for the first allied landings. So exasperated were they that, in July of 1942, General Marshall recommended shifting strategic focus from the European to the Pacific theater. They formally appealed to the president to choose their judgment over Churchill's – and Roosevelt's own. The president responded:

> I have carefully read your estimate of Sunday. My first impression is that it is exactly what Germany hoped the United States would do following Pearl Harbor. Secondly it does not in fact provide use of American troops in fighting except in a lot of islands whose occupation will not affect the world situation this year or next. Third: it does not help Russia or the Near East. Therefore it is disapproved as of the present.[67]

The president signed it "C in C," underscoring the unequal nature of their responsibilities. Roosevelt rarely put direction in writing; he was both giving unequivocal direction and pulling rank, emphasizing his expectation of compliance by subordinates. But a crisp reminder is not a crisis, and the military returned to planning Operation Torch for landings in North Africa. It's extraordinary how well the system worked given the colossal stakes and genuine disagreements over policy.

So well did it work, in fact, that it was perceived by the British as driven by Marshall rather than Roosevelt.[68] An official British historian of the war, John Ehrman, considered that it was Marshall "more than any one man conceived the American strategy." The US Army history records that "the President generally appeared at Allied conferences as the defender of the strategy worked out by the Joint Chiefs of Staff." Viscount Alanbrooke, chief of the imperial general staff, noted that "the President had no great military knowledge and was aware of the fact and consequently relied on Marshall and listened to Marshall's advice. Marshall never seemed to have any difficulties in controlling any wildish plans which the President might put forward."

Suspicion never abated among the US chiefs of British ambitions to use American forces for the purposes of maintaining the British empire: both Admiral King and General MacArthur were offered British forces to assist in the Pacific late in the war, and both declined.[69]

The Admirals' Revolt

Compared to the arguments over post-war strategy and budgets, the creation of the Department of Defense was congenial. A committee established by the joint chiefs of staff outlined plans for the establishment of a single Department of the Armed Forces with a civilian secretary and supporting staff, a single military commander of the entirety of the force reporting to the civilian secretary but who would also be the president's chief of staff, and the establishment of the Air Force as a separate military service.[70] The Navy's representative on the committee dissented internally from all the recommendations, the committee report included the dissent, and the Senate Committee on Military Affairs addressed many of the concerns as it drafted the 1947 National Security Act. In short, despite deep disagreements, the process worked to create a hugely consequential set of reforms establishing the modern defense and intelligence establishment.

But organizational issues were just the warmup for bitter inter-service disputes in 1949 over strategy, budgets, and force structure that would see serving Navy officers campaign publicly for the removal of the civilian leadership of the nascent Department of Defense. The precipitating factor was radically reduced military budgets, which were cut from $81 billion in fiscal year 1945 to $9 billion in 1948.[71] Moreover, the dawn of the nuclear age suggested the possibility of a revolution in warfare. In such a tightly constrained fiscal environment, President Truman opted for heavy reliance on long-range bombers armed with nuclear weapons as the backbone of the force. The Navy was cut from 1,166 warships to 343.[72]

The 1948 Key West agreement on military roles and missions assigned principal responsibility for strategic bombing to the Air Force. When Secretary of Defense Louis Johnson cancelled the large-deck carrier USS *United States* intended for the launch of long-range bombers, Navy Secretary Sullivan resigned in protest. A document produced anonymously by the Navy's civilian staff alleging fraud in Air Force bomber programs and insinuating conflicts of interest by the secretary of defense triggered a congressional investigation that ended up exonerating Secretary Johnson and the Air Force and revealing the Navy's instigation.[73]

With encouragement from the chief of naval operations, Admiral Louis Denfield, naval officers continued to publicly prosecute the case for more funding and to reverse the establishment of a unified Department of Defense.[74] House Armed Services hearings were a parade of World War II naval legends objecting to an over-reliance on strategic bombing and the Air Force's plans and capabilities: former Chief of Naval Operations Ernest King and former Marine Corps Commandant Alexander Vandegrift, Fleet Admirals Chester Nimitz and William Halsey, Admirals Raymond Spruance and Thomas Kinkaid. Admiral Denfield endorsed their views in his testimony. The Air Force civilian and military leadership countered, and the Army's World War II legends George Marshall, Dwight Eisenhower, and Omar Bradley weighed in to support unification; Chairman of the Joint Chiefs of Staff Bradley criticized the Navy for disloyalty. Subsequent to the hearings, Admiral Denfield was relieved as CNO for having lost the trust of his civilian leadership.

The intensity of dispute revealed in the hearings was exemplified by Admiral Radford, the Navy's commander in the Pacific, criticizing "a theory of warfare – the atomic blitz – which promises them a cheap and easy victory if war should come," and Air Force Chief of Staff Hoyt Vandenberg replying "Veterans of the Eighth, the Fifteenth, the Twentieth and other historic Air Forces know very well that there are no cheap and easy ways to win great wars."[75] Those squadrons had taken the highest proportion of casualties of any American units in World War II. The *New York Times* concluded: "there is not much doubt that many in the Navy still find it difficult to bend their necks to the yoke of the team. But this is even more true of the Air Force . . . Psychologically many in the services are not fully conditioned to teamwork – particularly to top-level teamwork in the politically-conscious and strife-laden atmosphere of Washington."[76]

Congressional oversight significantly improved administration policy, balancing affordability and military criticisms of strategic and budgetary decisions. Congress distinguished itself by the judiciousness of its findings, supporting unification, rebuking the DOD civilian leadership for preemptory decisions, supporting service autonomy in developing weapons systems, directing evaluation of weapons systems, criticizing the relief of Admiral Denfield as retaliation for his testimony, and chiding, "there has been a navy reluctance in the inter-service marriage, an over-ardent army, a somewhat exuberant air force."[77]

Secretary Johnson wasn't particularly good at the job, but, in his defense, he was only the second to hold the post and still needed to establish the authority of the office. The Navy's challenge was to consider him unqualified to make the decisions for which he was responsible; they objected that he made decisions "without due consideration of the uniformed service's opinions."[78] But civilian leaders in both the executive and legislative branches of the US government affirmed their standing as superior to the military and with the ability to establish and enforce compliance with their decisions.

The Navy had serious, substantive objections to national policy – the strategy, its execution, and budget.[79] Military officers have both a right and an obligation to make their views known during policy formation and either to carry out the policy decisions or resign their commissions. With the exception of some isolated cases of indiscipline, they made their case substantively and before Congress. While deeply unsettling for a Truman administration that was desperate to cut military expenditures, serving military members have a constitutional responsibility to provide

Congress with their military judgments. Six months after the hearings, North Korea invaded South Korea, which validated many of the Navy's criticisms of the budget austerity, the damage it had done to American fighting forces, and the over-reliance on nuclear forces.

Yet trust between the civilian and military leaders is also important to the American system of civil–military relations functioning well, and military leaders in senior positions opposing administration policy fundamentally compromise that trust. Moreover, the 1949 dispute was primarily over the budget, and only the civilian leadership is empowered by the American public to determine how much of the national effort to devote to military purposes. Military leaders lack the authority and responsibility to weigh and decide the aggregate preferences of American society. Only elected officials can make those decisions.

Admiral Denfield's relief is justifiable not on the basis of his congressional testimony but, rather, for his encouraging and rewarding officers leaking documents, holding unsanctioned press conferences to criticize presidential policy, publicly disavowing war plans and procurements he had approved internally, and himself taking numerous opportunities to undermine administration policy in ways that collapsed the trust of his civilian superiors.

I Shall Return

If Ulysses Grant's Solomonic decision during the constitutional crisis in 1866–7 is the hardest case to adjudicate in the annals of US civil–military relations, Douglas MacArthur's firing by President Truman in 1951 is the easiest. General MacArthur had a history of disregarding civilian authority dating back at least to the 1932 Bonus March. There is no question that he believed his strategy for war in Korea merited support despite its being contrary to the commander in chief's, and that he directly violated orders. There is no question that the president had a right, even a responsibility, to remove him from command. Moreover, MacArthur had flirted with running for president while in command in Korea and was unrepentant in retirement – worse, he believed that the military owed no allegiance to civilian leaders.

MacArthur was nominated for the Medal of Honor twice in his first fifteen years as a soldier, for reconnaissance during the 1914 US raid into Mexico and for action in World War I. His actions in combat also garnered a remarkable seven silver star awards in that war. He served as superintendent at West Point en route to chief of staff of the US Army and military advisor to the government of the Philippines. He retired from active duty in 1937 and continued in a civilian advisory role in the Philippines but was recalled to active military duty in 1941 to command the US Army in the Pacific, based in Manila.

The Japanese invasion of the Philippines drove MacArthur's forces back to Corregidor, from which he was rescued, but his Philippine and American troops endured starvation and atrocities so severe that the Japanese commanders were subsequently convicted of war crimes and executed. MacArthur was awarded the Medal of Honor (President Franklin Roosevelt believing the country needed "a hero, not a scapegoat").[80] Safely in Australia, MacArthur was elevated to the post of supreme commander of the Southwest Pacific, a placatory appointment further illustrative of civilian morale efforts and an additional headache for Admiral Chester Nimitz, who was actually orchestrating the war in the Pacific.

MacArthur's service was marred by the violence with which in 1932 he broke up an encampment of World War I veterans protesting for unpaid bonuses in Washington, DC (he insisted the American veterans were a "communist-led menace"), the unpreparedness of his forces for Japanese attack even after Pearl Harbor, and his easy willingness to be rescued from the Philippines while his soldiers endured the Bataan Death March. Omar Bradley, chairman of the joint chiefs of staff while MacArthur commanded in Korea, while admitting the latter's brilliance, criticized him for an "obsession for self-glorification, almost no consideration for other men with whom he served, and a contempt for the judgment of his superiors."[81] As early as 1932, Franklin Roosevelt paired MacArthur with Louisiana Governor Huey Long as "the two most dangerous men in the country."[82]

The zenith of MacArthur's career was as occupation authority in Japan after the war, a position to which he was promoted by President Truman. MacArthur wrote the Japanese constitution, ordered its economy, and was effectively godfather to modern Japan. While it's tempting to see his expansive responsibilities in post-war Japan as the key to his imperiousness and his belief that his own judgment should supersede that of elected officials, those tendencies were evident in his comportment throughout his career.

While in Japan, MacArthur politicked for the Republican presidential nomination in 1948, publicly criticized US policy, and looked to Republican ideologue John Foster Dulles for counsel, yet both military and civilian leaders in the Truman administration overlooked his norm violations and appointed him at the age of seventy as commander of UN forces in Korea.

MacArthur's Inchon amphibious landing of 75,000 troops in September of 1950 proved a colossal success, recapturing South Korea's capitol in weeks. It turned the tide of the war. Having preserved South Korea from collapse, MacArthur's force proceeded north in execution of his orders, which were the "destruction of the North Korean armed forces." Although his direction from the joint chiefs placed restrictions limiting his operations, Secretary of Defense George Marshall appended: "we want you to feel unhampered tactically and strategically to proceed north of the 38th parallel."[83] But both the civilian and military superiors did restrict Macarthur's tactical and strategic freedom of action. And MacArthur was compliant with numerous rejections of operational requests by the joint chiefs as "tactically unsound or logically infeasible" for aircraft to enter Manchurian airspace in hot pursuit or to bomb military bases, attack bridges and hydroelectric plants, blockade China's coast and attack its industry, and use Taiwanese troops to attack the Chinese mainland.[84]

What the secretary of defense was unquestionably clear on was the insistence that MacArthur should justify his decisions as militarily necessary. The administration was anxious to keep the Soviet Union and China out of the war, and the pivot from defense of South Korean territory to the pursuit of North Korean forces beyond the 38th parallel created international difficulties. Yet, as MacArthur drove North Korean forces toward the Chinese border, both the president and the joint chiefs gave him wide latitude in operational conduct, President Truman saying as late as November of 1951, "you pick your man, you've got to back him up. That's the only way a military organization can work."[85]

When he exceeded his orders by bombing Yalu River bridges and the joint chiefs ordered him to stop, MacArthur justified his refusal because Chinese troops were "pouring across all bridges" and threatened the destruction of his force. By so aggressively pursuing North Korean forces, the US had precipitated China joining the war – the very outcome limiting the war had been designed to prevent. As Lawrence Freedman concludes, "instead of being allowed latitude because he might bring victory, MacArthur now had to be given it to avoid defeat."[86]

MacArthur sought and received authority for a new offensive in November, but his estimate of 25,000 Chinese soldiers was low by a factor of eight, and, rather than end the war on American terms, it proved disastrous. He complained bitterly and publicly about not being able to attack Chinese territory, which resulted in orders not to comment publicly without State and Defense Department approval.

The Korean War was fought along partisan lines, Republicans objecting to both the strategy of a limited war and its unsatisfying lack of success – which they blamed on the president, not the military execution of the strategy. The election of 1950 had winnowed Democratic control of both the Senate and the House. Truman indulged MacArthur, even went to Wake Island to meet him when MacArthur declined to come to Washington to see the president, but the last straw was MacArthur writing the House minority leader, Republican Joseph W. Martin, a letter to be read in the chamber critical of Truman's conduct of the war.

Throughout the Korean War, MacArthur refused to return to Washington; in fact, he had not been since 1935, demanding that both his military and his civilian superiors travel to him for consultations – so, to the extent that lack of clarity in instruction or communications difficulties existed, it was MacArthur, as the subordinate to the chiefs and the president, that was at fault. Secretary of Defense George Marshall ought also to come in for criticism, given that it's the secretary of defense's fundamental responsibility to ensure that military plans are aligned with the president's political objectives.

When Truman fired MacArthur on April 11, 1951, he was able to cast the decision as "rank insubordination . . . If there is one basic element in our Constitution, it is civilian control of the military. Policies are to be made by the elected political officials, not by generals or admirals. Yet time and again General MacArthur had shown that he was unwilling to accept the policies of the Administration."[87] Truman overstates the case, probably for political reasons needing to overcome MacArthur's popularity, to brush under the rug his own culpability in selecting him and allowing him such latitude, and by this point personal resentment. Joint Chiefs Chairman Omar Bradley fretted that the chiefs' orders had been so crafted that relieving MacArthur might be unwarranted. He worried that "past orders had perhaps been too vague, and then, when ignored, not enforced."[88] But battlefield losses and command climate diminished both military support and public adulation.

Because MacArthur's popularity was still formidable and Truman was a shrewd and effective politician, when he relieved MacArthur, Truman released a ream of supporting documentation and twice emphasized his regret at having to enforce the subordination of the military to civilian control.[89] He understood he needed to win the political argument and made the case that "full and vigorous debate on matters of national policy is a vital element in the constitutional system of our free democracy. It is fundamental, however, that military commanders must be governed by the policies and directives issued to them in the manner provided by our laws and Constitution."[90]

MacArthur's clear transgressions are three: issuing public criticisms of the president's military and foreign policies, the violation of the JCS directive requiring DOD and State Department approval of same, and issuing a surrender ultimatum to North Korea that was not US government policy and contradicted the negotiations underway.

In hopes of garnering the 1952 Republican nomination for president, MacArthur publicly prosecuted the case not only against Truman's war strategy but even against the civilian leadership's legitimacy to set policy, claiming it to be "a dangerous concept, that members of our armed forces owe primary allegiance or loyalty to those who temporarily exercise the authority of the Executive Branch of the Government rather than to the country and its Constitution which they are sworn to defend. No proposition could be more dangerous."[91]

Lawrence Freedman summarizes the case succinctly: "Truman saw the issue as a general challenging the president's political judgment; MacArthur framed it as a politician challenging a commander's military judgment."[92] One reason the MacArthur case is so important in the study of civil–military relations is its establishment of the unequal nature of those two perspectives.[93] Truman firing MacArthur reinforced the supremacy of civilian authority. And both the military leadership and the broader American public supported that conclusion. It's the canonical case in American civil–military relations because Truman won the political argument.

One interesting civil–military aspect of MacArthur's story is the complicity of civilian policymakers in inflating his achievements: his recall to active duty to give luster to the war effort; the Medal of Honor for the defense of the Philippines even though it was unsuccessful and his troops suffered terribly after he was evacuated; and his selection at the advanced age of seventy to command UN forces in Korea.

Even with the clear case of insubordination, MacArthur's firing was treated at the time as a politicization of the military. Walter Lippman described it as "the beginning of an altogether intolerable thing in a republic: namely a schism within the armed forces between the generals of the Democratic party and the generals of the Republican party."[94] Not surprisingly, Truman got the last word, saying years later, "I fired him because he wouldn't respect the authority of the President. I didn't fire him because he was a dumb son of a bitch, although he was, but that's not against the law for generals. If it was, half to three-quarters of them would be in jail."[95]

Conclusion

The Spanish–American War in 1898 gets treated like the debutante ball for an America rising to international prominence: an upstart nation intervened in a war of liberation to aid independence from a major European power and then took possession itself. The US military, which had relied on Britain's Royal Navy for enforcement of the Monroe Doctrine for the previous seventy-five years, expanded in the space of just a few months to 280,564 sailors, Marines, and soldiers – all volunteers.[96] And while the war itself lasted just four months, its consequence was US control of Cuba, Puerto Rico, Guam, and the Philippines. Controlling insurrection against American occupation in the Philippines between 1898 and 1902 would be far more brutal and costly than the Spanish–American War, and the US would remain in occupation through 1946. But, again, even with the cataclysmic change of becoming an imperial power, there were no significant frictions between US civilian leaders and the military.

Professional education and the development of standing planning staffs took root in the years between the Spanish–American War and World War I. It emerged from within the uniformed Navy but was pressed into the ranks of the Army by civilian leadership enviously eyeing the superior performance of naval forces in 1898 and the new demands of developing an army of occupation. Motivated by an inability of the Army to recruit the forces deemed necessary for America's new global security commitments, Secretary of War Elihu Root created the modern Army structures of state militia organized into a National Guard and reservist forces compatible with the active-duty force. Confronted with the novel challenges of constabulary responsibilities, the Marine Corps developed a doctrine for the use of military force integral to civilian authority. The significant changes, though, were more welcomed than resisted and, in the case of the naval services, driven by the military.

Aggression from both Britain and Germany against American trade after 1914 precipitated a major military preparedness program designed to prevent a recurrence. The National Defense and Naval Acts legislated a doubling of the Army, a quadrupling of the National Guard, and making the Navy larger than Britain's world-dominating Royal Navy. Germany's recommencement of unrestricted submarine warfare and plot to foment war between the United States and Mexico brought the US into the war in 1917. When General Pershing cabled from Europe in 1919 that he anticipated the war requiring a million US troops, he underestimated the requirement by 100 percent. The Navy would expand to encompass 2,000 vessels and 600,000 personnel.[97] Conscription instituted in 1917 would draw from a pool of twenty-four million men, two million of whom would do service, a million of those on the front line of combat. Levying military forces at the scale required for World War I produced the modern American military.

There was one significant civil–military conflict during and immediately after World War I, emanating from the Navy. Admiral William Sims had become famous in 1902 for circumventing his chain of command and appealing to the president to force the naval hierarchy to adopt a significant military modernization. Appointed commander of US naval forces in Europe during World War I, Sims contradicted the president's policy that US forces should remain under national command, publicly critiqued administration policy, and launched a public relations campaign to discredit the secretary of the navy. Sims justified his activities as necessary to a cause higher than subordination to civilian authority, that of combat effectiveness. Congress, however, sided with the civilian leadership.

The inter-war years saw the US military grapple with how technology was changing warfare. Airplanes and tanks were invented but saw limited operational use during World War I, and sea power was severely constrained by arms control agreements in the 1920s; these created the prospect of dramatic changes in how wars would be fought, launching a rush toward innovation. Friction was enormous, but almost exclusively among uniforms rather than between the military and civilians.

A purported threat to civilian governance was alleged in 1933, when a decorated Marine veteran claimed business interests were conspiring to raise a force of a half million veterans to arrest President Roosevelt and install a fascist dictatorship. While the House of Representatives investigated retired Major General Smedley Butler's claims, no evidence was ever provided beyond his testimony, and Butler's political views and ambitions suggest he was intending to launch a political career on the claims.

World War II required a scale of US military forces never fielded previously or since. More than ten million Americans served under arms, and the leadership orchestrated wars in two major theaters, coordinating resources across the globe for a span of nearly four years. Military leaders had unprecedented opportunities to contest policy and resources, challenge civilian authority in both the executive and Congress, and appeal to an engaged public to relitigate disputes lost. And yet, the chiefs and field commanders did none of that. This was due partly to President Franklin Roosevelt's brilliance as a politician, partly to a military chief of staff with whom he could discuss the political and military realms, and partly to the starchy integrity of the military chiefs (especially Marshall). Trust among the chiefs and between them and Roosevelt is a rare model of accord, perhaps matched only by Washington with the Continental Congress and Lincoln with his late Civil War leadership.

A strident dispute between the military services contesting post-war military roles and missions in an environment of budget stringency spilled out into the public domain in 1949 and was termed by *Time* magazine "the Revolt of the Admirals." Navy leaders fought a rearguard action against the unification of the War and Navy Departments into a Department of Defense and sincerely believed President Truman's strategy of relying heavily on nuclear weapons and strategic bombing was unsound. Naval officers engaged in an underhand campaign to get the strategy and its associated budget reconsidered by Congress, but the consequence was a satisfactory outcome of better policy and reassignment of the chief of naval operations who had countenanced unprofessional conduct.

President Truman's firing of MacArthur is the canonical case for studying civil–military relations in the US, because MacArthur was so egregiously insubordinate but so popular during an unpopular war that the commander in chief had to proceed carefully in removing him. There have been no serious challenges by the military to their subordination since. But, whereas Sims in 1919 and the Navy leadership in 1949 commanded significant support from within the Navy, MacArthur was less representative than anomalous; his defenders were civilian political opponents of the president rather than military compatriots.

Chapter 6
The Modern Military

The Cold War necessitated the advent of the modern American military: a large, professional force at the ready, well-funded and bristlingly well-armed with high-technology weapons and innovative doctrines. But it was the domestic challenges of American society and policy that shaped the force: the moral stain of racial segregation, civilians asserting limited war strategies the military didn't believe in, losing the war in Vietnam, ending compulsory military service, discomfort with a statutorily empowered chairman of the joint chiefs of staff at a time when the military was uniquely popular with the American public, and straining the volunteer force by fighting wars of extended duration. The disparity between collapsing public trust in most institutions in American public life and sustained trust in the military unbalanced the civil–military relationship somewhat, increasing both reliance by politicians on the military to create support for their policies and creeping resentment by those politicians of the military for it.

The National Security Act of 1947 put in place the organizational structure for a peacetime military and intelligence force. Its intellectual architects were Senator Harry Truman and General George Marshall, who as early as 1942 saw the advantages of deeper and more routine coordination between the services – Senator Truman even writing that it was a necessity to prevent another Pearl Harbor.[1] The Act created the Air Force as a separate service, protected the Marine Corps as an independent service, eliminated the War and Navy Departments by unifying the two into a Department of Defense led by a civilian cabinet secretary, and created the joint chiefs of staff as a corporate body (which did not include the commandant of the Marine Corps).

Both the civilian and military leadership of the Army and Navy opposed the reining in of their autonomy (the Navy Department decrying "sacrifices of sound administrative autonomy and essential service morale").[2] Each of the services had independent plans and congressional allies who advanced them across a year of hearings and lobbied intensively to shape the legislation – so openly that it drew a public rebuke from President Truman. While antagonism was fierce as the services jostled for advantage, the maneuvering was only among the services and, as prior to policy being established, was fair game.[3] Legislation on the president's terms passed both houses of Congress on a bipartisan voice vote.[4]

Breaking the Color Barrier

> It is hereby declared to be the policy of the President that there shall be equality of treatment and opportunity for all persons in the armed services without regard to race, color, religion or national origin. This policy shall be put into effect as rapidly as possible, having due regard to the time required to effectuate any necessary changes without impairing efficiency or morale.

So reads Executive Order 9981, which President Truman signed on July 26, 1948. Integration of the American military trailed by eighty years the Fourteenth Amendment but preceded by at least twenty years an end to the abridgment of the privileges or immunities of Black citizens of the United States. Truman had to advance the policy by executive order because Congress refused to enact the recommendations of the President's Committee on Civil Rights, and, with the Democratic national nominating convention looming, Truman could not risk civil rights activist Philip Randolph staging a march to encourage draft resistance.

People of color had served in the American military from its inception. The first American killed in the Revolutionary War, Crispus Attucks, was a Black man, and more than five thousand Blacks fought in the Continental forces, mostly in integrated units.[5] During the War of 1812, General Andrew Jackson promised but did not provide freedom and equal pay to the 900 Black men who fought in the battle of New Orleans. More than 200,000 Black men fought in the Union forces during the Civil War, with a full quarter of sailors in the Navy being Black.[6] US forces contained more than 400,000 Black servicemen in World War I.[7]

Attitudes among their white counterparts varied widely. When during the War of 1812 Commodore Matthew Perry complained of "the motley set of blacks" assigned him on Lake Erie, his commanding officer, Commodore Isaac Chauncey, replied, "I have yet to learn that the color of skin, or the cut and trimmings of the coat, can affect a man's qualifications and usefulness. I have nearly fifty blacks on board this ship, and many of them are among my best men, and I presume that you will find them as good and useful as any on board your vessel."[8]

The Army created all-Black regiments in 1866: the 9th and 10th Cavalry and the 24th and 25th Infantry. Three of those four Buffalo Soldiers' regiments would charge up San Juan Hill with Teddy Roosevelt's Rough Riders, one soldier even being awarded the Medal of Honor. Typical of praise offered by some white officers of their Black soldiers was this award citation from Ranald Mackenzie, who commanded the integrated 4th Cavalry during the Remolina raid into Mexico: "Seminole Negro Adam Payne for habitual courage. This man has, I believe, more cool daring than any scout I have ever known."[9]

The backlash against Reconstruction, the persistence of racism, and the Supreme Court's "separate but equal" decision in 1896 dramatically reduced opportunities for African Americans. By World War I, a scant 1 percent of Navy sailors were Black, and they were restricted to menial positions. Harassment of 24th Infantry soldiers stationed in Houston was so intolerable that they rioted, killing fifteen civilians. Despite Black soldiers comprising 11 percent of the force, General Jack Pershing restricted Black units from combat assignments. He seconded them to French forces, where they served with distinction. One of those units, the 369th Infantry Regiment, called the Harlem Hellfighters, had more time on the front lines than any other American outfit. A million Black American men and women served during World War II, often with valor in units such as the Tuskegee Airmen, but they returned home to find little changed.

The service secretaries of both the Army and the Navy, and the service chiefs of the Army, Navy, and Marine Corps all opposed Truman's executive order, expressing concern about unit cohesion and civilians forcing the military to the forefront of a divisive social issue that would distract from its mission. Secretary of Defense James Forrestal (and his successors Louis Johnson and George Marshall) and Air Force Secretary Stuart Symington were advocates; if Air Force Chief Hoyt Vandenberg had concerns, they are unrecorded, and he pushed support for the policy through the chain of command so that it progressed "rapidly, smoothly and virtually without incident."[10]

Secretary of the Army Kenneth Royall did not consider "separate but equal" discriminatory and argued against the military being used for "social experimentation."[11] He was replaced for being an impediment to implementation of the president's order.[12] Army Chief of Staff Omar Bradley said the Army would have to retain segregation "as long as it was the national pattern." Bradley also said he opposed making the Army an instrument of social change in areas of the country which still rejected integration.[13] When the comments set off a press furor, General Bradley apologized to the president for undercutting established policy.

Bradley's successor, General Joseph Lawton Collins, and senior officers almost across the board argued tenaciously to maintain segregation and limit Black enlistments.[14] But the argument the Army took to support segregation (that states could not decide a matter of national policy for Guard units) would become the lever to advance integration. The Army retained a cap of 10 percent Black enlistment until 1950, but the urgency of personnel needs once the Korean War began – doubling the size of the Army in five months and creating the necessity for individual replacements in combat units – pushed the Army into acceptance of full integration in 1954.[15] When it happened, it proceeded almost without incident.[16]

The Navy complied in policy but not in practice, claiming progress despite the number of Black sailors prevented from becoming officers or non-commissioned officers and assigned only to kitchen, laundry, or valet duties. As Morris MacGregor's study of racial integration concludes, "while solemnly proclaiming its belief in the principle of nondiscrimination, the service had continued to sanction practices that limited integration and equal opportunity to a degree consistent with its racial tradition and manpower needs."[17]

The commandant of the Marine Corps, General Clifton Cates, defended segregation in 1950, saying the Corps "could not be an agency for experimentation in civil liberty without detriment to its ability to maintain the efficiency and the high state of readiness so essential to national defense," and sustained restrictions in enlistment, assignment, and promotion. Like Bradley, Cates objected to the military having to lead in changing the custom. But the cost and inefficiency of separate training and the need to rapidly expand the force due to fighting in Korea drove integration.[18] The combat performance of Black soldiers in Korea brought over Marine officers as supporters of integration, and General Cates officially announced a policy of overall integration in December of 1951.[19] Within six months, Commandant Lemuel Shepherd reported: "it was believed to be an accomplished fact at this time."[20] The number of Black Marines increased more than tenfold, to 17,000, between 1949 and 1953.

In the view of the DOD's Personnel Policy Board in 1949, "the Army had a poor policy satisfactorily administered, while the Navy had an acceptable policy poorly administered."[21] Defense secretaries and the President's Committee on Equal Treatment and Opportunity in the Armed Services pushed unstintingly using time-honored bureaucratic tactics (including threats to let Congress legislate a solution) to force a contested retreat on the Army and Navy without provoking a politically costly revolt.

In 1948, the Air Force was the only service actively supporting desegregation. Secretary Stuart Symington made the argument one of efficiency, but limited integration initially, partly to keep congressional support. To give a sense of congressional attitudes, Senator Richard Russell (D-GA), with unanimous support of the Senate Armed Services Committee, amended the defense bill to allow any white service member to refuse to serve in an integrated unit.[22] Yet the Air Force policy opened all jobs in all fields to Black servicemen. Symington and Vandenberg's leadership resulted by 1952 in fully integrated manpower practices, housing, schools, stores, and recreation facilities, often ignoring local segregation laws.[23]

The Army, Navy, and Marine Corps were clearly engaged in what Peter Feaver terms shirking – stalling compliance with civilian political directive.[24] It took years to bring their practices into alignment, and it would likely have taken even longer had the fierce necessity of wartime manpower needs not driven acceptance in front-line units. But, while there was considerable resistance to the president's policy, there was concordance in the services between civilian and military leaders: opposition from the Army, Navy, and Marine Corps, support in the Air Force. And, as the system is designed to work, the secretary of defense as a cabinet official enforced the president's policy on the department and fended off congressional action.[25]

It took until 1961 before a Black officer commanded a destroyer escort; racism remained so pervasive in the Navy that there were race riots aboard ships during the Vietnam War. Despite presidential authority, senior civilians in the Department of Defense pushing the policy through the bureaucracy, recognition by combat commanders of the value of Black service, and the advantages of compliance in the hierarchy of the military, racism remained a serious problem because it remained a serious problem in American society. In 1967 there were more than 150 riots in American cities touched off by white police treatment of Black citizens. The Department of Defense had to create a military school system to shield children of military servicemen and women from discrimination and abuse in the American south.

However, the arguments of Generals Bradley and Cates against pushing the military to advance policies that the broader American society has not adopted have continuing resonance. There is a tendency to use the success of desegregation in the military as justification for other socially progressive policies. Doing so exacerbates the civil–military divide, as many in uniform conclude that broader society fails to understand the exigencies of military life and is pushing onto them policies that civilians can avoid and that makes even more difficult the hard work the military does for the country.

A demonstration of the discipline in the American military that tempts elected leaders to propagate social policies by using the military as a vanguard can be seen in the 1957 integration of public schools in Little Rock, Arkansas. Governor Orval Faubus deployed Arkansas National Guard troops to prevent enrolled Black students from attending the high school. President Eisenhower privately advised the governor to change the Guard orders to "continue to preserve order but allow the Negro children to attend."[26] When Faubus failed to do so, Eisenhower declared Arkansas in violation of the Constitution, invoked Title 10 authority under the Insurrection Act, and federalized the entire Arkansas National Guard, taking them out of the governor's control and removing them from the equation.[27]

Eisenhower deployed a thousand troops from the 101st Airborne along with troops from that same Arkansas National Guard to protect Black students in the face of vitriolic abuse by white citizens opposed to integration. He insisted they were there "not to enforce integration but to prevent opposition by violence to order of the court."[28] The very soldiers whom the governor had deployed to prevent integration were ordered to enable it, and did so. Soldiers were stationed at Little Rock High School for the remainder of the school year; Governor Faubus closed all four of Little Rock's high schools the following year rather than allow integration to proceed. During a stalemate between federal and state civilian authorities, American soldiers stood obedient to civilian control in complex circumstances and in the face of public opposition.

Armageddon

After the 1949 Soviet nuclear test, President Truman initiated the review of strategic objectives and plans that would become NSC 68; President Eisenhower's Project Solarium validated the approach.[29] Military strategy placed main but not sole reliance on nuclear forces that could substitute for conventional forces.[30] In both the Truman and Eisenhower administrations, thinking about nuclear weapons was shaped predominantly by military leaders who had fought in World War II; nuclear operations were more "the result of war planning than of deterrent planning."[31] Each service developed independent target lists, the Navy jealously guarding its autonomy from the Air Force.

Civil–military friction was over the size and role of conventional forces, President Eisenhower demanding of his military leaders "why we should put a single nickel into anything but developing our capacity to diminish the enemy's capacity for nuclear attack."[32] The president believed warfare in the nuclear age dramatically reduced the role of conventional forces, since troop concentrations, staging areas, and points of embarkation were ideal targets for atomic weapons.[33] In Eisenhower's view, Army units that were not forward-deployed as trip wires for nuclear escalation would remain in the continental US to restore order in American cities after the nuclear strikes that would comprise a US–Soviet war.[34]

Army Chiefs of Staff General Matthew Ridgway and his successor, General Maxwell Taylor, fundamentally opposed this reduced role for the Army.[35] The Army and Navy staged Operation Sagebrush in 1955 with 140,000 troops and airmen to demonstrate that nuclear weapons use would increase manpower because of higher casualty rates, greater depth of operations, and contested logistics.[36] General Ridgway testified repeatedly before Congress that the conventional force reductions jeopardized the Army's ability to carry out its missions.[37] General Taylor assessed the Army needed to be more than doubled, to twenty-eight divisions.

While the Eisenhower administration reconsidered its reliance on nuclear forces in 1957 and again in 1958, the president rejected Ridgway and Taylor's alternative as too expensive.[38] General Taylor reluctantly restructured forces into pentomic divisions, but both he and General Ridgway would later become even greater public critics. Taylor's book *Uncertain Trumpet*, written after his retirement and castigating both the strategy and force reductions of Eisenhower's administration, would become the template for the buildup of the Army during the Kennedy administration and see Taylor recalled to active duty to become Kennedy's military representative (essentially the role Admiral Leahy performed in the Roosevelt White House).

The Army did to President Eisenhower what the Navy did to President Truman in the Admirals' Revolt: its officers disagreed profoundly with the president's strategy and force structure decisions, argued unsuccessfully against policy internally, testified before Congress in opposition while in military service, and became even more active political partisans upon retirement than did Navy leaders. But in neither case did the military's lobbying effort produce different strategy or force structure decisions. The Navy's objections in 1949 have received more attention than have the Army's in the 1950s for two reasons: the ominous titling by *Time* magazine of the Navy effort a "revolt" and the greater difficulty for the Army in the mid-1950s of overriding the credibility of a president associated with military victory in World War II.

Army end strength wasn't the only civil–military issue associated with nuclear weapons, however. Extending civilian oversight fully into the details of nuclear planning would take another forty years.

General Curtis LeMay had moved the Strategic Air Command headquarters to Omaha, Nebraska, in 1948 in part to base nuclear-capable bombers deep in the geographic heartland of the country but also to reduce civilian oversight by being far from Washington, DC. Military leaders considered civilian oversight an "unnecessary, unwanted, and illegitimate intrusion on military prerogatives."[39] Civilian discomfort with the military's exclusive domain of nuclear planning is famously summed up by one of Secretary McNamara's "whiz kids" rebutting an officer's argument with "General, I've fought just as many nuclear wars as you have."[40]

The vexing dilemmas of warfare in the nuclear age pushed the Kennedy administration to seek limited response options and drive into the Single Integrated Operational Plan (SIOP) withholds for urban and allied targets – an important shift from the Truman and Eisenhower strategic bombing approach toward targeting narrower military capabilities.[41] But by 1973 both the pre-emption of Soviet nuclear forces and counterforce targeting were rendered impossible when the Soviets developed survivable second-strike forces.

The Carter administration's review of targeting policy shifted away from a long-war focus on preventing economic recovery (famously ridiculed in the movie *Dr Strangelove* as the mine shaft gap) toward attempting to target what Soviet leaders considered essential to fighting and winning a nuclear war. The process revealed that, because the military was still wholly in control of targeting, civilian policy directives were not being adequately reflected in war plans. As late as 1985, the president and secretary of defense believed they had nuclear options that did not exist.[42]

Part of the problem was that, absent civil–military debate and review over targeting, the military often didn't understand the intent of policy. But, in addition, a major driver of the extent of the nuclear target set was the inter-service tacit agreement that any nuclear strike had to involve all three legs of the nuclear triad: Air Force bombers and land-based missiles plus Navy submarine-launched missiles. The involvement of civilians in the review of targets enabled a 40 percent reduction in the weapons requirement by surfacing over-coverage, under-coverage, and tacit agreements.

The Army's efforts to reclaim both strategy and force structure restrictions and the extension of civilian oversight in nuclear strategy and planning required the military to adopt policies they found deeply unsettling to their military judgment. In both cases they tried to establish their judgment as superior to that of their civilian leadership. In the case of the Army, their efforts were stemmed by the president's authority – formal in setting the budget, informal in sustaining congressional support to fund it – and by his experiential advantage trumping theirs. In the case of nuclear strategy and forces, adding civilian involvement both ensured civilian policy was reflected in planning and objectively improved the military plan at lower resourcing.

Quarantine

The Cuban missile crisis is the closest the US has come to nuclear war. President Kennedy's war council famously excluded the military leaders other than the president's former White House military advisor, now chairman of the joint chiefs of staff, General Maxwell Taylor. Extensive military plans and preparations were undertaken, but the joint chiefs were not included in policy deliberations.[43]

On October 14, 1962, a U-2 overflight of Cuba revealed the construction of Soviet missile installations. Military leaders advised a strike of five hundred sorties to ensure all the missile sites and retaliatory assets were targeted.[44] The president's men wanted "a middle course between inaction and battle" and settled on a maritime blockade, cagily termed a quarantine to elude the fact that a blockade is an act of war.[45] While the joint chiefs were not included in the executive committee, President Kennedy did meet separately with them to hear their case for the strike option. He simply wasn't persuaded by it.

President Kennedy consulted congressional leaders and made a solemn address to the nation explaining the discovery and the quarantine and emphasizing that any missile launched from Cuba would be considered as an attack by the Soviet Union. There ensued two weeks of highly secretive negotiations conducted through informal political channels that struck the deal of removing Soviet missiles from Cuba and US missiles from Turkey and the commitment by the US not to invade Cuba.

In the meantime, however, the Air Force carried out intelligence overflights and put nuclear bombers on airborne alert, the Navy effected the quarantine, and the Army and Marine Corps prepared for invasion. Military preparations for both offensive strikes and defensive protections were advanced; to give the crisis the perilousness it merits, the leading participants believed war was imminent. President Kennedy made numerous operational decisions that the military vehemently disagreed with, but no decision by the president was either refused or evaded. Objections weren't leaked to the news media or Congress. Military leaders continued to advocate for a policy the president did not choose, but the president's policy succeeded.[46]

Still, bitterness ensued and trust was shattered (if it had ever existed) between the Kennedy administration's best and brightest and most of the military leadership; deep-seated antipathy characterized civil–military relations from that time forward.[47] Civilian leaders seemed to want more than just compliance with political direction; they wanted agreement with their perspective, which the military leadership other than General Taylor did not share. What President Kennedy concluded from the crisis was that "the first advice I'm going to give my successor is to watch the generals and avoid feeling that just because they were military men their opinions on military matters were worth a damn."[48]

But the Cuban missile crisis wasn't a civil–military crisis. The president can organize his advisory councils in any way he wants; there's no constitutional or statutory requirement for him to include military leaders in his policy deliberations. President Kennedy did have military advice from General Taylor, who was the only uniformed officer with whom the president was comfortable and who supported the civilians' efforts to establish a wider range of choice in warfare than nearly all the experienced military believed possible. Kennedy gave them opportunities for counsel and harnessed their military preparations as political leverage but didn't take their advice – and his political judgment was borne out.

The Things They Carried

The Vietnam War wasn't the first war the United States lost (the War of 1812 bears that distinction), but it was in very many ways the most painful. Commenced during the Kennedy administration, it was mostly fought with mounting effort but without conviction under the Johnson administration. Although more than 16,000 American forces were already in South Vietnam by 1964, and 122 American combat deaths had occurred the previous year, President Johnson campaigned in 1964 insisting: "We are not about to send American boys 9 or 10,000 miles away from home to do what Asian boys ought to be doing for themselves."[49] The number of US troops fighting in Vietnam would rise to 543,000 by 1969, and by the war's end the US would have suffered 58,200 fatal casualties.[50]

As Army chief in the Eisenhower administration, Maxwell Taylor (rather like MacArthur) believed military leaders needed to be punctiliously committed to the Constitution rather than deferential to civilian superiors, but once in the Kennedy White House he considered civil–military relations in crisis; there was a deep distrust between President Kennedy and the military for their complicity in the Bay of Pigs debacle that could be overcome only by "an intimate, easy relationship born of friendship and mutual regard between the president and the Chiefs."[51] Exasperation in the White House at the military's unhelpful recommendations during the Cuban missile crisis led the administration to select military leaders who either supported their approach or were not assertive in shaping policy decisions.[52]

Rather than exercise his role, as Admiral Leahy had, as a conduit and translator between the military and civilian leadership and bringing the two together, General Taylor supplanted the joint chiefs, providing his own judgment rather than either including or representing theirs.[53] When appointed chairman of the joint chiefs of staff, Taylor continued to shield the president from military criticism while limiting the chiefs' involvement in policy deliberations. The military was also aggrieved by Secretary McNamara and his civilian subordinates, who viewed their responsibility solely as forcing the president's political objectives and as a new way of doing defense analysis on a military the civilians perceived as recalcitrant.

The resultant concentration of activity in the White House and the Office of the Secretary of Defense set the pattern of operational involvement for the Vietnam War.[54] H. R. McMaster's detailed review of decision-making about the war exonerates the military leadership, other than Taylor, of blame for the major policy decisions on involvement in Vietnam: backing a coup against the Diem government, overly optimistic evaluations of progress, an intensification of involvement, covert actions in North Vietnam, the ambiguous objective, a graduated escalation, the response to the Gulf of Tonkin attack, troop increases, and the Americanization of the war.[55]

But McMaster condemns military leaders for not publicly disavowing the president and secretary of defense. He believes that the president and secretary of defense lied to the American public, and the military ought to have publicly denounced their civilian leadership as misrepresenting the conduct of the war. And there was surely regret by many of the architects of the war, both civilian and military. Military leaders such as the Army chief of staff, General Harold Johnson, later bitterly regretted they were not more forceful in objecting to President Johnson and Secretary McNamara's choices.[56] But their regrets are not for the same reasons, or for the reasons McMaster portrays.

McMaster's central condemnation is that, "uninterested in the Chiefs' advice, but unwilling to risk their disaffection, Johnson preserved a facade of consultation, concealed the finality of his decisions on Vietnam policy, and promised that more forceful actions against the North might be taken in the future."[57] But another way of saying that is that the president (and the secretary) gave the chiefs the formal opportunity to make their case in policy formation, declined to adopt their advice because it wasn't consistent with his domestic priorities, kept his own counsel, provided the resources their military judgment advised to make the strategy work, and was open to reconsidering his decision in the future. All of which are the elected leader's prerogatives.

Dereliction of Duty is questionable as a guide to civil–military policy. It is a more modern version of the Prussian stab in the back excuse but blaming the top military leaders, as well as the president and secretary of defense, for betraying the fighting men and the American people. McMaster argues that "the war in Vietnam was not lost in the field, nor was it lost on the front pages of *The New York Times*, or on the college campuses. It was lost in Washington, D.C., even before Americans assumed sole responsibility for the fighting in 1965 and before they realized the country was at war."[58] He is vituperative about President Johnson prioritizing domestic policy goals over the war he inherited from his predecessor and misrepresenting the costs of the war. But those are the president's prerogatives, both to determine what proportion of the nation's effort to commit to the conflict and to craft a political strategy for sustaining it. What McMaster blames the military leadership for is attempting to make a politically selected bad strategy successful. He impugns them with bartering their support for the president's war to gain increased budgets and force structure.[59]

McMaster's preferred posture for the military was to create a unified JCS position in opposition to the civilian leadership and publicly object to the president and secretary of defense's characterization of the war.[60] But the chiefs had numerous opportunities to provide their counsel during policy formation and internally even after policy had been decided by the president. Since the time of George Marshall it has been the norm that, if given the chance to provide their advice within the system, senior members of an administration to include military officers resist public criticism of the policy on which the president decides. Because the president has a right to receive counsel in private that he does not take, and only the president has the right and responsibility to aggregate preferences for the American people.

Nor does the US military have a tradition of resigning in protest at policy, because that also undermines civilian control.[61] Even the best military advice might be wrong or might be beyond what a president wants to risk or commit. Yet again, Peter Feaver captures the decision rule: political leaders have a right to be wrong.[62] But the belief is widespread in the military that the chiefs ought to have contested more vociferously the president and secretary's characterizations, worked end-runs to the Congress or internal bureaucratic feints to prevent the policies being enacted, or leaked their views to the press.[63]

It is not a dereliction of duty not to sabotage the civilian leadership's policy. McMaster's recommendation fails the George Marshall test; it would set military officers up to pass public judgment on a president's weighting of domestic and foreign demands that few genuinely have either expertise or authority to judge.[64] It would collapse civilian trust and probably lead to the exclusion of military leaders from policy councils – which would likely produce even worse military outcomes for the nation.

Given General Taylor's centrality in the disaffected relationship between the civilians and military, what *Dereliction of Duty* describes is less a civil–military problem than just a badly functioning administration.[65] The fundamental friction between most of the military leadership and the civilians was a disagreement over "graduated response" in warfare. Most military leaders – especially those with extensive combat experience – remained deeply skeptical of the limited uses of military force. But it also was not their decision to make.

The administration vetted and selected for promotion senior officers who were either advocates of their graduated pressure approach or were considered socially and politically comfortable with the Kennedy, McNamara, and Johnson circles of advisors. And the services themselves considered those officers capable, otherwise they would never have achieved their exalted ranks. But the Vietnam War also illustrates the price political leaders pay for politicking around military advice: despite its many civil rights and social policy achievements, the war was the ruin of Lyndon Johnson's presidency.

The End of Compulsion

The draft has been used sparingly in America because it was always unpopular; Alexis de Tocqueville reports:

> In America conscription is unknown; they enroll men there for money. Forced recruitment is so contrary to the ideas and so foreign to the habits of the people of the United States that I doubt that one would ever introduce it into the laws . . . I have heard American statesmen avow that the Union will have trouble maintaining its rank on the seas if it does not resort to Impressment or to maritime conscription, but the difficulty is to oblige the people, who govern, to suffer impressment.[66]

Unless conscription is universal, fairness is a problem. But conscription in America has never been universal – the economy needs to work to support war efforts, and some people are exempted for family, religious, or health reasons. New York City was aflame for three days and more than a hundred people died in 1863 as fury erupted at the Civil War levy; there was anger that Black men, for whose freedom the war was being waged, were not subject to conscription and resentment at those wealthy enough to pay the $300 substitution fee. Twenty-one thousand Americans were punished for desertion in World War II, the war with the greatest public support. The peacetime draft was permissive; in 1958, 57 percent of potential inductees were rejected, nearly half for mental unfitness.[67] But, as the Vietnam War drove the need for forces, the services deepened reliance on draftees.

President Nixon campaigned in 1968 on ending the draft, saying that

> a system of compulsory service that arbitrarily selects some and not others simply cannot be squared with our whole concept of liberty, justice and equality under the law. Its only justification is compelling necessity . . . the

only way to stop the inequities is to stop using the system. It does not work fairly – and, given the facts of American life, it just can't.[68]

Nixon also argued that the nature of war in the nuclear age was unlikely to require mass armies and that "our likely military needs in the future will place a special premium on the services of career soldiers." He equated the draft to "a huge hidden tax" of foregone earnings for draftees. He attested that 93 percent of draftees did not remain in service, thus taking the $6,000 of investment in them out of the force, and that the benefits accorded a volunteer would retain more recruits.[69] And he argued it would increase "morale, efficiency and effectiveness" in the force.

Nixon also addressed what he considered three spurious arguments against a volunteer force: "The first is that a volunteer army would be a black army, so it is a scheme to use Negroes to defend a white America. The second is that a volunteer army would actually be an army of hired mercenaries. The third is, a volunteer army would dangerously increase military influence in our society." There were numerous arguments that garnered serious policy consideration from within the military against ending conscription. Most concerning was that the threat of being drafted encouraged voluntary enlistments (since by enlisting you could choose your branch of service), a volunteer force might not produce the needed education and skills, it was dramatically less expensive than paying recruits (draftees were paid a third of minimum wage), and service encouraged civic virtue.[70]

The Gates Commission that Nixon established conducted an elegant series of analyses evaluating the "determinants of volunteerism," the potential for alienation of the military from broader society, civil–military relations, the economics of the US labor market, the costs of stable volunteer forces at a variety of end strengths, other countries' experiences, and alternatives to the volunteer force. It identified and rebutted nine explicit objections to their recommendations. While it acknowledged the long-standing American concerns about a standing army becoming a threat, it dismissed the social arguments against a volunteer force:

> an all-volunteer military is not expected to differ significantly from the present mixed force in its size, composition, and relations with civilian society. Its subordination to the nation's political leaders will change not at all. The

belief that volunteers will be more aggressive, will have greater autonomy from the civilian leadership and will exploit international tensions to their own advantage springs, not from any rational evidence, but from an irrational fear of relying on the neglected mechanism of freedom to preserve and protect our nation.[71]

It also analyzed and dismissed concern about Black Americans becoming disproportionately represented in the force.[72]

Weighted with prominent economists such as Milton Friedman and Alan Greenspan, the Gates Commission concluded that, when implicit costs were made transparent, a volunteer force was not more expensive than a conscripted one.[73] It recommended raising military salaries by 67 percent to attract the talent and numbers needed by the services and ending conscription in 1971, provided that the Vietnamization program enabled large-scale reduction in US forces fighting in the war; White House and DOD concerns about the effect on the war persuaded Nixon instead to introduce the changes incrementally.[74]

The Army was the service most affected by the draft, as it had the largest proportion of draftees and was the largest service. Army leaders worried – and still worry – about the viability of what came to be known as the all-volunteer force. Both civilian and military leaders worried pay increases would be insufficient to produce the necessary end strength, and that has proved true: the shrinking of the US military starts with the end of conscription. The Army leadership particularly feared that a volunteer force wouldn't draw from all sectors of society and therefore be less skilled.[75] And, initially, that was the case: the AVF recruits proved less committed, less skilled, poorer, and with greater minority representation.

The Gates Commission substantially underestimated the cost of recruiting and retaining the quality force that the military wanted, and Congress hesitated to incur the costs of making military service genuinely competitive in the labor market. Without the urgency of adaptation during war, it took nearly a decade for the system to adjust and address deficiencies in its recruiting and retention policies, and the military services never adopted many recommendations such as reducing changes of station and eliminating up or out promotions.

Chief of Staff of the Army William Westmoreland ushered in a series of quality of life improvements to make service "more enjoyable, more professionally rewarding, and less burdensome in its impact on our people and their families."[76] Soldiers would henceforth have weekends off, and civilians would be hired for kitchen work and groundskeeping.[77] The 1984 GI Bill, with increased pay, education and health benefits, serious market research, and creative advertising ("Be all you can be" and "The few, the proud, the Marines"), brought into the force the men and women the services wanted. In 1983, quality recruits exceeded recruiting goals, and Secretary of Defense Caspar Weinberger declared victory.

One advantage offered by conscription not taken into account in the Gates Commission analyses is that conscription prepares the society for war. The broad populace has some experience on which to draw but, more importantly, has some familiarity with military issues that is lacking in societies where only a small portion of citizenry do military service.

What is striking is how little vehement dissent there was from military leaders about the dramatic changes which ending conscription entailed. There was no equivalent to the 1959 revolt of the admirals or the Army and Marine Corps' opposition to desegregation, which indicates that the military understood the disadvantages of compulsory military service better even than the politicians, who saw electoral benefit, and the economists evaluating the labor market. Worried as they were, and worried as they remain, military leaders appreciated the advantages of having in the force people who wanted to be there.

Enforced Revolution

The most consequential reform of the modern American military was forced upon it by the Congress. As with so many revolutions, the outcome became far more radical than its original purpose. While the failed operation in 1980 to rescue American hostages being held in Iran, the operational inadequacies of the US military evident during the 1983 invasion of Grenada, and the bombing of US Marine barracks in Lebanon that same year exposed the need for defense reform, what set in motion the most far-reaching revisions to the organization and operation of the US military since the 1947 National Security Act was political concern about the optics of waste, fraud, and abuse of taxpayer dollars by the Defense Department.

The Reagan administration came into office determined to restore American military power, which they claimed during their electoral campaign had atrophied during the Carter administration. They initiated "a free-spending crusade that lifted the nation's military industry out of the doldrums after the Vietnam War."[78] Defense spending had been increasing in the final years under Carter, but the Reagan administration ramped it up to levels not seen since the panicked surge undertaken during the Korean War: defense spending increased by 40 percent in the Reagan years.[79] Per capita defense spending hit $6,000 (at the time of writing it hovers around $2,000).[80] Procurement catapulted from $71.2 billion in 1980 to $147.3 billion.

The creation of the President's Blue-Ribbon Commission on Defense Management, more generally known as the Packard Commission, was precipitated by public outrage over costly defense procurement – but not the big-ticket items such as aircraft carriers or the $2 billion B-2 bomber. What sparked the political momentum for defense reform in the mid-1980s was press reports of $600 toilet seats and $7,000 coffee makers. Set up by President Reagan in 1983 to quell public criticism, the Packard Commission had an expansive mandate, to

> study defense management policies and procedures, including the budget process, the procurement system, legislative oversight, and the organizational and operational arrangements, both formal and informal, of the Office of the Secretary of Defense, the organization of the Joint Chiefs of Staff, the Unified and Specified Command system, the Military Departments, and the Congress.[81]

And it duly recommended significant changes: the adoption of two-year appropriations for defense spending, a requirement for the president to produce a national security strategy, the creation of an undersecretary for acquisition, measures to increase unity of command and the interoperability of forces, the establishment of the chairman of the joint chiefs of staff as the president's principal military advisor, and the operational elevation of combatant commanders.[82] But the Packard Commission was principally interested in financial efficiency and accountability.

It was the Congress that drove the most important and enduring change – military services operating in unison – with its implementation of Packard Commission recommendations.[83] Bipartisan legislation sponsored by Barry Goldwater (R-AZ) and Bill Nichols (D-AL) segregated military responsibilities, giving service chiefs sole responsibility for the recruitment, training, and equipping of the force and reserving operational use of the force to unified and specified combatant commanders, with the chairman of the joint chiefs of staff as the principal military advisor to civilian leaders.[84] The legislation also incentivized development of a unified military perspective by requiring joint professional military education and assignment to a joint staff prior to elevation to flag rank.

What is now the principal operational advantage of US forces was obdurately resisted by the Marine Corps and Navy leaders, who argued it would severely restrict their fighting ability. Complaints about the inadequacy of Defense Department practice didn't cut strictly along civil–military lines, however, because Secretary of Defense Caspar Weinberger opposed the legislation while, after retirement, JCS Chairman David Jones was an ardent advocate for the changes.[85] Nor were attitudes uniform in the Congress: the legislation passed by a single vote. But an activist Congress utilized its constitutional prerogative for raising armies and maintaining navies to dramatically change the US military for the better.

A Riveting Spectacle

The American military created by a volunteer force, intensive professional education and training, significant increases in defense spending during the Reagan administration, and the 1986 Goldwater–Nichols defense reforms was on grandiloquent display during the 1991 Gulf War. In less than six weeks of combat operations – five weeks of air and naval bombardment and just one hundred hours of ground campaigning – the president's objectives were achieved. It was probably also the best-run war the US ever fought: President Bush cut a striking figure declaring that Iraq's invasion of Kuwait "will not stand," the United Nations Security Council gave its endorsement, political objectives were clearly defined and not expanded once success was evident, the president did not just commit the necessary forces but included a wide margin for error, forty-two other countries contributed forces or funds, 956,000 troops were gathered and fought, regional countries participated, and Secretary of State James Baker's diplomacy resulted in the US recouping two-thirds of the cost.[86] The American military was the envy of the world.

The 1991 Gulf War showed the extent to which the US military had reformed and professionalized itself since the end of the Vietnam War and the clumsy operations in Panama and Grenada. It flew 100,000 sorties with only seventy-five aircraft losses. It deployed and supported 540,000 troops to the Middle East. It integrated air, maritime, and land components into large-scale, sequenced, joint operations. It was armed with technological marvels such as precision-guided munitions. US forces suffered only 146 killed in action and 458 wounded. It made television stars of General Norman Schwartkopf, the regional combatant commander for the Middle East, and General Colin Powell, the chairman of the joint chiefs of staff.

While there were occasional problems (Secretary Cheney directing General Powell to confine his comments in NSC meetings to strictly military topics), there was only one civil–military incident of note in the expanse of a military operation involving 500,000 US forces, and it was briskly dispensed with. Air Force Chief of Staff Michael Dugan was fired by Secretary of Defense Cheney for telling reporters the US would target Saddam Hussein and his family, quoted specifically as saying "I don't expect to be concerned" about political constraints. In championing what the Air Force could contribute, General Dugan discussed a range of targeting and seemed to speak for the CENTCOM commander as well when he said: "air power is the only answer that's available to our country."[87] General Dugan wasn't insubordinate; he was parochial and indiscreet. And he was summarily dismissed with no objections from the military.

General Powell had an unusually political career. He'd been a White House fellow in the Office of Management and Budget working for the future defense secretary Frank Carlucci, as a brigadier general he served as the military assistant to the defense secretary Caspar Weinberger, and as a lieutenant general he became President Reagan's national security advisor after the Iran Contra scandal. He fit so comfortably into the Republican establishment that he was seriously considered as President Bush's running mate in 1992 and was encouraged to run for president as the Republican nominee in 1996. Those experiences, and the enhanced authority accorded the chairman of the joint chiefs of staff by the 1986 Goldwater–Nichols reforms, made Powell a particularly influential chairman.[88] Wanting Powell confined by the textbook military norms is the basis for much of the civil–military criticism of his tenure.

While working for Weinberger in 1984, and in response to the attack in Lebanon that killed 241 US Marines, Powell helped craft a set of conditions to be met by political leaders before committing military forces. The Weinberger Doctrine challenges civilian leaders to clarify their goals, commit troops only with the military objective of victory, and endeavor to garner public support. The doctrine drew strong criticism at the time from Weinberger's cabinet colleague Secretary of State George Shultz as enfeebling diplomacy without the threat of military force, but President Reagan endorsed the approach.[89]

As chairman, Powell reformulated the principles to limit the use of military force to

1 when the objective is important and clearly defined;
2 when all nonviolent means have failed;
3 when military force can achieve the desired political objective;
4 when the costs and risk are acceptable, in terms of expected gains;
5 when the consequences have been thought out.

In particular, his criteria were designed to ensure political leaders provided force decisively and overwhelmingly relative to the political objectives – to give a wide margin for error, a substantial buffer against the fog of war.[90] And he staked his claim to set those parameters: "we owe it to the men and women who go in harm's way to make sure that this is always the case and that their lives are not squandered for unclear purposes."[91]

Powell's criteria raised two concerns. First, whether they unduly limited the uses of force important in the post-Cold War security environment, such as intervention in the Balkans. Military historian Hew Strachan castigated Powell: "thanks to Colin Powell and his intellectual legacy, American military thought at the dawn of the new millennium had become quite explicit about its separation from the context of policy."[92] Analysts of both the humanitarian left and the neo-conservative right considered his criteria too constraining.

The decade after the end of the Cold War saw endless debates about appropriate or effective uses of military force, as the circumstances were newly permissive and American military power seemed so dominant. Powell was an active participant in those debates, developing the Base Force to put a floor under force structure and budget cuts and arguing against involvement in the Balkan wars, Somalia, and Haiti. So the first line of argument about the Powell criteria is a substantive one about strategy for the use of force.

There was particular objection to Powell publishing his opposition to intervention in the Balkans in October of 1992, because the issue was being actively contested by the candidates in the presidential election. Powell argued: "President Bush, more than any other recent President, understands the proper use of military force. In every instance, he has made sure that the objective was made clear and that we knew what we were getting into."[93] While Powell was supporting the president's policy, he did so in a partisan way in the heat of a presidential campaign. His view would be understood as that of the military as an institution supporting the Republican candidate. He also slapped back at his critics: "So you bet I get nervous when so-called experts suggest that all we need is a little surgical bombing or a limited attack. When the desired result isn't obtained, a new set of experts then comes forward with talk of a little escalation. History has not been kind to this approach . . . we have learned the proper lessons of history, even if some journalists have not." The edge of dismissiveness in Powell's comments gives a sense of the resentments of both civilians and the military as the military's approval ascended far beyond that of politicians, journalists, and even scholars in the heady days of American power at the end of the Cold War.

The second criticism of the Powell criteria was the inappropriateness of military leaders establishing conditions by which their civilian superiors would be constrained.[94] Russell Weigley, author of *The American Way of War*, argued:

> General Powell's intervention in the policy debate would have been proper only if he was voicing a professional military judgment to the effect that his knowledge as a military expert assured him that limited military intervention was incapable of attaining the desired objectives. He was doing no such thing. His opinions in the case were much more political than professional.[95]

But the best strategists agree that "a political sensibility is an essential part of a professional competence, enabling officers to understand the contexts in which they operate, and how the way they act affects these contexts."[96] Powell's diversity of political experience did give him broader scope than most military leaders. If he had been only national security advisor and never chairman of the joint chiefs of staff or a senior military officer, there would have been interest in his views on what would make a military operation successful. To limit him to the constraints applied to military officers who hadn't had his broadening experiences is to undervalue what he as an individual could contribute.

The second attenuating condition is that, twenty years into an all-volunteer force that was small relative to the population, there were few civilian leaders with experience or expertise in military issues. As the American model of service extended further in time from conscription, the military began to believe it had a responsibility to educate both political leaders and the public on military issues. That view was hotly contested, military historian Russell Weigley arguing that the appropriate role for the military is "silent support of civilian decisions at the intersection of policy, diplomacy, and strategy."[97] But Weigley's strictures would leave the military only with mute obedience, the very unbalancing of the American system that McMaster argues produced a war-losing strategy in Vietnam.

Moreover, military officers spend about a quarter of a twenty-year career in professional education. They study warfare, history, and strategy in ways that most civilians – even those in senior national security policymaking positions – do not. And, as conscription receded, an American public little exposed to those issues came to be deferential to military explanations. It is common for 30 to 40 percent of civilian respondents to have no opinion on military issues and to look to military leaders and veterans for understanding.[98] Powell was responding to that.

Powell did view himself as representing the military's views about military issues – not just operations, but its culture and values too. He considered those as subjects the public and civilian leaders knew little about. He would argue that he was in bounds because, although he actively worked to shape policy, he did so before policy had been decided upon and with partners on both sides of the political aisle. For example, on the policy that would become "Don't Ask, Don't Tell," he worked closely with the Democratic chairman of the Senate Armed Services Committee, Sam Nunn (D-GA), before President Clinton took office to get legislation in place before the president could issue an executive order.

Powell took that approach on two issues that generated considerable civil–military friction: the assignment of women to combat units and homosexuals serving openly in the military. On both those issues, he worked behind the scenes with the Congress between President Clinton's election in 1992 and his inauguration in January 1993 to build support in Congress for what he represented as the military's view. He was accused of "leading a military preemptive assault upon the president-elect's campaign promise to lift the military's ban against homosexuals in uniform, an assault that persisted after the inauguration of President Clinton on 20 January 1993 . . . General Powell followed the partisan effort with a military resistance against the promised change, again veiling what was in fact a highly political stance in the guise of professional military judgment."[99] He succeeded in forestalling both policies. But he also enforced the boundary between acceptable pre-decisional activism and the discipline demanded of the military once civilian leaders made their decision. When, during a speech at the National Defense University, he was asked by an officer opposed to serving with homosexuals what to do if the president lifted the ban on homosexual service, Powell was unequivocal: the officer could either salute and carry out the policy or resign his commission.

Public adulation of the military was amplified by the fact that public confidence in just about every other political, professional, and civic institution of American life collapsed at about the same time. While public trust has never been particularly high – Americans, after all, have a government founded by people who distrust government – trust in the federal government fell precipitously in the mid-1960s and in 2023 averaged around 35 percent.[100] And they trust Congress, the judiciary, and politicians even less.[101] However, confidence in the military has been sustained at well over 50 percent.[102] The gap between the military as consistently the most trusted institution in American life and the abjectness of public attitudes toward politicians and the federal government has sent politicians scurrying to hide behind uniforms; in many cases they resent having to do so.

Some of the criticism of Powell can be attributed to discomfort with the newly expanded powers Goldwater–Nichols vested in the chairman of the joint chiefs of staff. But General Powell also aggressively used those powers and his political celebrity, especially after the 1991 Gulf War, in ways that did constrain civilian leaders' political running room. As Weigley complains, Powell was able to "use his uniform as an instrument of advantage in a policy debate."[103] Civilians had used Powell's uniform to quell criticism of the Reagan White House after Iran Contra, and Powell used it to constrain what he believed were bad policies in the making by civilian leaders. Given the political salience of his views, and the canny effectiveness of his tradecraft in working to get policy outcomes, it is perhaps not surprising that no president since has selected so powerful a chairman of the joint chiefs of staff.

The Long Wars

The volunteer force was not designed to fight long wars. As crafted by the veterans of the Vietnam War, the Army and Air Force were structured to require the commander in chief to call up reservists to deploy and sustain the active-duty component. The design was both a practicality of structuring to put expensive but rarely used elements in the reserve component and a challenge to civilian leaders to incur the political cost of calling up reservists in order to go to war. In the wars of the twenty-first century, that constraint has been erased; yet, despite changing the terms of reserve service, there was almost no protest or refusal to deploy – less, in fact, for the 2003 war in Iraq than there had been during the 1991 Gulf War.

But objections to the invasion of Iraq came from within the active-duty military and the veterans' community. Whether to conduct a preventative war is a strategy question, properly understood as the president's prerogative. A panoply of high-ranking veterans advised publicly against going to war. The initial military concerns in policy councils about the degree of risk implicit in the war plan were substantive, and a reminder that the US military passes the crucial civil–military test of carrying out to the best of their abilities policies they don't agree with.

Secretary of Defense Donald Rumsfeld was a two-time defense secretary, former White House chief of staff, successful business turnaround specialist, and bully. He was notorious for issuing "snowflakes" (so named because they fluttered down in profusion), random queries addressed several levels down into the staff with no contextualizing of why the question was being posed or action ordered. He likewise injected chaos into the military planning system in the run-up to the war by going through the military's time-phased force deployment data (TPFDD) and eliminating elements he considered unnecessary. The TPFDD isn't a policy document; it ensures, for example, that port handlers are on site before ships arrive. This is what the US military is brilliant at. Rumsfeld ardently believed the precision and range of US weaponry, coupled with increased surveillance and communications connectivity, had transformed military operations, allowing those to substitute for mass of forces.[104] By meddling in the TPFDD, Secretary Rumsfeld was not only creating havoc in the planning process but, even more importantly, was not spending his time doing the work that only the secretary of defense can do – ensuring the president's political objectives translate into military operations.

Secretary Rumsfeld and CENTCOM commander General Tommy Franks produced a war plan commencing with a three-brigade "rolling start" into Iraq.[105] The joint staff's director of operations (J-3) resigned, and the joint staff's director of plans (J-7) attempted to do so (he was dissuaded by the director of the joint staff) and aggressively alerted the NSC to raise alarm. The chief of staff of the Army, General Eric Shinseki, asked to replace the CENTCOM director of war plans with an officer more resistant to the risks Rumsfeld was building into the plan. He also dented the Bush administration's credibility in the run-up to the war by testifying before Congress that the troop to population ratio employed to size forces in the Balkans would suggest a dramatically larger invasion force than the Pentagon was telegraphing.[106]

General Shinseki was also the only military leader who voiced their concerns directly to the president. Before the military commanders' conference with the president in the winter of 2003, NSC staff advised President Bush to directly address military concerns. Secretary Rumsfeld intervened before the meeting, characterizing military concerns as antiquated and asking for the president's support. President Bush opened the meeting with the joint chiefs and combatant commanders by praising Secretary Rumsfeld and then asking whether anyone had concerns about the war plan for Iraq. This obviously prejudiced responses: the commandant of the Marine Corps and chief of staff of the Air Force both replied that their service could carry out everything assigned to them in the war plan. Only the chief of staff of the Army voiced concerns about the plan, detailing several. The president seemed not to know how to reply – just thanked General Shinseki and moved on. If the commander in chief had asked: "Do any of you share these concerns?" or "Don, that sounds reasonable, why don't we resolve those problems before this kicks off?," a much better outcome would have been possible. But the failure wasn't down to Bush alone – the room was full of civilian experts in positions responsible for ensuring the president's political objectives get translated into military plans that achieve the objectives. Everyone in that room except General Shinseki failed the country that day.

But there was no clear civil–military divide over the 2003 Iraq War; as with the Kennedy administration, the Bush administration, at least in its first term, just functioned poorly. Military leaders such as General Franks and the chairman of the joint chiefs of staff, General Richard Myers, supported Secretary Rumsfeld's approach to "transformation." The initial months of the invasion seemed to bear out Secretary Rumsfeld's approach.[107] Until the insurgency.[108] But disbanding the Iraqi army and allowing a broad de-Baathification removed bases of potential support the US military had anticipated relying on for keeping order.

While the military was divided over war policies and restrained by the norm of accepting decided policy and making it work, the veteran community was active in condemning the management of the war. Former CENTCOM commander General Tony Zinni and the J-3 who had resigned, Lieutenant General Greg Newbold, publicly called for Secretary Rumsfeld's firing, as did many others.[109]

Disentangling active duty from veteran activism is difficult, largely because the public makes no distinction, but also because veterans' political weight comes from being perceived as a proxy for attitudes of the active-duty force, so they often purposely conflate the two to maximize their perceived authority. Restrictions on the military to prevent them overtaking civilian authority do not constrain the political activity of Americans when they have left military service: the other term for veteran is citizen. The person in the Bush administration who best understood the latitude of veteran activism was President Bush himself. When cautioned by his chief of staff and national security advisor that he ought not fire Secretary Rumsfeld for at least six months because of civil–military concerns resulting from veteran activism, the president replied that veterans should be treated like any other political pressure group.[110]

Changing the strategy to surge forces in Iraq in 2007 was likewise contentious: military leaders supported the approach (in some cases grudgingly), but it was bitterly contested politically.[111] The counterinsurgency concept had emerged from civilian analysts outside the government and the bottom-up experience of Marines and soldiers fighting in Iraq. The Bush White House, discredited from having managed the war badly and having replaced Secretary Rumsfeld with an Iraq War critic (during confirmation hearings, Robert Gates had acknowledged the US was losing the war) only after a disastrous showing in the 2006 congressional election, had the political leadership in the White House sending the military to Capitol Hill to make the public case. The primary fissure over the surge wasn't civil–military, it was civil–civil.[112]

Where civil–military friction was palpable was over President Obama's decision to withdraw from Iraq. The military had persevered through confused political direction both from Washington and from the Coalition Provisional Authority in Iraq; there was inadequate resourcing for expanding missions, and in Fallujah they experienced the fiercest combat since Vietnam.[113] The strategy and additional forces from the surge, coupled with the Sunni "awakening," broke the back of the insurgency by 2009, but Barack Obama had won the Democratic nomination for president, deriding those who'd supported the war and pledging to end it.[114] The Bush administration strengthened Obama's case by agreeing in August of 2008 to withdraw coalition forces by 2011. Despite anguish and specific warnings from intelligence analysts and the military, there were no military resignations and no hesitance in carrying out either commander in chief's policy of bringing to an end American military involvement in Iraq.

There was also civil–military friction over what to do about Iran's advancing nuclear programs, together with its destabilization of governments in the region, threat to Israel, arming and funding of proxy terrorist organizations, interdiction of shipping in the Straits of Hormuz, and appalling domestic human rights record. The Bush administration dismissed one CENTCOM commander, Admiral William Fallon, for publicly opposing war with Iran, and the Obama administration dismissed another, General James Mattis, for pressing (much like Powell) the civilian leadership to consider the consequences of their declaratory policy.[115] Demonstrating just how deeply engrained the rule of "serving at the pleasure of the President" is, in neither case were there objections from the Pentagon, although both Fallon and Mattis were venerated within the military.

The war in Afghanistan wasn't freighted with all the concerns the Iraq War had raised, but it, too, created civil–military disputes as the war dragged on inconclusively. President Obama had attempted to balance withdrawing from Iraq with a surge in Afghanistan, but disputes between the White House and the military leaking into public (which the president's staff accused the military of having done) put the White House resentfully on the defensive.[116] General Stanley McChrystal's *Commander's Initial Assessment* was that

> the overall situation is deteriorating. We face not only a resilient and growing insurgency; there is also a crisis of confidence among Afghans – in both their government and the international community – that undermines our credibility and emboldens the insurgents. Further, a perception that our resolve is uncertain makes Afghans reluctant to align with us against the insurgents . . . The key take away from this assessment is the urgent need for a significant change to our strategy and the way that we think and operate.[117]

White House allies claimed the military sought to "box the President in" by recommending troop increases and speculated that CENTCOM commander General David Petraeus had political ambitions.[118] Using a veteran to counter the legitimacy of military criticism, National Security Advisor and retired Marine Commandant James Jones downplayed the need for additional troops and warned against the military presenting the president with a fait accompli.[119] Despite bitterness over the leaking of the McChrystal report, the dispute was between the White House and the Pentagon, not civilians and the military. Secretary of State Hillary Clinton, Secretary of Defense Robert Gates and Under Secretary for Policy Michèle Flournoy were of the same view as the military.

The Obama administration, like the Kennedy and Johnson administrations, didn't trust the military and didn't want to bear the political cost of revealing their true policy objectives. The result was similar to civil–military friction over nuclear targeting: the military didn't have the framing to understand what the politicians were trying to do; nor could they provide effective military advice because they were responding to what they thought the White House wanted.

Unlike in Iraq, commanders were fired during the war in Afghanistan: first General David McKiernan was relieved by Secretary Gates in order to provide "new leadership" consistent with President Obama's strategy, and then, much more publicly, General Stanley McChrystal was fired for derogatory comments made by his command group about Vice President Biden. Although McChrystal in particular was widely admired in the military, in neither case was there consternation from within military ranks over the dismissals.

There was, however, one significant military radicalization from the long wars – that of Lieutenant General Michael Flynn. He had been a highly regarded tactical intelligence officer in Iraq, promoted to head the Defense Intelligence Agency, but was retired early in 2011. He frothed at President Obama claiming al-Qaeda had been defeated and that the Islamic State were junior varsity terrorists.[120] Flynn would lead cheers of "lock her [Clinton] up" at the 2016 Republican national convention, feature prominently in the Trump administration's outreach to Russia during the twenty-two days he was national security advisor, become an incendiary Trump political surrogate, and four years later advocate for the military taking over election security. His arc of activity in many ways echoes that of General Smedley Butler.

President Trump thrashed in consternation at continuing involvement in Afghanistan but was stayed from complete withdrawal of forces by Pentagon warnings that the Taliban would revert to pre-war dominance and again pose a threat to the US. He did set in motion the denouement that would occur in 2021, first sidelining the Afghan government to negotiate an agreement with the Taliban. He drew down US forces from 13,000 to 8,600 by mid-2020, ahead of complete withdrawal by the summer of 2021, and further curtailed support to the Afghan National Security Forces (which had also been restricted under President Obama). Although the Taliban did not meet their obligations, President Biden elected to proceed with the withdrawal at the height of the fighting season over the advice of the military and Pentagon civilians. The debacle of August 2021, with the abandonment of Afghan allies, American veterans frantically working informal networks to get known Afghans to safety, the lethal attack on Abbey Gate, and the terrible sight of Afghans clinging to landing gear as planes took off was a searing conclusion reminiscent of the fall of Saigon.[121]

While President Biden blithely insisted Afghanistan was always going to end this way ("the idea that somehow there's a way to have gotten out without chaos ensuing, I don't know how that happens"), the view is resented in both civilian defense and military circles.[122] The chairman of the joint chiefs of staff General Mark Milley and CENTCOM commander General Frank McKenzie both testified before Congress that the president misrepresented their position by saying they supported the withdrawal.[123] Which they are required to do, unless they are cagey enough to avoid getting trapped into admissions damaging to the president's policies by Congress, as has been the case with General Eric Shinseki and so many other military leaders. Congress is full of professional politicians, after all – they have tradecraft just as do other professions, and it is their job to draw out weaknesses in the activity of the executive.

What they did not do was put their judgment about the policy above the president's, disastrous though it proved, and which McMaster's *Dereliction of Duty* advocates they should do. But the difference between complying with the constitutional requirement to inform Congress and advocating policy priorities that are properly the president's to determine is slim. And it is not often that a military officer is politically adroit enough to navigate between that Scylla and Charybdis without compromising the trust of the executive leadership.

In both the Trump and Biden administrations, the military and defense civilians were on the same side of the argument. The schism lay along the Potomac, or perhaps even along the boundaries of the White House compound, since in both the Trump and Biden administrations the major policy decisions about America's long wars were the president's own, over the objections of both military and DOD civilians and often also senior diplomats.

Conclusion

The post-World War II issues that animated civil–military relations were varied, consequential, and stress-tested America's constitutional arrangements. What is striking is how very well the American system has held up under strains for which it wasn't designed. The American military wasn't designed to lead such social changes as racial integration, remain subordinate to elected politicians enduringly less trusted by the public than are the military, or sustain rotations of forces across decades of war. Yet it has.

Opposition to racial integration by both civilian and military leaders in 1949 highlights the recurrent concern by the defense community about advocates of social change in America using the military as a test bed. While racism was surely motivating opposition in many cases, integration's opponents also had legitimate concerns about unit cohesion and were exasperated at having to deal with problems that made even more challenging the already demanding work of fighting wars.

Because the military is a hierarchy where rules can be enforced in ways much more difficult in broader society, it will generally show a positive result to experiments conducted in its ranks. That is, the military's hierarchy facilitates compliance, as does its culture of accepting the legitimacy of civilian leaders to frame the social policies that govern it and making work anything civilian authorities decide, whether it's bad strategy, insufficient resources, or social policies. So there's a bias toward success of any social experiment.

But that's not the story, or at least not the whole story, of racial integration in the US military. Because the case also touches on an important boundary condition of civil–military relations, which is that it's fair, and their responsibility to the nation, for military leaders to engage in policy formation – to give media interviews and argue their views in policy councils. But, once the commander in chief determines a course of policy, it's unfair for the military to impede its implementation. And that's what both the civilian and military leaders of the Army, Navy, and Marine Corps did by trying to forestall an end to racial segregation.

The Army retained segregated units and imposed a ceiling on Black enlistments, the Navy's policy went unimplemented, and the Marine Corps continued to defend the utility of segregation until the urgency of the Korean War gave the ground forces a military necessity for Black troops; at that point, combat commanders in the fight requested and received authority to put Black troops in as individual replacements and were impressed with the results.

What the Navy did to President Truman, the Army did to President Eisenhower, testifying before Congress in opposition to his strategy, force structure, and budget. We don't remember it as a "revolt" in the same breathless way because there was no denting President Eisenhower's credibility on military issues, and because both civilians and the military were grappling with novel problems of how nuclear weapons might change warfare. An even wider civil–military gap opened up during the Kennedy administration as civilian oversight extended into nuclear planning. Targeting wasn't fully civilian directed until 1985.

Friction between civilians and the military in the Kennedy administration wasn't just about nuclear strategy, however. Abrasive management by Secretary McNamara and his whiz kids and distrust of military judgment emanating from the White House would have major consequences in both the Cuban missile crisis and the Vietnam War. Abrasive management by Secretary Rumsfeld would have major consequences in both the Iraq and Afghanistan wars.

In the Cuban crisis, the White House relied on General Taylor to the exclusion of the joint chiefs even before it was clear the president was dissatisfied with their advice. The disagreement was significant and substantive: how to coerce a nuclear-armed adversary without triggering a nuclear exchange. The military's preferred approach was to go first and go big to prevent any prospect of retaliation; the president was groping for limited war options which the chiefs genuinely didn't believe existed. And the president was vindicated, with a creative solution that worked.

It raises the uncomfortable problem of trust. President Kennedy and his advisors just didn't trust the military leadership. It's often attributed to the Bay of Pigs debacle, but General Taylor's appointment suggests the distrust was always there. Kennedy observed the formalities of granting the chiefs a hearing, but they weren't trying to solve the problem on terms he was going to seriously consider. Moreover, compliance by the military with the president's policies doesn't appear to have been adequate to engender trust; the White House wanted agreement, not just compliance. And so the White House moved into senior military positions officers congruent with the White House perspective. Which is their right, but also how we come to Vietnam.

Selecting senior military officers who share the White House perspective axiomatically excludes those who do not. Presidential administrations are stocked with hundreds of national security specialists who commit to advance the president's policies. What the military, diplomats, and civil servants offer is a balancing perspective from their expertise, which is often different from that of the president's team. If a White House also chooses only military and civil servants (or even Cabinet members) who align with their views, it produces less internal friction but also less breadth of perspective. And the reason to choose military officers ignorant of their views not just on politics but also on the issues of their expertise is that it helps prevent mistakes. Diversity of thought and expertise also can shield the White House when things go wrong, and that's especially true with the military.

President Johnson and Secretary McNamara not only adroitly manipulated the military leadership into alignment with their policies but also presented them as public advocates. But it is difficult to see clear abrogation of the civil–military compact. As with Kennedy and the Cuban missile crisis, the military was offering advice the political leadership simply rejected. And as with the military leaders of the Cuban missile crisis, the military leaders of the Vietnam War let the president make the public case for policy choices and did their best to make them work. During and immediately after the Vietnam War, the American public blamed the military along with civilian leaders; with time, the balance has shifted in public attitudes to place the weight of condemnation onto politicians who make the strategy and resourcing choices.

H. R. McMaster would have those Vietnam War generals publicly rebuke the president and secretary over policy, which would create a very different kind of relationship between civilians and the military. Distrust between the two camps was a significant problem in the Kennedy, Johnson, and Obama administrations; what it produced was exclusion of the military from important policy deliberations and plans that did not address the political objectives of the civilians, because the military didn't fully understand those political objectives or the constraints under which the civilians were operating, intellectually or politically. McMaster's recommendations also encourage a politicized military, one that considers its own judgment superior to that of elected officials and positions itself as defending the republic from its politicians. An example of what McMaster's recommendation produces would be Lieutenant General Flynn.

Ending conscription gave the military the ability to further professionalize. The transition was rockier than was envisioned by the Gates Commission, and the military was anxious over recruitment and the racial composition of qualified troops, but within a decade quality recruits exceeded recruiting goals. Military professionalization created out of the troubled force of the Vietnam War a fighting force so far advanced that in the 1991 Gulf War it produced an unexpected rout.[124]

The 1991 Gulf War also catapulted Chairman of the Joint Chiefs of Staff Colin Powell into the limelight. His role representing military interests assertively in policy councils, creating congressional obstacles to initiatives before they became decided policies, and speaking publicly on military issues was that of a much more activist chairman who, like George Washington, was an effective military leader because of his exposure to politics. Powell's activism discomfited, especially as he was a military leader setting conditions civilian politicians needed to meet, solid as the advice was and is.

The two wars the US has fought in the twenty-first century brought strain on a force not designed for such extensive campaigns. In the case of the 2003 Iraq War, there was no clear civil–military divide; the problems were predominantly civilian in nature, and military leaders took positions on both sides of the arguments over the invasion plans and the 2006 surge. The Obama administration pressed to have agreement from its military leaders rather than just competent compliance. In both Iraq and Afghanistan, decisions about bringing the wars to an end pitted the White House against civilian and military leaders in the Defense and State Departments.

What is striking about all these cases is how little opposition the military actually engages in, even over enormously consequential military issues. They make their views known in policy counsels and in congressional testimony, they often get angry and even resentful, and then they get to work trying to carry out whatever the civilians have decided on. Rarely did military officers resign, although they were on several occasions fired. There's not a single case from the expanse of time from 1951 to the present when the military leadership refused to do what they were told.

The United States has created a large military in peacetime (the Defense Department is the country's largest employer) that has a broad expanse of influence and is often at odds with its civilian superiors but has not once organized itself to intervene in the political life of the nation. It is, as George Washington fervently hoped it would be, the first military in a thousand years not to be a threat to civilian governance.

Chapter 7

How Worried Should We Be?

It is a truth universally acknowledged that politicians will hide behind the military for as long as the military is more popular than are the politicians. American politicians have been doing so since the inception of the republic, and even as support for the military declines it remains so far above public attitudes about other political and civic institutions that most politicians seek opportunities to associate themselves with the military and use the military as props in political advertisements. Veterans, Guardsmen, and reservists have a distinct advantage as candidates for political office.

In a time of ferocious partisanship and a populace evenly spread between political parties, elections feel incredibly consequential to much of the American public, and even slight advantages are perceived to have electoral impact. In those circumstances, politics pervades many more aspects of civic life; issues and organizations not only come under greater scrutiny but become totems of partisan struggle. And so it is with the American military: the services find themselves accused of being, and sometimes actually are, political pawns for social activists of both liberal and conservative bent.

The result of being sucked into the political maw is less public support for the military as an institution, greater concern shown by parents and other influencers in potential recruits' lives, and the possibility of increased divisiveness within the military itself as political identities and even political activities become important signifiers.[1] Such politicization is cause for genuine concern, especially if the military perceives itself culturally superior to the broader society.[2]

The scholarly term for such condescension by a military toward the society it is protecting is "praetorianism," named for the legionnaires who were bodyguards and became power brokers in ancient Rome. It's the attitude becoming dangerous that was benign in Phil Klay's story "Psychological Operations," quoted at the beginning of this book.

Keeping that sense of superiority from becoming an excuse to usurp civilian power has been a rarity in world history. And, as Peter Feaver and Richard Kohn point out, the US has "the unbroken record of civilian control and the nearly unbroken record of worry about civilian control."[3] We always worry about it, especially since the small percentage of the population engaged in military service is likely to feel set apart from broader society by their service.

But do we need to worry? The Trump era has posed particular problems that the military, as many other institutional constraints on political power in the United States, have weathered admirably well. One of the revelations of the Trump era, though, has been how much of accepted political behavior in the American system is traditional rather than constitutional or legislated.[4] Veterans and even, in some instances, active-duty members of the services have transgressed norms against political activity, with a resultant drop in public confidence in the military.[5] This suggests a reduction in return on investment for political activism, although that may not prevent veterans from engaging in ways damaging to the relationship between the military and broader American society. Without valuing our unique state of high respect, military members dismissing the norm of two and a half centuries will imperil the country's confidence.

The main restraint on the American military becoming a destabilizing weight in American politics and a danger to civilian supremacy in policymaking is the professionalism of the military itself. Military equipoise in these circumstances will require political sensibility at a time when the country is in the throes of an unusual degree of politicization and politicians are using the military like a dog's chew toy. Especially since the demands of recruiting a volunteer force may necessitate an inclusiveness that is divisive in some quarters of society. It will also require greater civilian restraint than has been in evidence recently. As unfair as it is to repose responsibility for fixing a problem principally of politicians' making on the military, that may well be the only tool amenable to control – but expecting the military to compensate for the recklessness of politicians could well stoke the very praetorianism it is intended to prevent.

The Data

Polarization is a constituent feature of America's two-party political system, and it's commonplace to assert that polarization is more intense currently than ever before. But it's also true: the two political parties are further apart than they have been at least in the last fifty years.[6] Demonstrated by legislators' votes, both parties are more ideologically cohesive and have moved further from the center. People of both parties actively dislike one another; Republicans have become particularly indulgent of threats and even acts of politically motivated violence. This even though the public largely agrees on national priorities.[7]

There is, however, significant partisan difference on foreign policy priorities other than on China, on which there is broad bipartisan concern.[8] Partisans of both stripes favor multilateral solutions, although Republicans are more skeptical about international organizations.

Republicans are also less supportive of active international engagement, and Republican political leaders are strikingly less concerned about Russia than are either Democrat or Republican voters. Democrats rank climate as a priority, while most Republicans do not.

Indicators of growing stress on civil–military relations emerge from the corrosion in Congress. Norms of bipartisan behavior in Congress have broken down. It used to be the case that the Senate refusing presidential national security nominations was a rarity; it is now common for presidential appointees to major ambassadorial posts and civilian defense appointees to be kept in confirmation limbo for more than a year – actually reducing civilian oversight of the military.[9] The National Defense Authorization Act, with its sixty-two-year record, is the only legislative vehicle predictably passed, and even that bipartisan norm is fracturing. Moreover, in eleven of the last thirteen years Congress has failed to pass the budget on time, imposing the managerial and financial burdens of the legislative maneuver of continuing resolutions that prevent program changes and paralyze military adaptation in a fast-changing world. Perhaps most alarming to the military has been the novelty of senators refusing to act on military promotions in order to protest administration policies, an unprecedented level of using the military as a political lever over policies the military have had little to no ability to influence.[10]

Media sorting, in which people choose media that conform to their politics, and social media exacerbate tensions by amplifying divisive messages and allowing malign foreign actors to mask their identity and participate in domestic American political space. And artificial intelligence may both expand and accelerate the chaos. Previous technological innovations in communication (the printing press, newspapers, telegraph, radio, television) have upended the politics of their time initially, so it is likely that we are living through the churn as society figures out how to tame or marginalize these media. But, for now, American politics is whipped up into a frenzy of loud and antagonistic voices.

That political frenzy has significantly influenced how the American public perceives its military. As surveys conducted for Peter Feaver's book *Thanks for Your Service* demonstrate, "public confidence in the military is already shaped by partisan considerations."[11] Public confidence in the military has dropped by fourteen percentage points in the past six years.[12] The decline began in 2009 (falling eight percentage points in the first nine years) but has been especially pronounced since 2018. The main driver has been attitudes of conservatives. Republicans have historically been, and remain, the political partisans with the highest level of support for the military; it's just that support has declined from an exo-atmospheric 91 percent approval down to 58 percent. Support from political independents has declined almost as much. While support for the military increased among Democrats once President Biden took office, at 55 percent approval Democrats remain the political partisans expressing the least confidence in the military.[13]

Some civil–military experts argue that the decline in public approval of our military isn't necessarily a bad thing for civil–military relations.[14] And the outsized adulation that materialized in the 1990s could well have been unhealthy, impeding accountability.[15] But high approval is essential in a free society because the military have the guns, and, when servicemen and -women sign the oath, they are agreeing to an unlimited liability clause: they are offering their lives. There should be a distinction between high confidence and caricature; terming every serviceman or -woman a hero captures the Marvel Comics characterization of Americans in military service.

When military service touched more lives during wars and conscription, attitudes were less deferential – the military that won World War II also produced Joseph Heller's *Catch-22* and Kurt Vonnegut's *Slaughterhouse 5*. And it should be concerning that the policy decision of a small force relative to the population is frequently described by the military with the praetorian "We're the 1%." It is uniquely and endearingly American but somewhat embarrassing to many servicemen and -women to be offered boarding on airplanes ahead of families with small children or to be routinely applauded in sports stadiums, and many struggle to figure out how to respond when thanked for their service. Those are performative gestures that don't serve to better connect our military with our broader society.

Even when public support for the military was sky high, it was both costless and often shallow – especially for Americans who have no connection to the military.[16] Satirical newspaper *The Onion* perfectly captured the combination of socially expected support for the military and the shallowness of that support in 2003 with the headline "Area Man Supports the Troops He Didn't Go to High School With."[17]

Support for the military continues to be high relative to that for other political and social institutions in American life. Only small businesses are rated higher. Still, the military worries about the decline. It is a genuine culture shock, because there is no one currently on active duty that experienced a time when the American military wasn't venerated by the public. Healthy views should understand what the military does and does not do in our country. The public needs to understand that our military is a disciplined, merit-based organization obedient to the Constitution and that is the reason why it has not been a threat to our democracy.

Citizen or Soldier?

Reasons for the decline are surprisingly uncorrelated with attitudes about or success in the twenty-first-century wars.[18] Surveys conducted in 2014 showed that the main drivers of admiration for the military were the result of its reputation for opportunity and as a conveyor belt into the middle class.[19] The Reagan Institute polling asks what the current basis for attitudes is:

> Previous Reagan Institute polling revealed the reason behind the decline in confidence as a growing perception of politicization of military leadership.

This year's survey found that a plurality of Republicans (38%) think the military is too focused on social issues at the expense of a focus on warfighting, while almost half of Democrats (47%) think the military is appropriately balancing a focus on warfighting and social issues.[20]

While comportment of the military's most visible active-duty and veteran leaders isn't the main cause of public perception about politicization, those leaders have made significant mistakes that have fueled fires that politicians have ignited. As a result, the public thinks less well of military leaders than it does of the military as an institution.[21]

A significant reason why the public makes no distinction between the military and veterans is that high-ranking veterans who accept political appointments continue to act like and believe they should be treated as military officers rather than as partisan politicians; thus the military's non-partisan prestige effectively shields them while they advance the political agendas of the elected leaders.

President Barack Obama appointed a large number of high-ranking veterans to prominent political jobs, including the former commandant of the Marine Corps Jim Jones to national security advisor, the former chief of staff of the Army Eric Shinseki to Veterans Affairs, and the former CENTCOM commanders David Petraeus to CIA director and John Allen to special envoy for countering the Islamic State. President Donald Trump appointed the same number, but to even more consequential portfolios: the former CENTCOM commander James Mattis to secretary of defense (requiring congressional waiver of the legislative ban on recently serving military to that position), the former defense intelligence director Michael Flynn to national security advisor (he was succeeded as national security advisor by active-duty Lieutenant General H. R. McMaster), the former SOUTHCOM commander John Kelly to first homeland security advisor and then White House chief of staff, and the retired Major General Keith Kellogg to Vice President Pence's national security advisor. President Joe Biden likewise required a congressional exemption to appoint another recently retired high-ranking veteran as defense secretary, the former CENTCOM commander Lloyd Austin.

The 1947 National Security Act that created the job of secretary of defense included a restriction on recently serving veterans from appointment to the post in order to ensure civilian control of the military and prevent service parochialism by the secretary.[22] In addition to the Senate's general requirement for confirmation of high political appointees, the National Security Act requires both houses of Congress voting to exempt a recently serving veteran from the restriction. That exemption has been granted three times: for George Marshall in 1950, James Mattis in 2017, and Lloyd Austin in 2021. When the Congress voted to exempt George Marshall, the legislation included this sense of the Congress:

> It is hereby expressed as the intent of the Congress that the authority granted by this Act is not to be construed as approval by the Congress of continuing appointments of military men to the office of Secretary of Defense in the future. It is hereby expressed as the sense of the Congress that after General Marshall leaves the office of Secretary of Defense, no additional appointments of military men to that office shall be approved.[23]

In addition to preserving civilian control over the US military, there are other practical political reasons not to appoint recently serving veterans to the job as secretary of defense. The Pentagon is packed to the rafters with capable military officers who can give good military advice to political leaders; that doesn't need to be the expertise of the secretary. In fact, the secretary's main job is dealing with Congress over authorities and funding, and most military leaders have limited experience of the wheeling and dealing that constitutes legislative activity. The most effective secretaries have often been experienced legislators such as Elihu Root, because wrangling Congress is so central to running the Department of Defense. Trust is at a premium in advising the president effectively, so existing relationships that are less common across the civil–military divide facilitate the secretary in that quadrant.

Political sensibilities that guide an appreciation for the president's decision space are also likely to be in greater supply among civilian appointees, as was evident in the friction between President Kennedy and the military leadership during the Cuban missile crisis and in Lieutenant General McMaster's awkward attempt to defray concern about President Trump revealing sources and methods of intelligence collection to the Russians in a White House meeting.[24] The White House naturally sent the national security advisor out to defend the president's actions. While

Brent Scowcroft or Colin Powell could perhaps have handled that, a civilian national security advisor steeped in the politics of Washington would have been more likely to throw a brushback pitch, defending the president's right as he sees fit to share intelligence with other countries as a normal part of diplomacy. General McMaster cautiously half-defended the president, which exacerbated the political difficulty. Having an active-duty senior officer politically defending the president was also problematic by putting the military's integrity as the defense of a questionable use of intelligence.

There is no restriction on veterans serving in high political roles other than that of defense secretary; to ban them would not only infringe on their rights as citizens but also rob the public of experienced national security practitioners in civic life. But they were appointed to provide reflected glory and to shore up support for or legitimate the president's polices – in President Obama's case to shield him from criticism for ending American involvement in the Iraq War, in President Trump's case to calm concerns about his unorthodox behavior and views, and in President Biden's case to shield him from criticism for ending American involvement in Afghanistan. Nor is the public wrong to associate those veterans and active-duty military in high political positions with the policies of an administration – as the public would consider any other high political appointee. The assumption by the public of their political inertness ended with active-duty military service.

The justification offered by those accepting appointments and their supporters has been twofold: first, a sense of responsibility to accept when a president "calls you to service" and, second, to shape policies in ways that attenuate the president's worst judgments. In President Trump's administration, they were termed "the adults in the room," preventing reckless or illegal actions. But, having been elected to the highest office in the land, presidents deserve political appointees who will carry out their policies. In the case of both Barack Obama and Donald Trump, as candidates they had campaigned on the policies they attempted to enact, so had a political mandate.

The American political system has a constitutional remedy for presidents who commit high crimes or misdemeanors, and that remedy lies with the Congress to impeach or the Cabinet to invoke the Twenty-Fifth Amendment and declare the president unfit. It contains no provision for the military or veterans to shield the republic from the bad behavior of a president – the military are not the guardians of American democracy against the civilian officials whom Americans elect.[25] Nor should free societies embolden their militaries to be their political salvation; that is the well-trodden historical path to militaries threatening freedom.

President Trump seemed initially to think military leaders were only knife in the teeth killers, aligned with his attitudes on torture and derisory about allies, rather than strategists of geopolitics and master logisticians. The veterans in his administration got a rude awakening as to just how ruthlessly Trump would use their legitimation (which ought to have been evident from his campaign conduct when a candidate) when just a few days into his tenure the White House surprised Defense Secretary James Mattis by having the president sign in the Pentagon's Medal of Honor hallway the ban on Muslim travel.[26] Signing the executive order in the Pentagon created a national security backdrop for the policy and associated the military with a deeply divisive policy contrary to its own proclaimed values. A professional politician as defense secretary might have seen that coming in ways someone habituated to the fair play of the military did not.

There may be no difference in performance between civilian appointees and their veteran counterparts, but the public expects more of those it associates with military service, and the arguments for high levels of public approval of the military are justified to a considerable extent by the distinction that we want high approval of those who could bring violence to bear.[27] So veterans are held to a higher standard, and that has positive consequences for the military as reflected in the higher degree of public confidence. But the benefit of higher approval comes with public expectations of better comportment.

Lafayette, We Are Here

Like Secretary James Mattis, National Security Advisor H. R. McMaster, Chief of Staff John Kelly, and Vice-Presidential National Security Advisor Keith Kellogg, Chairman of the Joint Chiefs of Staff Mark Milley volunteered for the job. But Mark Milley had an organized campaign to get the chairmanship. He garnered the appointment as chairman in a way that clearly telegraphed both what he was in for and his willingness to play by Trump's rules.[28] He encouraged Secretary of the Army Mark Esper, Secretary of State Mike Pompeo, and presidential friend David Urban to advance his candidacy to become chairman of the joint chiefs of staff, even though he was not the secretary of defense's choice and the serving chairman, General Joe Dunford, had the president's confidence. Sent to the White House by the secretary of defense as the nominee to be supreme allied commander, Europe, he emerged as the nominee to be chairman an embarrassing nine months before his predecessor's term concluded.

President Trump asked General Milley why he wasn't there as the nominee to be chairman. There is a textbook civil–military answer to that question, which is "Mr. President, that's a conversation for you to have with the Secretary of Defense." And whatever General Milley replied to the president, he became the nominee for chairman then and there, without consultation with the secretary of defense. Nor can General Milley plead innocence of expectation that President Trump might behave in such a manner, as he'd been Army chief of staff since Trump took office and was touted at the time of his elevation to chairman as having "a very good relationship with the President."[29]

It must grieve General Milley that, in a forty-two-year military career of considerable achievement, and having attained its highest rank, there is a near certainty the picture that will accompany his obituary will be of him in combat fatigues striding with President Trump in a politically contrived photo opportunity in June 2020 through a public square that had been forcibly cleared with tear gas of peaceful protesters. In the heat of social justice protests following the police killing of George Floyd, that choice seemed to align the military with efforts to violently repress protests and with the president's incendiary rhetoric.[30]

General Milley and Secretary of Defense Mark Esper had been arguing in policy counsels against the president's desire to invoke the Insurrection Act so that he could supersede the Posse Comitatus restriction on the domestic use of the military for law enforcement, deploy military forces to quell protests, and issue orders for those military forces to shoot protesters.[31] When political operatives suggested the members of the Cabinet walk through Lafayette Square, the chairman accompanied them.

Australia's military leadership demonstrate a different possibility. When their civilian minister launched into a political tirade at a press event in their company, General Angus Campbell quietly told the minister it wasn't appropriate for the military to be there, and they left.[32] General Milley's defenders argue he couldn't have known the Lafayette Square event would be a political stunt. And, in his defense, American military officers get extensive education on many aspects of their professional responsibilities (organizational, legal, operational), but not on what to do when those responsibilities are in conflict.[33] Still, to create a hypothetical military parallel, if General Milley had an experienced combat commander excuse behavior catastrophically damaging to the war effort by failing to anticipate enemy action years into a war, he probably would relieve that commander.

To his great credit, within days General Milley acknowledged the damage his behavior had done and apologized in a commencement address to the graduating National War College class:

> As many of you saw the result of the photograph of me at Lafayette Square last week, that sparked a national debate about the role of the military in civil society. I should not have been there. My presence in that moment and in that environment created a perception of the military involved in domestic politics. As a commissioned uniformed officer, it was a mistake that I've learned from, and I sincerely hope we all can learn from it.[34]

He advised officers to "hold dear the principle of an apolitical military that is so deeply rooted in the very essence of our republic" and "embrace the Constitution . . . it is our North star." It strengthened civil–military relations that he remained on active duty and worked to repair the damage. But his march through Lafayette Square did do damage, especially to the relationship between the military and the public. It created the perception for the first time in a very long time that the American military might be used against the American public, the very circumstance the Posse Comitatus law had been put in place to prevent.

Nor was the damage confined to the relationship with the public. General Milley's indiscreet commentary to colleagues who proudly reported it to the press with the chairman as savior of the republic, and Milley's own interviews to practically every journalist writing about the Trump administration, collapsed confidence in policy circles that anything could be considered confidentially in his presence. The

White House became so suspicious of him they had civilians reviewing National Security Agency intercepts to catch him undercutting civilian leadership.[35]

It was Secretary Esper (himself a veteran who politicked for the job) who did the most to restrain President Trump during that intense episode in the summer of 2020. Although he, too, stumbled, telling governors to "dominate the battlespace," he corrected his mistake, working with White House lawyers, consulting with governors about their authority over National Guard forces, conferring with members of Congress and the attorney general, and giving a press conference on June 3, 2020, outlining the legal requirements for invocation of the Insurrection Act and why he opposed the president doing so.[36] It was the proper way for defense expertise to be brought into the fraught moment, a civilian politician driving up the political price to the president for actions he considered dangerous and damaging. The nation didn't need its military leadership to make that case.

Nor was General Milley's retirement speech free from political commentary as he snidely extolled the virtue of the military over the commander in chief, saying, "We don't take an oath to a king or queen or a tyrant or dictator. We don't take an oath to a wannabe dictator. We don't take an oath to an individual. We take an oath to the Constitution."[37] That is the posture that causes the public to believe the military is becoming involved in politics.

General Milley established other problematic precedents – for example, drawing the military into the political fracas that was the debate over critical race theory. In a June 2022 congressional hearing on the defense budget, the secretary of defense was challenged on military reading lists that included content about critical race theory. Again, there is a textbook civil–military answer: what the chairman ought to have done is to have let the civilian secretary engage on that politically fraught issue. But he did not. Instead, General Milley subjected the members of Congress to the following disquisition:

> I've read Mao Zedong. I've read Karl Marx. I've read Lenin. That doesn't make me a communist. So what is wrong with understanding – having some situational understanding about the country for which we are here to defend? And I personally find it offensive that we are accusing the United States

military, our general officers, our commissioned, noncommissioned officers of being, quote, "woke" or something else, because we're studying some theories that are out there . . . I want to understand white rage, and I'm white, and I want to understand it. So what is it that caused thousands of people to assault this building and try to overturn the Constitution of the United States of America? What caused that? I want to find that out.[38]

The general himself and the American military would have been better served had Milley taken the advice of the legendary criminal defense attorney Clarence Darrow that "no man was ever convicted on the basis of testimony he did not give." Many of both his personal difficulties and the civil–military infractions were the consequence of Milley assuming an exaggerated role of instructing the country. To give a feel for his sense of intellectual grandiosity, during the social justice protests in the summer of 2020 he gave a speech explaining: "What we are seeing is the long shadow of original sin in Jamestown, 401 years ago."

In the fateful budget hearing that devolved into a dispute over the arcane legal notion of critical race theory, the secretary of defense had already provided the Department of Defense's answer: "We do not teach critical race theory. We don't embrace critical race theory, and I think that's a spurious conversation. We are focused on extremist behaviors and not ideology – not people's thoughts, not people's political orientation. Behaviors is what we're focused on."

By answering the question about critical race theory, General Milley made it fair game for every other general to have to answer the question before Congress – and they are routinely asked it now on the questionnaires for promotion of two-star generals and above. It dragged the military into a divisive social issue on which the military has no particular expertise but now will have to develop a politically safe answer or be screened for their views on an obscure academic legal subject on which virtually none of them have competency to genuinely take a position.

Milley's advocates initially tried to justify his statement by saying that he didn't want to leave the first Black secretary of defense unshielded in a racially tinged interrogation. But that ignores the civil–military awkwardness of the chairman placing himself between the secretary and hostile political inquiry, supplanting the civilian response of the department and defining a wider role for himself. And surely the first Black secretary of defense has the experience of navigating choppy political waters of race issues and doesn't need someone who's spent their whole professional life in uniform to handle the politics of it for him. General Milley's advocates' last line of defense of his comportment in the hearing was that "he's a hockey player," as though that childhood and collegiate experience justifies leaning into an argument damaging to the profession.[39] As Doyle Hodges concludes, "Milley's rationale is laudable, his actions were not."[40]

Mark Milley was the architect of much of the difficulty he experienced as chairman of the joint chiefs of staff. The contrast is stark to the quiet suasion of his predecessor, who operated in the same difficult circumstances. None of which justifies the threats made against him by the former and current commander in chief. Donald Trump's fulminations that General Milley should be executed for treason are both unfounded and genuinely dangerous – to the health of American democracy by normalizing political violence, to the American system of civil–military relations by attempting to replace professionalism with personal loyalty, and to the physical safety of General Milley and his family.[41]

Arson and Arsonists

General Milley can be somewhat exonerated for his mistakes because he was operating in an environment that imposed a stratospherically high degree of difficulty.[42] The agent of chaos imposing that degree of difficulty was President Donald Trump. As Jim Golby has chronicled, "Trump enthusiastically embraced and indeed encouraged the politicization of the military, accentuating and exaggerating it at almost every opportunity."[43] In addition to appointing an active-duty general officer to a political post, Trump used his commander in chief responsibilities as campaign stops, encouraging assembled troops to agree with him that "We had a wonderful election, didn't we? And I saw those numbers – and you like me, and I like you."[44]

Nor were President Trump's efforts restricted to simple public support. Risa Brooks demonstrates a more sinister and dangerous strategy by the president and his supporters, which is to create a coalition within the military committed to keeping him in office.[45] Trump recruited both active-duty and retired military to publicly endorse him, asked military audiences to lobby their members of Congress in support of his policies, and pardoned servicemen who had been convicted of serious crimes – including war crimes – by courts-martial and then included them in campaign events.[46] In doing so, he was trying to normalize the military as a partisan force and create loyalty that was personal to him. He was also attempting to reach past the senior leaders who serve to discipline the rank and file by ridiculing "the generals" and accusing them of stupidity, cowardice, and betraying the fighting forces.[47] He has since said he would fire all the "woke" generals, threatened General Milley in particular with incarceration for treason, and even suggested he should be hanged.[48]

General Milley's Lafayette Square mistake served the valuable purpose of alarming the military leadership as to what President Trump and his acolytes were capable of. In the five months leading up to the election, military leaders, including General Milley, thought carefully about how to keep the military out of political reach.[49] They frequently repeated the mantra that "there is no role for the United States military in a contested election."[50] This assertive "pre-bunking" inoculated the military against suspicion of complicity when President Trump suggested the military should "safeguard" voting machines and vote counting.[51] The 2020 presidential election was in no way affected by military involvement; the American military's unbroken record of civilian control remains unbroken – even when civilian control was stressed in novel, reckless, and dangerous ways.

The final months of the first Trump presidency were even more chaotic than its beginning, in part because "the adults in the room" had left the building. They were replaced by civilians of breathtaking recklessness, including veterans such as Chris Miller and Douglas Macgregor. When a surprise presidential directive to withdraw all forces from Afghanistan was circulated, both civilians and the military in the Pentagon scrambled to force reconsideration and consultation, but only intervention by the national security advisor and White House counsel stayed the order.[52] Friction was intense, but not along civil–military lines. As with earlier Afghanistan debates, the line fell along the Potomac:

> In the view of Trump's mistrusting inner circle, this was typical of Pentagon leadership: Delay key decisions by disputing that strategic meetings had led to consensus, insist the process was still ongoing, and leak apocalyptic scenarios

to the media. These were the tactics Trump allies believed military leaders had perfected to obstruct presidents over the course of decades.[53]

The eventual Trump administration agreement negotiated with the Taliban was announced without any warning to Congress or to allies with troops in Afghanistan.

One other, less fortunate, result of the Lafayette Square imbroglio is that elected officials in the District of Columbia, governors of surrounding states, and the military itself wanted the military kept far from future protests. Since the District of Columbia isn't a state, there isn't a local elected official like a governor to assume authority over the National Guard. That responsibility lies formally with the president, but has by law been assigned to the secretary of defense and operationally is exercised by the secretary of the Army. Having been concerned that the military would be called in over DC Mayor Muriel Bowser's objections during the summer 2020 protests, elected officials had their hackles up when the Pentagon suggested trouble was brewing for a rally organized by President Trump on January 6th. Much criticism has been avalanched on the Pentagon unfairly for its slow response to developing insurrection on January 6th; the pace of military response was the result of decisions made to prevent a repeat of fears manifest during the summer of 2020.[54]

There is also a public misapprehension of extensive military and veteran involvement in the insurrection. Of the 2,500 people who stormed the Capitol, three were active-duty military and an additional three were reservists or Guardsmen.[55] And of the 1,476 people charged by federal officials, one hundred are veterans, most of them long past their military service. What has given the mistaken impression of a serious problem with insurrectionists in the military is that military service is an easy public record to check, and political reporters on tight deadlines initially over-weighted military service in their accounts.[56]

Research by the University of Chicago Project on Security and Threats indicates that insurrectionist views are no longer fringe elements of American politics, but mainstream: only 14 percent were militia members, but half of the people charged for storming the Capitol are business owners and half have some college education.[57] Extrapolating the findings of their research to the American population at large would suggest 21 million Americans are "active and dangerous," and as many as four million potential insurrectionists might have done military service. But those are projections, not data, and they would anyway reflect veteran involvement, not a threat posed from within the military forces.

In the aftermath of January 6th, the military had a force-wide stand down requiring units to discuss extremism; the services increased vetting recruits for extremism, and troops being assigned to guard the Capitol were screened for potential extremist ties. But determining what constitutes cause for concern is vexingly difficult: What of political speech, even in the military, justifies grounds for separation? Who decides? And how to ensure recruiters are cognizant of emergent worrisome groups?

There is little data about, and therefore little actual evidence of, extremism as an institutional problem in the military, but there is a vigorous campaign by extremist groups to recruit veterans as members – not principally for their tactical skills, but to capitalize on the public confidence in the military to legitimate their political ideologies.[58] Extremist groups see the advantage gained by mainstream politicians through military association and are copying an effective tactic. Servicemen and -women may be acutely vulnerable to recruitment in their transition out of military service, as they leave a community and may not feel reconnected to broader society.

Support for insurrectionist tendencies among veterans has revealed that prior military service increases by 15 percent support for restoring Trump to the presidency by force.[59] Nor are the findings explained by political support for Trump, which makes the support for anti-democratic violence even more worrisome; that is, it isn't political preference but a preference for determining political outcomes. While veterans are not the military, the study provides an important warning of praetorianism that may be developing in the ranks or being normalized through its adoption by veterans.

It is tempting to believe that Donald Trump is insufficiently strategic to devise and enact a plan to use the military against constitutional authority; but that is to underestimate the protean instincts that have made him a successful politician, and the authoritarian ambitions he and many around him hold. And, as Lindsay Cohn and Steve Vladeck emphasize, "The authorities governing the domestic uses of force are notoriously open-ended."[60] It also avoids understanding how the military has been politicized to support authoritarian rule in other countries.

And it had a significant effect on American public attitudes about the military: the most careful assessor of civil–military survey data, Dr Peter Feaver, concludes the decline in public support for the military is largely the result of attacks on senior military officials by President Trump and Republican opinion leaders.[61]

Within the first month of his second term, President Trump fired the chairman of the joint chiefs of staff, the chief of naval operations, and the USAF vice chief. Secretary of Defense Hegseth fired his senior military aide Lieutenant General Jennifer Short, and the administration is suggesting more firings are to come. While no reason was given for the dismissals, the optics are that the administration is airbrushing women and minorities out of the leadership picture. But every senior military officer serves at the pleasure of the president and can be relieved for any reason or no reason at all. The American system of civil–military relations relies heavily on fostering trust between the civilians and the military, and anyone elected president deserves senior military leaders they trust and have confidence in. It's very important for the functioning of the system that the president can fire any military leader, just as Lincoln fired Generals Scott, Halleck, and McClellan, Truman fired MacArthur, and Obama fired McKiernan, McChrystal, and Mattis. The appropriate response of the military is to accept even unfair civilian decisions, because they are the tests of subordination to civilian supremacy. The Trump administration looks poised to squander an enormous amount of military talent in ways harmful to individuals; but the bench of talent in the American military is very deep.

More worryingly, the Trump administration has fired the service legal advisors, has appointed to civilian roles in the department former military officers who were relieved of command for disobeying their chain of command,[62] and has reinstated servicemen and -women who refused the legal order to be vaccinated during the Covid pandemic. Most worrisome of all is the threat both by the Trump administration and their advocates in Congress, such as Senator Tuberville, to penalize serving officers for having complied with legal orders in the previous administration. These moves reinforce suspicion that President Trump is seeking to weaken good order and discipline in the force and reward behavior that encourages politicized activity – even to create the impression the military would become a partisan force defending illegal presidential acts. They are ignoring – and Congress has so far been complicit – George Washington's caution that "an army is a dangerous instrument to play with."

Donald Trump as commander in chief is what Dr Pauline Shanks Kaurin terms "the unprincipled principal": someone with no normative or moral commitments.[63] The president admires authoritarian power, is indifferent about damage to institutions of which the office he holds traditionally has been guardian, and routinely flouts norms of presidential conduct. The American public pays little attention to the subject of civil–military relations because it trusts in the professionalism of our military.[64] But it is unreasonable to expect a military derived from broader society to remain perpetually constrained by norms when its political leaders openly flout them. In civil–military relations, as in so many other areas of American politics, we are buying risk.

Is There a Crisis?

Nor was Donald Trump the only politician to shove the military into the glare of politics recently: candidate Biden confidently asserted that, if President Trump attempted to remain in office instead of transferring power, the military would, "I promise you, I'm absolutely convinced they will escort him from the White House with great dispatch."[65] It followed a growing trend to cite escalating lists of retired generals as endorsements. Both parties' candidates used military images in campaign ads, both party conventions utilized high-ranking veterans as validators. President Biden also brazenly strode across the line of appropriate uses of the military by having uniformed Marines stand sentinel behind him as he gave a midterm election speech in 2022 about fighting for "the soul of the nation . . . Donald Trump and the MAGA Republicans represent an extremism that threatens the very foundations of our Republic."[66]

Three of the best analysts of civil–military relations, Risa Brooks, Jim Golby, and Heidi Urben, are deeply concerned that these political developments have unbalanced civil–military relations. They argue:

> over the past three decades, civilian control has quietly but steadily degraded. Senior military officers may still follow orders and avoid overt insubordination, but their influence has grown, while oversight and accountability mechanisms have faltered. Today, presidents worry about military opposi-

tion to their policies and must reckon with an institution that selectively implements executive guidance. Too often, unelected military leaders limit or engineer civilians' options so that generals can run wars as they see fit.[67]

Nor is their view an isolated one. Military historian Russell Weigley sees a pattern of "quarrelsomeness" among the military with civilian leadership, from MacArthur through Vietnam to the 1990s.[68] He had by the mid-1990s come to the conclusion that "conflict and bickering between soldiers and civilians have become perennial impediments to the formation of a coherent American foreign and military policy."[69]

Mara Karlin perceives "a crisis of meaningful civilian control … the military's tendency to blame civilians rather than simultaneously engaging in more serious introspection; the resurgence of the Powell Doctrine (and its exceedingly narrow criteria for using military force); the popularity of the phrase 'best military advice'; and efforts to minimize civilian oversight in crucial areas."[70] Michael Desch argues that "the end of the Cold War has coincided with a deterioration of the relationship between civilian authority and the military institution in the United States."[71] Heidi Urben's research shows partisanship weakening among Army officers, but the officer corps becoming ever less representative of the broader public's demography. She raises the concern that "their commitment to civilian control may be conditioned on their partisanship and which party controls the White House at the time."[72] Even Peter Feaver and Richard Kohn, two of the most establishment-friendly civil–military experts, are concerned that "the military establishment in the superpower era has enjoyed remarkable power – in fiscal, political, and prestige terms – far in excess of what the Framers of the Constitution would have thought was proper or safe for the preservation of a free republic."[73]

My own sense is that the concerns are overworked. The American military continues to pass the two essential tests of civil–military relations: presidents can and do fire military leaders with impunity, and the military carries out civilian-determined policies to the best of their abilities with the resources provided. Most civil–military scholars fear a military powerful and uncompliant, while I think the bigger fear is a military buffeted ceaselessly by civilian politics and thereby made ineffectual. In this way, I suppose my view is uncomfortably close to Samuel Huntington's. Where I differ from Huntington is that I don't believe the solution is for American society to become more like the military. I believe the political system is churning through a febrile moment to which civilian politics needs also to be the solution.

Presidents have always worried about military opposition to their policies: draft riots accompanied Washington's call for militia during the Whiskey Rebellion, Adams feared the New Army would drive the country to war with France, Jefferson cashiered the military leadership for being Federalists, Monroe fretted about firing Jackson, Johnson tried to send Grant to Mexico to marginalize him, Custer's insubordination derailed Grant's Indian policy, Wilson fretted about firing Sims, Roosevelt and Truman fretted about firing MacArthur, Bush and Obama worried about military opposition to their policies on Iraq. But those concerns represent the normal functioning of civil–military relations in a country where the military is respected and therefore a political force, even if it is subordinate to civilian authority.

Nor am I persuaded by Brooks, Golby, and Urben's arguments about selective implementation of orders by the military. For example, one area of concern identified by these authors, and given further credence by the 2018 congressionally mandated National Defense Strategy Commission, was that the chairman's joint staff has become too dominant within the Pentagon. Their report says that "the Commission was struck by the relative imbalance of civilian and military voices on critical issues of strategy development and implementation. We came away with a troubling sense that civilian voices were relatively muted on issues at the center of US defense and national security policy, undermining the concept of civilian control."[74] But, tellingly, the authors also concluded that the secretary has the authority needed to ensure effective civilian control – he just chose not to use it. So the problem wasn't the military, it was that the secretary preferred to rely on his military advisors rather than his civilian staff. And, in the specific case they reference, it ought to be factored in that so many of the Republican civilian defense experts took themselves out of consideration by participating in the "never Trump" letter campaign, and that the chairman of the joint chiefs of staff was personally close to and a longtime military subordinate of the secretary. The most recent 2023 commission review did not highlight civil–military relations as problematic.[75]

Georgetown law professor Rosa Brooks also finds unpersuasive the arguments in support of there being a crisis. While acknowledging differences between the civilian and military sides of the equation, she's skeptical as to whether the "differences make a difference." She concludes: "when it comes to civil–military relations, perhaps things are not as bad as they seem. Or, at any rate, often the things that are bad have less to do with civil–military relations than with other challenges – from widespread civic disengagement to abuses of executive power."[76] In the same vein as Rosa's and my conclusions, Richard Betts argues that "civil–military relations are not an outsized problem as conflicts in a democracy go."[77]

Not only is the military not really the problem, it also isn't really the solution. General Milley erred when suggesting it was his responsibility to "land the plane" of preserving democracy.[78] They cannot substitute for the constitutionally prescribed checks on the power of the president; nor should they. It is not their job to protect the country from a president the country elects. Democracy in America stands or falls on the basis of what Congress, the courts, and civil society do.

But President Trump's return to office may yet produce a civil–military crisis. Re-election does validate his actions, and his second-term administration appointments for national security portfolios in intelligence and defense are dangerously reckless and unqualified. As candidate and president-elect, Donald Trump had already proclaimed that he would fire all the "woke" generals and have the military conduct mass deportations. His supporters have recommended setting up boards of veterans to evaluate serving officers for past as well as future adherence to the president's current predilections. Dark intimations swirl of recalling Jim Mattis or Mark Milley to active duty for court-martialing. News reports suggest that appointees – which could even include military officers – will be required to agree that the 2020 presidential election was stolen and that the January 6th insurrection was justified.[79]

The president has no obligation to seek or accept military advice, and, given the president's resentment of "the generals" and the dearth of national security experience in his confidants, marginalization of military leaders is likely – as is firing enough of them until they find someone who agrees to carry out policies that confront the American public with the potential for domestic violence conducted by our military. The Founders' fears of a standing army restrict the active-duty force from domestic use, but National Guard units may be offered by Republican governors and utilized under Title 32 authority (so technically under state authority when a governor chooses to use them to carry out federal policy).

"Lawful but awful" orders of many varieties are likelier than not, given the president's expressed enthusiasm for invoking the Insurrection Act and threatening to use federal institutions to take revenge on political opponents. Military compliance with such orders will shock the American public, who wrongly believe their military can refuse to carry out immoral orders, when they have that recourse only for illegal orders.[80] And that will have a damaging impact on recruiting, both in numbers and in the beliefs of people who choose to serve, politicizing the military from within.

Good Order and Discipline

In *The Soldier and the State*, Samuel Huntington infamously claimed that an effective military was incompatible with American society and advocated for society to become more like the military. That is both undemocratic and unlikely. Nor should Morris Janowitz's recommended solution to America's civil–military gap of erasing the sphere of military expertise untrammeled by civilian involvement be advised. There is no work around or best practice that can substitute for trust between civilians and the military in the US system.[81]

The challenge of civil–military relations remains how to "reconcile a military strong enough to do anything the civilians ask them to do with a military subordinate enough to do only what civilians authorize them to do."[82] But contemporary problems of civil–military relations are less the result of military insubordination than they are civilian–civilian disputes with efforts to recruit military legitimation by both sides. As a result, the American military will need to understand "command as politics."[83] That does not mean, nor should we in a free society want it to mean, the American military getting "into a position where it can distort national priorities, pick and choose the threats with which it wishes to deal, or else, and most seriously, take over the running of the country." It does mean, as Lawrence Freedman argues, that "a political sensibility is an essential part of a professional competence, enabling officers to understand the contexts in which they operate, and how the way they act affects these contexts."[84] It also requires civilian leaders having the humility to allow the military's professional judgments to carry weight in policy deliberations on issues affecting not just the war but also the composition and practices of the military itself.

Eliot Cohen's *Supreme Command* is a long-form refutation of the Huntington model, demonstrating that some of modern history's most successful wartime leaders – Lincoln, Clemenceau, Churchill, and Ben Gurion – all violate the strict divisions Huntington advocates for effective military operations under civilian control. Cohen's purpose is to show that only with deep engagement by politicians in the military realm can strategy be molded to political constraints; without subjective control, the political and military elements of strategy cannot be fused and will fall out of alignment.

Cohen's unequal dialogue harkens back to Washington at Newburg acknowledging that Congress is terrible at its job, but civilian superiors being good at their work is not the basis for the Army's subordination: the American military aspired to be the first army in a thousand years that wasn't a threat to democracy.

Cohen also contributed a humorous but prescient insight during the 2000 US presidential election, which was to say that it was important for George W. Bush to be elected president so that the military could learn to hate Republicans again.[85] Cohen surmised that the civil–military frictions of the late 1990s were transitory, the result of society becoming more socially tolerant and the military's discomfort with a Vietnam War draft dodger elected commander in chief. Those frictions would – and did – dissipate as post-Vietnam servicemen and -women rose through the military to leadership positions, and Republicans' policy choices in office frustrated their military counterparts.

Getting civil–military relations right requires balance. Lawrence Freedman summarizes it best:

> it is not that the civilians and military must stick to their own spheres of influence, and not interfere in the other's, but that they must engage constantly with each other. Even while recognizing the vital importance of civilian primacy, the military must advise on the realism of political objectives. Even while acknowledging the importance of professional judgments, the civilians must check that operational plans support those objectives.[86]

Several scholars have recommended ways to rebalance the system to strengthen the civilian side of the civil–military equation, thanking other professions for their service and increasing funding for non-defense departments of national security.[87] Those are earnestly meant but nowhere near the scale of effect necessary to shield the military from the political pressures under which contemporary politicians have them.

Recommendations for attenuating current concerns about civil–military relations focus predominantly on the military itself: increased teaching about norms of civil–military relations, senior leaders consistently modeling non-partisanship, and ceasing veteran political endorsements – and these are beneficial (if, in the case of veteran endorsements, unenforceable). They will also over time reinforce public perceptions of the discipline and professionalism of the force, which will help recover public support for the military.

I believe that's already happening. General Milley's successor as chairman of the joint chiefs of staff, General C. Q. Brown, maintained a much lower profile and, after his firing, other military leaders are likely to be even more circumspect. Stung by decreasing public support, military leaders are searching for ways to reclaim the lofty status that benefits both morale and recruiting. They are also eager to find ways to get out of the bright, hot lights of congressional castigation.

While it's neither their job nor appropriate, as the concerns about the Powell Doctrine reveal, for the military to police civilian behavior, Risa Brooks, Jim Golby, and Heidi Urben are absolutely right that, "when politicians endorse military insubordination that serves their interests, they do long-term damage to the principle of civilian primacy."[88] Unfortunately, politicians of both parties view their short-term advantages of politicizing the military too appealing to prioritize that longer-term benefit of a positive relationship between the military and the American public. It's important to recognize, though, that only Republicans are encouraging outright insubordination.

The politicians are the real problem in civil–military relations, and it is more difficult to see how to address that side of the equation. We Americans get the military we deserve, and unless political elites cease dragging the military into non-military issues for partisan advantage we will have an increasingly partisan military. Where, then, does that leave us? Even if there isn't a crisis, maintaining civil–military relations with a military strong enough to protect the country without becoming a threat to democratic governance merits both attention and effort. The American experience suggests several lessons for military leaders.

Adopt the Marshall rule

Military leaders such as Custer, Sims, or MacArthur, believing themselves better strategists and more adroit operators than actual politicians, were proven wrong. Smedley Butler publicly fumed at the operations Presidents McKinley, Theodore Roosevelt, Taft, and Wilson authorized, which he considered immoral. The chiefs of the Vietnam era agonized over whether they should have exposed the rosy assessments by President Johnson and Secretary MacNamara. Many of their successors of the Iraq and Afghanistan wars had similar recriminations regarding the descriptions of both political and military assessments. George Marshall had no such concerns, even though he believed President Roosevelt misled the public about the extent of support for Britain and other judgments during World War II. Marshall in uniform lived the axiom that politicians had a right to be wrong.

Another way of characterizing it is that Marshall did not put his own assessment above that of the president. He and the World War II chiefs understood the war they were fighting was a political undertaking and required the strength of the nation, and they deferred to the president on how to describe it to the American public. And while his personal comportment suggested distrust of Franklin Roosevelt's legendary manipulations, Marshall did not parade his personal virtue as a contrast to the president's.

In our current moment, too many military leaders and, even more so, high-ranking veterans seem to believe the country cannot do without their evaluation of the suitability of policies, candidates, or elected leaders. They draw on the public admiration of the military in recommending candidates or policies, often perceiving themselves as morally superior to the tawdry politics rampant in our time. It is somewhat reminiscent of the disapproval of civilian leaders captured in the landmark 1990s Triangle study of military attitudes. But the institution of the military would be better served were they to adopt the Marshall rule, because such endorsements rarely affect voting or policy decisions, but they do cause the public to consider the military a partisan political actor and they do cause civilian leaders to distrust the military.

The problem of an unprincipled principal creates the dilemma of whether the military should obey democracy-destroying orders. Avishay Ben Sasson-Gordis argues, "militaries do not have a duty to obey orders that severely undermine the processes that produce legitimacy, accountability and trust across transfers of power," and advocates for institutional leaders disobeying them.[89] This approach will lead to individual military leaders making highly subjective determinations of what orders to obey, when the American system is built on the presumption of legality and morality of orders.[90] Yet the procedurally clear direction that "the military possesses no autonomy of any kind not derived from civilian political institutions," outlined by Richard Kohn, could make the military a tool of repression by such a president.[91] Pauline Shanks Kaurin argues that, instead, military leaders should "use pragmatic appeals oriented to the context, individual, or power of personal relationships to try and navigate the boundaries," acknowledging it as an unsatisfactory solution. Her approach is less likely to create dangerous precedents, but there is simply no good practice to recommend in the circumstances of a president this willing to violate the norms and challenge the institutional and political restraints that have governed American civil–military relations.

The American system of civil–military relations is not fireproofed against an unprincipled principal. The Founding Fathers openly worried that the system of their design breaks down without virtue, and we are now testing that proposition.[92] The military will – and should – obey legal orders. Leaving them to determine whether orders are ethical is a recipe for dysfunction of the organization. The arena where issues of policy and propriety are designed to be evaluated in the American system is fundamentally civilian and fundamentally political. There is only so much that can be done to protect institutions, including the military, from an elected president, provided Congress is complicit. Moreover, it is not the military's job to save the republic. Not only can our military not save American democracy, it can't even save itself from democracy. The institution of the military is derivative of American society and dependent on the political system to govern it.

Stay Out of the Culture Wars

To the extent possible with their dual responsibility to both the Congress and chief executive, military leaders should be clear about issues of their professional expertise and respectfully decline to state their views on subjects beyond it. They should feel freer than many recently to have no opinion on a subject, even under examination. An excellent civilian example was provided by Secretary Mattis when pressed for his view on football players kneeling during the national anthem. He looked exhausted, said something to the effect that he had a really demanding job and wasn't able to inform himself on every issue, and left it at that.[93]

Public demonstrations of restraint amidst the cultural maelstrom reinforce what the public admires about our military. General Milley's congressional grilling in September of 2021 at which Republicans called for his dismissal, and even shockingly accused him of treason for reports of post-election phone calls with Chinese counterparts, provides a valuable example.[94] He calmly explained his actions and stoically sat silent while politicians raged.

In a more complicated case, a promising Army major general, Patrick Donahoe, was investigated for misconduct and subsequently retired in 2022 after arguing over social media. Tucker Carlson had slurred women's service, and Donahoe, who was widely followed on Twitter, defended their contribution.[95] What ought to have happened is for the civilian leadership of the Department of Defense to have done so; divisive social issues are what civilians are there to litigate. But both the Office of the Secretary of Defense and the secretary of the Army were silent. Many in uniform believed it important to engage to defend the institution's values and support women in uniform – and many women in uniform appreciated Donahoe and other prominent soldiers standing up. But the tenor of debate probably was damaging to public attitudes about the military, since the public expects more of its military than of celebrities.

Staying clear of the culture war shrapnel is, of course, easier said than done. Members of Congress can demand answers and resent cuteness designed to avoid statements on the record. The invidious practice of individual senators placing promotion holds to penalize the carrying out of policies the military was legally bound to enact is especially difficult to deal with. It could only be prevented by either a groundswell of shame accruing to the practice or the Senate changing its rules to require, for example, a majority of the Armed Services Committee members to hold a nomination back from a vote. But culture wars are a political reality, and the less the military feeds the flames the less it will be singed.

The military doesn't have to be a champion of social change to benefit from it. That is the lesson of ending segregation in 1948. President Truman wanted the change to affect the 1948 presidential election but could not get a congressional majority for legislation, so he enacted the policy by executive order. The Army, Navy, and Marine Corps chiefs opposed it for defensible, practical reasons. When General Bradley publicly criticized the policy, he recanted and apologized, but each of the services excepting the Air Force shirked execution of the policy in a variety of ways until the manpower needs of the Korean War and proven service by Black Americans gave them a reason to embrace the change. It entailed an enormous bureaucracy, including creation of a DOD school system, to fully enact a policy in advance of social change in the country. That, too, merits remembering as we valorize the military as a lever for social change.

Enforce your rules

One commonality in all of the examples of charismatic military leaders asserting the superiority of their judgment over that of their civilian masters is that, because the military rightly considered them top performers at combat, their military superiors protected them from penalties for misbehavior. Instead of making examples of them, the civilian and military leadership mostly exempted them from the rules. So Hamilton was allowed command of the New Army even though he proposed to use it to subvert President Adams's policy. Wilkinson's career prospered despite several courts-martial, as for a decade did Fremont's – and even later Fremont was only subtly forced into retirement, the Army leadership not directly confronting his challenges to President Lincoln but instead finding his administration of military responsibilities deficient. Numerous officers were political candidates while on active duty. Custer was repeatedly resuscitated by Sheridan, even after President Grant had him arrested. Smedley Butler was shielded from accountability because of his father's congressional stature. William Sims was even allowed to publish defamatory statements about President Wilson's conduct of the war before being reduced in rank and office by Secretary Daniels. Jackson and MacArthur ought to have been disciplined by their military superiors or, failing that, by the civilian leadership of the War Department; instead, the responsibility and political consequences fell to the president. Counter-intuitively, the recent military leader best known for expansive political maneuvering was sharply reined in by the civilian leadership: Secretary Cheney did enforce on Powell narrower constraints of operation, ordering him to restrict his NSC participation to military advice.

The firing in 2024 of a four-star Army general for manipulation of the command selection process suggests the culture of preferential treatment persists.[96] And it took the civilian leadership to impose even that compliance with the Army's own rules. The respect that accrues to the military from the American public because it considers it different and better than most other institutions of public life rests on a foundation of procedural legitimacy – that is, on the belief that the military has rules by which individuals within the institution are governed. When those rules are excepted, it fosters cynicism both within the military ranks and outside them. Americans want a military that is different and better than society at large – but with the discipline to remain subordinate to civilian control.

When the Law Conflicts with the Commander in Chief, Choose the Law

The American experience of civil–military relations would be profoundly different had anyone less exemplary than George Washington laid its foundation. As Lin-Manuel Miranda lyricized it in the musical *Hamilton*, "Washington's the president / Every American experiment sets a precedent."[97] Washington was unerringly committed to a strong military subordinate to civilian leadership. Even when his army was starving and deserting, he pleaded rather than demanded of the Continental Congress. When resources necessary to winning the war were not forthcoming, he devised an approach that needed less. He set the standard that elected leaders determine the objectives and resourcing and that it is the military's job to figure out a strategy for succeeding at the objectives with the available resources. And no general in American history has had to achieve more with less than did George Washington.

Ulysses Grant also understood he was exemplary in 1866 because of the unprecedented animosity and constitutional confrontation between the president and Congress: a nation reeling from the murder of its president, his successor vacillating wildly on policies toward the defeated Confederate states and threatening to disband Congress, Congress legislating retributive policies and threatening to impeach the president, the military occupying the southern states and exercising governance there. Hostility was deep between Grant and President Johnson, but, to avoid a constitutional crisis and the derailing of Reconstruction, Grant allowed himself to be thrust by the president into the middle of the political dispute. Grant was wrong to believe the military could be the solution to a political crisis. Confronted with a steep fine and the threat of imprisonment, Grant reconsidered and elected to obey the law rather than the commander in chief.

Military leaders made a different choice in 1861 – they chose to obey the commander in chief when Lincoln suspended habeas corpus and the courts declared it unconstitutional. But deference to commander in chief while fighting an actual armed insurrection with half the country attempting to enact the unconstitutional provision of succession has a different flavor than political stalemates do.

American military leaders may not have things as difficult as did Washington or Grant, but circumstances are likely to be plenty demanding in our own time. After the Lafayette Square incident in 2020, military leaders did an excellent job of reinforcing both their commitment to the Constitution and their commitment not to become a means of illegal intimidation in the political sphere. They took advance action to neutralize anticipated political uses of the military, and it redounds much to their credit. The Navy's training question of what to do when caught between a rocky coastline and a stiff onshore breeze may prove useful.[98]

Reinforce the Difference between the Military and Veterans

Veteran partisanship is taken by both politicians and the public as a proxy for military attitudes. This is not only an incentive for political activism but, as Michael Robinson's research demonstrates, it delegitimizes military advice within policy circles: "with repeated forays into the political arena, retired military elites complicate the integrity of the larger institution with civilian leaders who rely on their objective counsel."[99] The last several chairmen of the joint chiefs of staff have tried to cajole and shame their fellow "Princes of the Church" into silence on political and social issues to little avail. But veterans are citizens and entitled to draw on their professional expertise as they engage in the rough and tumble of American politics. What most benefits a healthy civil–military relationship is leading politicians, and especially the president, making the distinction between veterans, to whom constraints do not apply, and the active-duty military, to whom they do.

My guess is that the only way to cut this Gordian knot is for the military leadership to disavow that the veterans are an accurate reflection of uniformed attitudes, as Suzanne Nielsen and Don Snider recommend.[100] "She doesn't speak for the military" will be a tough line for military leaders to take, but it's the only solution likely to have any effect. It would be even better for the political leadership to make the distinction, as President Bush did in 2006 with the "generals' revolt" over the Iraq War. But that's unlikely for as long as the military is more popular than politicians, which is likely to be forever.

Even though the incentive structure is misaligned (individual veterans gain the benefit while the military as an institution bears the damage), political endorsements by veterans may be a problem that is solving itself. While escalating numbers of retired general officers sign letters advocating for candidates or policies, those endorsements have little political salience – all they do is reduce confidence in the military as an institution.[101] So, the more endorsements become normalized, the less effect they will have. But it should be cause for concern that military iconography is coming to be used less as patriotism than for encouraging violence.[102]

Legalized Insubordination

Constitutionally, Congress is the more important governmental force in military issues. It legislates and funds, creating the framework within which the military operates. Think you want to exclude female soldiers from combat units? That requires congressional action. Want to eliminate commissaries or the DOD school system, or return troops to the US that are deployed in allied countries? Congress will have to fund that.

The system is designed to force public debate and check errant power. President Adams had to endure Congress creating the New Army and demanding his negotiating correspondence. President Monroe sweated congressional investigation of his orders to Jackson. President Polk had to finesse congressional investigation of his initiation of the Mexican War. President Wilson had his secretary of the Navy dragged before Congress to defend his wartime decisions. The so-called Admirals' Revolt was an appeal to Congress to overturn the president's defense budget. While Truman's executive order ending segregation in the armed forces shows that presidents can circumvent Congress, Congress has the power to override with legislation or funding. Congress created the modern military, ending conscription and enacting the Goldwater–Nichols reforms.

Powell's political genius was to get Congress to do the work of advancing policies he considered important for the military before President Clinton made policy decisions. President Eisenhower fumed that undercutting the president's policy to Congress was legalized insubordination, but it's also fair game in the American system. Working Congress continues to be important for the military as both accountability and a check on executive power. Working Congress without alienating the administration is the challenge.

Trust is the Coin of the Realm

The Continental Congress had it with Washington, Adams did not have it with Hamilton, Jefferson did not have it with the revolution's veterans, Monroe did not have it with Jackson, Polk did not have it with either Taylor or Scott, Lincoln had it with Grant but lacked it with McClellan and Fremont, Johnson had it with Grant then lost it, Grant lacked it with Custer, Wilson lacked it with Sims, Franklin Roosevelt had it with the wartime chiefs, Truman lacked it with MacArthur, Kennedy lacked it with any but Taylor, Johnson lacked it with all, Bush and mostly Cheney had it with Powell, and Obama, Trump, and Biden mostly did not have trust in their military leaders.

But trust is the emollient that makes the American model of civil–military relations work best. Without it, military leaders often cannot know enough of the political reasoning and limitations that guide civilian decisions, as was evidenced in both the Cuban missile crisis and the development of nuclear strategy and targeting. And because the American system of civil–military relations is an unequal dialogue, fostering trust falls more to the military than to civilians. As unsettling as was President Trump's firing of General Brown and other military leaders, he was within his authority, and anyone elected president of the United States deserves to have a military leadership they trust. Washington's shining example of listening carefully to the political constraints under which the civilians are operating, of entreating rather than demanding, and of making the best of what is made available, continues to be the best guide to building trust.

A Closing Thought

America's Founding Fathers would be astonished to behold an American military so powerful, so respected, and so restrained from exercising that power to control the functions of government in our country. Their fear of a standing army was not borne out – instead, the creation of a professional military in the United States actually removed the incidences of charismatic military leaders attempting to subvert civilian supremacy. But the American system of civil–military relations will falter if we continue to rely on the military alone to prevent civil–military relations from becoming dangerously unbalanced. Our military is drawn from our society, and it will not perennially remain politically inert and more disciplined than the rest of American society. We must ourselves become more restrained about pulling the military into social and political disputes and allow them to focus more on the work of fighting and winning the nation's wars.

Epilogue: Disputing the Canon

While the classical writers Herodotus and Thucydides in ancient times and Clausewitz in the nineteenth century have much to say about civil–military relations, the field of study in America during modern times has been defined by two texts: Samuel Huntington's *The Soldier and the State*, which was the first important work focused on the American military, and Morris Janowitz's *The Professional Soldier*. Both say as much about the times in which they were written as they do about the military itself, and both are motivated by a policy agenda of what the military's purpose should be.

Deference to the two canonical texts of American civil–military relations partly has its origin in the Cold War expansion and enduring demands on the American military establishment. When militia were considered largely adequate to security demands and the American military was surged only as the country engaged in wars, there was little intellectual interest in its composition, culture, and relationship to broader American society.

Three factors made the subject of civil–military relations of increased scholarly attention by the mid-1950s: the mobilization of such a large proportion of citizens to fight World War II, the first time in eighty years the state made such a demand on the populace; the consequent determination that the magnitude of the Soviet challenge and the advent of surprise nuclear attack necessitated a robust standing national security establishment; and the dismal performance of American forces in the early stage of the Korean War barely five years removed from the triumphant performance of defeating Nazi Germany and imperial Japan.

The national security mood at the inception of interest in civil–military affairs is captured by the 1954 Doolittle Report, which argued that the US risked annihilation because it was fighting by rules our enemies were unconstrained by.[1] President Eisenhower commissioned the classified study, which recommended "an aggressive covert psychological, political, and paramilitary organization more effective, more unique, and if necessary, more ruthless than that employed by the enemy." The report argued that "we are facing an implacable enemy whose avowed objective is world domination by whatever means and at whatever cost. There are no rules in such a game. Hitherto acceptable norms of human conduct do not apply. If the United States is to survive, long-standing American concepts of 'fair play' must be reconsidered."[2]

The Doolittle Report is of a piece with indicators of the anxiety attendant on the dawn of the US–Soviet confrontation: the 1953 Soviet test of an atomic bomb, US concessions in negotiations with North Korea to end the war and secure the release of American prisoners, and McCarthyism calling the loyalty of American diplomats and defense officials into question. It is in this context of fear about the successes of Soviet power and anxiety about the ability of free societies to protect themselves that the field of civil–military relations got its start.

Canonization

The Soldier and the State is generally regarded as the single most important text in the canon of civil–military relations, read in military staff colleges, assigned in every graduate course on the subject, referenced in every serious work of scholarship. The wellspring of mystification is that, in a book of 466 textual pages, Huntington never once – not once! – attempts to grapple with the main concern animating the subject of civil–military relations in free societies: how to prevent a capable military from becoming a threat to civilian governance. He completely ignores praetorianism, which had been the death knell of every free society in history. His subject is the ways in which free societies, politically and socially liberal societies, are a threat to military professionalism. His reverence for the profession, and the military professional as he defines it, surely accounts for some of the book's popularity among military readers. Huntington's message is that the military is fundamentally a conservative institution, and its broadly liberal society is letting it down by not appreciating and emulating its strictures.

The Soldier and the State was not the only book of academic rigor written about the American military, but there were relatively few in the mid-1950s and most were focused on either military history or war strategy. Its moment in time is the advent of the nuclear age, the shock of American military failure in the Korean War, and the emergence of civilian strategists of military issues. Huntington's book is unique in that it focuses exclusively on the internal character of the military and its relationship to broader society.

And Huntington does get one hugely important thing right, which is that we need a military of professionals who can effectively impart expertise unique to them and crucial to sound national security policymaking. There is an inherent tension between the culture and structural dimensions of an effective military and a free society; civil–military relations as a field of study is about how much independence a military should have and how to ensure it doesn't accrue more than that. Huntington's theorizing neither newly discovers those elements nor identifies better practices short of apocalyptically changing American governance and society to achieve his desired ends.

Not only is Huntington's theory puzzling in many respects; where it is clear, it is dangerous. His fundamental view, the ideology that animates the entire book, is that "the tension between the demands of military security and the values of American liberalism can, in the long run, be relieved only by the weakening of the security threat or the weakening of liberalism."[3] And it is the weakening of liberalism that he advocates. Huntington's critique is that

> The only theory of civil–military relations which has had any widespread acceptance in the United States is a confused and unsystematic set of assumptions and beliefs derived from the underlying premises of American liberalism . . . it is obsolete in that it is rooted in a hierarchy of values which is of dubious validity in the contemporary world.[4]

He theorizes two types of civilian control of the military: objective and subjective.[5] He writes "civilian control in the objective sense is the maximizing of military professionalism . . . it is that distribution of political power between military and civilian groups which is most conducive to the emergence of professional attitudes and behavior among the members of the officer corps."[6] But he equates complete autonomy with professionalism. What his theory intends is wholly separate spheres for civilian and military responsibilities, in which the political leaders have no influence over either what the military does or how they do it. It is the Prussian model, but with an American twist: where military leaders unyieldingly and publicly judge the policies of their elected leaders, but comply with them.

The alternative to objective control is its opposite – subjective control – in which the military has no unique sphere of activity or culture independent of broader society. "Subjective civilian control achieves its end by civilianizing the military, making them the mirror of the state."[7] The theory comes into focus by contrasting the two: "The essence of objective civilian control is the recognition of autonomous military professionalism; the essence of subjective civilian control is the denial of an independent military sphere . . . Objective civilian control is thus directly opposed to subjective civilian control."[8]

The enduring popularity of *The Soldier and the State* may have to do with Huntington's description of the military as a profession, one with the characteristics of expertise, responsibility, and corporateness.[9] He describes its representative, advisory, and executive functions.[10] And he establishes a useful lexicon of vertical (subordinate to superior authority) and horizontal (hemmed in by civilian authorities at same level of authority) control.[11]

Huntington believes the military role should be cast narrowly, providing advice only on the strictly military aspects of a problem. But the arrow goes in only one direction: the military informs civilians, but civilians are restricted from informing the military. For example, he criticizes a chairman of the joint chiefs for going "beyond a military role: he represented the political views of the Administration to the Joint Chiefs as well as the military views to the government."[12] His objective control would have the military providing advice on the narrow aperture of strictly military issues absent any political context. Huntington terms the model he advocates 'balanced'; in it, neither the president nor the secretary of defense would have any military responsibilities, and below the secretary authorities would split into military and administrative lines. In his judgment this would maximize both military professionalism and civilian control.[13]

Huntington argues that political and social liberalism are inherently corrupting to military professionalism; the risk is that "the satisfactions of professional performance and adherence to the professional code are replaced by the satisfactions of power, office, wealth, popularity, and the approbation of nonmilitary groups."[14] But he acknowledges no political risk in a militarized society: "In a society dominated by an ideology favorable to the military viewpoint, on the other hand, military power may be increased to a much greater extent without becoming incompatible with a high level of professionalism."[15] Huntington considers the risk of liberal society even more dangerous than corrupting the military. He sees American society as destroying it: "The essence of this [liberal] policy is sustained opposition to military values and military requirements. Liberalism's injunction to the military has in effect been: conform or die . . . This is a policy of extirpation."[16]

It is unclear what practically Huntington wants the military to do differently from what American military leaders have traditionally done. He identifies obedience as the cardinal military virtue and, in exploring its limits, concludes:

> The superior political wisdom of the statesman must be accepted as a fact. If the statesman decides upon war which the soldier knows can only lead to national catastrophe, then the soldier, after presenting his opinion, must fall to and make the best of a bad situation . . . General MacArthur forgot that it is not the function of military officers to decide questions of war and peace.[17]

The liberal view he castigates would come to the same conclusion. Clausewitz comes to the same conclusion.

But Huntington considers the very structure of American governance an impediment: "The real constitutional stumbling block to objective civilian control is the separation of powers."[18] It's a staggering confession that his preferred view of civil–military relations is unconstitutional, or at least extra-constitutional.[19] He considers that "civilian control has at times existed in the United States, but it has emerged despite rather than because of constitutional provisions."[20] Divided responsibilities to both the commander in chief and Congress are an inducement to politicization of the military for Huntington: "the conflict of constitutional ideologies and governmental loyalties divides the officer corps and superimposes political considerations and values upon military considerations and values. The nature of an officer's political loyalties becomes more important to the government than the level of his professional competence."[21]

Yet Huntington's ideal for military leaders preserving their professionalism is resort to Congress to make their dissents publicly known. He considers General Matthew Ridgway's comportment the professional standard: "the general emphasized his acceptance of higher-level executive decisions fixing the size of the Army which obviously did not accord with his own judgment. In 1954 he gave his own views in executive session; in 1955 he presented in public his military opinion."[22] Which is exactly what the Navy leadership did in 1949. So, again, it's not clear why civil–military relations are in crisis, or what Huntington would have either the civilians or the military do differently.

Moreover, the strict separation of professional responsibilities Huntington argues for is almost sure to produce political leaders who won't know enough to make good decisions, even on the basis of sound military advice, and military leaders producing policy options and recommendations unencumbered by political and economic constraints, and therefore of little use to civilian policymakers. This is especially true in an all-volunteer force small relative to the size of the civilian population, in which most elected leaders have little direct experience of the military and in which most military leaders spend their professional lives.

Huntington concedes that "present in the minds of the Framers when they wrote it and perpetuated in its provisions was an essentially subjective approach to civil–military relations."[23] He absolves the framers of American governance from blame for liberalism's danger to the military profession by explanation that their work predates military professionalism, which he clocks to nineteenth-century Prussians. But it is just not true of the Founders that "they were more afraid of military power in the hands of political officials than of political power in the hands of military officers."[24] As Huntington ultimately concedes, "The Framers identified civilian control with the fragmentation of authority over the military."[25] And nothing in his account demonstrates that has served the country poorly.

To the contrary, Huntington's account of American military history provides a number of intimations of military praetorianism resulting from the very model he advocates. For example, he praises Alexander

Hamilton's professionalization of the New Army in 1799 but averts his eyes from the latter's plan to turn it against Thomas Jefferson's political faction in Virginia or to march on for conquest of French and Spanish territories beyond US borders in contravention of President Adams's policy.[26] Huntington seems not to connect the objectively controlled military created by Sherman's reforms with budget demands "out of place in the long, quiet years of the 1880s and 1890s ... [when] the United States actually had little need for military force."[27] Nor does he criticize General Leonard Wood politicking a presidential run while chief of staff of the Army or military campaigns against pacifism in the 1920s; instead he idealizes military motives as "being designed exclusively for the purposes of military security."[28]

Huntington's version of American history is awry in several other respects. He considers that "not only did every group in American society normally feel economically secure but also American society as a whole normally felt politically secure."[29] He argues that "the outstanding historical fact of American civil–military relations has been the extent to which liberal ideology and conservative Constitution combined to dictate an inverse relation between political power and military professionalism."[30] He brushes away the number of military men who have played leading roles in American political life, saying "the role of the military hero in America is indeed conclusive proof that political power and military professionalism are incompatible in the American climate ... all the great national heroes of American history, with the possible exception of Washington, have been liberals, and the professional soldier, consequently, has had little durable appeal."[31] The two periods of American history in which he considers society had a proper balance in civil–military relations were the political program of the revolutionary era Federalists and during William Tecumseh Sherman's tenure leading the Army.

These contortions are necessary to arrive at his conclusion that Alexander Hamilton, John C. Calhoun, and William Tecumseh Sherman were the only truly military-minded professionals, even though that requires him to describe the author of the *Federalist Papers* and the vice president to both John Quincy Adams and Andrew Jackson as "isolated from the mainstream of American intellectual and political development."[32]

Huntington titles the time frame 1940 to 1955 "the crisis of civil–military relations."³³ And he doesn't mean Truman firing MacArthur during the Korean War – that isn't even covered.

He expends twenty pages describing "the military mind." Yet any definition of the military mind that excludes George Marshall, Ernest King, Dwight Eisenhower, and Douglas MacArthur seems odd at the least and categorically ineffectual for advancing theory.³⁴ He excludes those wartime military leaders for "sacrificing their military outlook and accepting the national values. The military leaders blended with the liberal environment; they lost their alien and aloof character and emerged as the supreme embodiment of the national purpose."³⁵

It is very odd that a scholar with living memory of World War II would consider a military of ten million citizens under arms and complete comity between the president and its entire military leadership that wins the war to be a civil–military failure. And yet Huntington does.³⁶ Although he describes civil–military relations as "a remarkable harmony . . . there were no conflicts, ill-feelings, or clashes of policy or personality serious enough to cause anyone to be fired or to quit in disgust," he concludes: "something is wrong with a system in which, during the course of a four-year major war, the political Chief Executive only twice overrules his professional military advisors. This can only mean that one of them was neglecting his proper function."³⁷ He seems to think that a single source of civilian oversight vested in the commander in chief is the only way to achieve objective control, yet he denigrates the performance of Franklin Roosevelt exercising his authority in that way.

Huntington's real objection is to the policy: he considers "military victory in the most efficient manner" the wrong objective.³⁸ He vehemently disagrees with the policy and seems to think the military should not have allowed the president to choose it. He believes the military ought to have insisted the president fight on against the wartime ally the Soviet Union: "the derangement of American civil–military relations was simply the institutional reflection of a deeper malady: the ignorance and naïve hopes which led the American people to trade military security for military victory."³⁹ So the military was effectively carrying out policies determined by the president and consistent with public attitudes, but that constitutes a crisis of civil–military relations. For that to occur, Huntington asserts, the military must have compromised their military judgment:

If their views had not been altered, the military leaders might have warned the country of the permanence of the struggle for power, the improbability of postwar harmony, the weaknesses of international organization, the desirability of preserving a balance of power in Europe and Asia, and the truth of history that today's allies are frequently tomorrow's enemies. . . . The trouble with American policy making was not too much military thinking but too little.[40]

These intellectual tangles make *The Soldier and the State* an imperfect messenger for conveying the fundamentals of civil–military relations in America. But it is not a work of neutral scholarship: Huntington has ideological views that he smuggles into theory as explanation. "Conservatism is at one with the military ethic."[41] And this purporting to be neutral while advocating a political agenda is what makes Huntington so problematic. He seeks to associate the military with political conservatism and to make society's values more closely approximate those of the military: "the requisite for military security is a shift in basic American values from liberalism to conservatism. Only an environment which is sympathetically conservative will permit American military leaders to combine the political power which society thrusts upon them with the military professionalism without which society cannot endure."[42]

If your view of civilian control is something the Framers, who worried desperately about a military overthrow of the civilian government, wouldn't recognize, you have an odd theory. The American military has been reliably subordinate to the political control of elected leaders for nearly 250 years and remains a bristlingly effective fighting force. How is that not success?

The impetus for sweeping socio-political change Huntington advocates is that "changes in technology and international politics have combined to make security now the final goal of policy."[43] Yet he does not attempt to specify what those changes are – he asserts but does not prove a necessitating basis. It is a work innocent of acknowledgment that economics, alliance politics, or even the routine compromises of domestic politics have any place in determining the military's role or counsel. And it ignores how well the American system of civil–military relations has actually worked.

No Quarter

Morris Janowitz's *The Professional Soldier* is the flip side of the coin to *The Soldier and the State*. Huntington's model emphasizes the military as distinct and separate from society; Janowitz considers the military establishment "as a sort of self-contained organ, as a vestigial appendage, rather than a creation of contemporary society."[44] He worries that "a civil or military service whose political beliefs were widely at variance with those of the electorate would present a danger to political democracy, for such a service could not be counted on to remain loyal to the concept of political neutrality."[45] Janowitz goes so far as to believe that "the military can only be controlled by being effectively integrated into the larger society, not merely by being professional."[46]

Janowitz argues for the complete convergence of military and civilian spheres and makes the full-throated case for what Huntington terms subjective civilian control. He posits that allowing the military a separate sphere produces "absolutists – men who thought in terms of traditional conceptions of military victory," and proposes that what the country needs from its military is "pragmatists – men concerned with the measured application of military force and its political consequences."[47] He concludes that both necessitate greater civilian involvement in military decision-making, because "the more technical-minded officers are a hazard to the conduct of foreign policy; the more political-minded require more elaborate direction than is supplied by traditional forms of civilian supremacy."[48]

For Janowitz, it is not the liberal nature of society but the expansion of military roles in (then) recent wars that is blurring the distinction between the civilian and the military, driving the need for greater influence of civilian mores into the military.[49] He considers that

> In the past the military profession has been considered deficient in its ability to judge the political consequences of its conduct ... the behavior of the American military was not so much unpolitical, as inappropriate and inadequate for the requirements of a worldwide system of security. The growth of the destructive power of warfare increases, rather than decreases, the political involvements and responsibilities of the military. The solution to international relations becomes less and less attainable by use of force, and each strategic

and tactical decision is not merely a matter of military administration, but an index of political intentions and goals.[50]

Presaging what General Charles Krulak would thirty years later term the strategic corporal, Janowitz assesses that "the prescribed career of the future is one that will sensitize the military officer to the political and social consequences of military action ... even the most junior officer, depending on his assignment, may be acting as a political agent."[51] Janowitz believes that "the technical character of modern warfare requires highly skilled and highly motivated soldiers," but that, to achieve this, "the military commander must develop more political orientation, in order to explain the goals of military activities to his staff and subordinates."[52] It is a politicized version of commander's intent: the force needs not just to be comprehending of the military objectives but to become proficient in judging the political consequences of its use of force.

Janowitz produces the data to demonstrate that Huntington's assertion of "the military mind" represents only one part of military attitudes. The American military isn't the monolith Huntington represents it as.[53] In assessing it internally, Janowitz concludes that "the military establishment requires a balance between the three roles of heroic leader, military manager, and military technologist."[54] He acknowledges the necessity of heroic leaders such as MacArthur, Halsey, Patton, Wainwright, Doolittle, and LeMay. But he argues that World War II also necessitated and produced military managers, whom he counts as Marshall, Eisenhower, Bradley, Arnold, Smith, Leahy, and King.[55] For Janowitz, modern warfare "required communications skills, trained the officer in negotiation, had strong political overtones, and involved relating the military to some outside organization."[56]

Interestingly, like Huntington but for different reasons, Janowitz considers General Matthew Ridgway his model's ideal. Whereas Huntington celebrated Ridgway for making clear his advice first privately to the executive branch and then publicly to the Congress, Janowitz celebrates him as "the innovating officer who fused both images, but in which the military manager was ultimately dominant." Ridgway had staff assignments through the 1930s and no combat experience before becoming assistant division commander; he went on to command the 8th Army in Korea, become supreme allied commander in Europe, and serve as chief of staff of the Army. What Janowitz sees in Ridgway is a diversity of experience, maintaining his operational proficiency, and not only pushing back on orders he believed would not achieve their objective but developing politically acceptable alternatives for civilian leaders to choose.[57]

Developing political sensibilities ought not produce a politicized military, according to Janowitz:

> Under democratic theory, the "above politics" formula requires that, in domestic politics, generals and admirals do not attach themselves to political parties or overtly display partisanship. Furthermore, military men are civil servants, so that elected leaders are assured of the military's partisan neutrality . . . but partisan neutrality does not mean being "above politics" to the point of being unpolitical . . .
>
> Civilian supremacy in the United States has operated because military officers function under rules which reduce or eliminate the ability to influence the electoral contests for national political leadership. Civilian supremacy also requires that military leaders operate under prescribed rules in offering advice and in stating dissenting opinions with regard to national defense policies. The strain on contemporary political institutions arises rather from the lack of clarity regarding the rules for governing the behavior of the military as a "pressure group" in influencing both legislative and executive decisions about foreign policy.[58]

Janowitz introduces the concept of "unanticipated militarism," which again presages debates of the 1990s, because it envisions a military determining the public standard for civilian accountability. Military officers publicly establishing criteria against which civilian decisions would be judged created a furor when Joint Chiefs Chairman Colin Powell did so at the end of the Cold War. For Janowitz, unanticipated militarism "develops from lack of effective traditions for controlling the military establishment, as well as from a failure of civilian leaders to act relevantly and consistently."[59]

The Professional Soldier, too, is a product of its time, that time being the debate over military strategy in the early nuclear age, the competition for policy influence between military leaders who had fought in World War II and emerging civilian strategists who questioned the applicability of military experience (as President Wilson had), and the expansion of civilian scholarship of the military in sociology and other academic departments (in part due to Janowitz's founding of the Inter-University Seminar on Armed Forces and Society).

Acknowledging that Huntington's characterization of the military mind accurately describes traditional military thinking, Janowitz believes that, "if the military is forced to think about avoiding wars, rather than fighting wars, the traditions of the 'military mind' based on the inevitability of hostilities must change, and the military decision-making must undergo a transformation as well."[60]

For Janowitz, the nuclear age changed everything, including the military itself. He argues that "total war is a prenuclear notion ... the interpenetration of the civilian and the military is required as more and more of the resources of the nation state are used in preparing for and making war. It became appropriate to speak of the 'civilianization' of the military profession." So, for Janowitz, both the nature of war in the nuclear age and the scale of societal effort necessary for security justify much greater civilian involvement in military affairs than had traditionally been the case. That is, even if Huntington's model of objective control had been suited to warfare in an earlier age, contemporary conditions necessitate something different.

The military leaders Huntington's objective control would produce are what Janowitz terms "absolutists." What Janowitz advocates is the marginalization from influence of absolutists, those World War II veterans who question the efficacy of limited uses of military force calibrated by often complex political objectives. He believes "the military profession must now recognize the fact that the power of destruction is so great that it is dangerous to generalize from past experience."[61] Janowitz favors "pragmatists" who see military force in the nuclear age as integral to political warfare, who accept limited outcomes because of the apocalyptic enormity of the newfound destructiveness of such weapons.

Janowitz acknowledges that military culture tends to "lean to the right," and that the self-conceptions and professional ideology of the military officer have served as a powerful counterforce to civilianization."[62] He also acknowledges that "the armed forces have incorporated many operations which could be performed by civilian agencies, and which decrease the effectiveness of military units." But he advocates "the idea of a constabulary force, the notion that a soldier may have an effective career without ever fighting."[63]

Janowitz is litigating grand strategy, not just civil–military relations. He argues for the supremacy of the strategy of flexible response over the Eisenhower administration's heavier weight on nuclear weapons and decisive military victory. Like Huntington, he perceives a military crisis: "the military face a crisis as a profession: how can it organize itself to meet its multiple functions of strategic deterrence, limited warfare, and enlarged politico-military responsibility?"[64] But, whereas Huntington considers the crisis a result of the ascendance of too little traditional military thinking, Janowitz considers it to be the traditionalists having too much success.[65]

Janowitz believes the nuclear age requires a military that ceases to fight to victory but, instead, considers its core function constabulary duties. The model Janowitz advocates is that "the military establishment becomes a constabulary force when it is continuously prepared to act, committed to the minimum use of force, and seeking viable international relations rather than victory because it has incorporated a protective military posture."[66] He would reshape the military from a force that dominates the escalation ladder to one that dampens the prospect of escalation. He would have its leaders consumed with arms control and limited wars. The problem with Janowitz's preferred model is that it creates a military for the kind of war you want to fight instead of the kind of war an enemy could force on you.

Because his study is of the military rather than warfare, and because he is focused on the nuclear age, Janowitz misses an important corroborating example that might strengthen his case. In fact, the United States had a military force with constabulary duties as a core function and took proficiency at constabulary duties as a central doctrinal and operational responsibility. That force is the United States Marine Corps. But, whereas limited or small wars were but one mission of one part of the US military, Janowitz envisions constabulary duties and the political involvement outlined in the *Small Wars Manual* to be both the central focus for the entirety of the US military and the ethos that shapes military culture.

The Professional Soldier is a much better book than *The Soldier and the State*. It describes and transparently applies its methodology, utilizes academically rigorous practices of sociology in structuring interviews and producing data to support its claims, provides detailed histories of events to illustrate the theories in action, and is straightforward about the preferences for which it advocates. It is a snapshot of the interplay within the military and between civilians and the military across the 1950s. But, like Huntington, Janowitz has a political agenda he is advancing, along with the scholarship of who the military are and what their relationship is to the political superstructure of American government.

Whereas Huntington is unconcerned about praetorianism, Janowitz centers it as the purpose of study, because "few nations have succeeded in both adequately solving the political problems of civil–military relations and maintaining political freedom."[67] But the civilianization of the military that Janowitz advocates could also lead to a dangerous praetorianism. He acknowledges "the possibility of an inbred force which would hold deep resentments toward the civilian society and accordingly develop a strongly conservative, 'extremist' political ideology."[68]

The central thing Janowitz understands is that "civilian control of military affairs remains intact and fundamentally acceptable to the military; any imbalance in military contributions to politico-military affairs – domestic or international – is therefore often the result of default by civilian political leadership."[69] The basis for healthy American civil–military relations is that "the military think of themselves as civil servants in national service, and that is an essential ingredient of civil control."[70] What Janowitz gets right is that Washington's example of subordination to civilian authority is a defining feature of the modern American military.

And Janowitz places responsibility for maintaining that virtue in the military not only with the military itself. Civilian leaders, too, have responsibility for how the military sees itself in relation to broader American society: "In the United States the task of civilian leadership includes not only the political direction of the military, but the prevention of the growth of frustration in the profession, of felt injustice, and inflexibility under the weight of its responsibilities."[71] Janowitz further expands responsibility to American society more broadly for sustaining a military connected to society, writing that "outdated and obscure conceptions of the military establishment persist because civilian society, including the alert political public, prefer to remain uninformed."[72]

Janowitz's model of a military much more integrated with society and more penetrated by civilian ideas of warfare was more fashionable before the Vietnam War than after. The humbling of civilian strategists detailed in David Halberstam's *The Best and the Brightest* and the persistent willful incomprehension evident in Errol Morris's documentary film *The Fog of War* serve to validate Huntington's argument for distinctive military judgment.

Conclusion

It is clearly true that the function our military performs necessitates some unique practices divergent from those of our society more broadly. But strict separation of culture and structure to the highest level of authority as Huntington advocates will produce a military ignorant of the political and economic constraints under which elected leaders operate. And it is surely preferable for civilian leaders to consider proficiency in military affairs a prerequisite for good national security policy – but it is just as surely the case that they do not.

Strict segregation of civilian from military will produce civilians dismissive of military equities from lack of comprehension. Civilian leaders will only understand military judgment if military leaders find an amenable way to convey it to them. So, on both the civilian and military sides of the equation, Huntington produces sub-optimal outcomes. Nor is it an advantageous solution to eradicate the entire cultural and intellectual gap between our military and the rest of American society, as Janowitz advocates. A military optimized to one kind of war will surely be confronted by adversaries forcing upon it the kind of war it is unprepared for.

Janowitz and Huntington are caricatures of each other's positions, which makes them a useful pedagogical pairing. As Suzanne Nielsen and Hugh Liebert point out, "Janowitz helps to correct Huntington's weaknesses, not to justify Huntington's banishment."[73] And Janowitz pays tribute to Huntington's *The Soldier and the State* as "the first time since Alexis de Tocqueville that American military institutions were being analyzed as an aspect of the American political process." But both advocate for extreme models at variance with what has actually worked, and worked well, in American history.

Huntington's formative civil–military experience was the Korean War, while Janowitz's was the strategy debates of the 1960s. And while Janowitz updated *The Professional Soldier* in 1988 to incorporate findings on how the American military changed as the result of the tectonic shift from mass conscription to a smaller professional and volunteer force, his book remains fundamentally an appeal for the military to eschew military victory for more limited political aims. Their successors were products of the Vietnam War, in which the frustrations of limited war took their largest human and policy toll, and the consequence of which was the elimination of conscription and the establishment of a volunteer force.

The successor generation of scholars refined the concepts, conducted extensive field surveys of both public and military attitudes, and made policy recommendations to correct emergent imbalances. Nearly all of those scholars are products of military education, either as servicemen and -women themselves, as faculty at institutions of military education, or as fellows allowed to work in military staffs. By contrast, very few institutions of civilian higher education invest in scholarship on these issues. It is one more example of civilians expecting the military to take responsibility for what should be a shared concern.

Acknowledgments

This is a work of deep indebtedness. First and foremost to General Colin Powell, who, as chairman of the joint chiefs of staff, took this unpromising PhD student into the joint staff in 1990 that I might learn. I was Powell's science project, proof that you could teach any dog to talk. And what I learned fallen among the officers of his joint staff was that mostly what the American military are is great teachers, because they live in an environment in which you can't be good at your job unless you can make everyone around you good at their job – and I had none of the experience that had trained all of their judgment. I was the weak link in every chain, so Major Jim Warner, Lieutenant Colonel Robert Burkhardt, Commander Peter Daspit, Lieutenant Colonel Greg Newbold, Colonel D. L. Johnson, Colonel Steve Randolph, Colonel Jim Riley, Brigadier General John Jumper, Major General John Admire, Lieutenant General John Shalikashvili, Lieutenant General Barry McCaffrey, and so many others invested in teaching me. I went for one year and stayed for four; it was then and remains now the best education of my professional life.

I also had the great good fortune to teach for several years in the Social Sciences Department at the US Military Academy, where the study of civil–military relations is so seriously considered that much of the scholarship of the field is in one way or another connected to it. It was an honor to teach young men and women who chose to be soldiers when their country was at war. It was also a joy – to give a sense of the place, the History Department solemnly sports T-shirts emblazoned with "we make the history we teach" and is rebutted by the Social Sciences Department's playful "we make up the history we teach." Americans of little association with our military miss out on both its earnestness and its humor.

I'm particularly grateful to Jim Mattis, who buoyed me through the writing of this book by reading each chapter as I finished it, pointing

ACKNOWLEDGMENTS

out where I'd missed examples he knew that I didn't, and imparting the perfect balance of criticism and encouragement.

All three of the anonymous pre-publication reviewers who made this a much better book subsequently revealed themselves: Heidi Urben, scholar, soldier, and leader of the civ–mil academic community, who encouraged me to write this book; Frank Gavin, who cheerily pressed the relevance point; and Peter Feaver, who gave such detailed and constructive notes that I forgive him for wrongly claiming to have originated my idea that General Milley should be graded like Olympic diving, with a degree of difficulty factored into his score.

I'm also grateful to scholars from whom I learn so much on the subject:

- Michael Robinson, former student and now distinguished colleague, who turned his critical attention to the concluding chapter and required me to take credit for ideas of his own;
- Richard Kohn, whose account of the establishment of US civil–military relations during the founding generation is unsurpassed and who kindly nudged my thinking;
- Matt Waxman, who generously shared both his thinking and his ground-breaking manuscript in progress on the history of war powers in American government;
- Phil Klay, writer of great literature and powerful essays on morality and war, who was a careful critic of the manuscript and especially the concluding chapter, which strengthened it considerably;
- Peter Lucier, Marine veteran and activist, soulful writer about the moral burdens of warfare and generous commentator on legal issues raised in this text, whose "Marine French" was wonderfully encouraging;
- Walter Haynes, another former student and ruthlessly critical thinker who read the opening salvo on Washington;
- Ryan Evans, magic maker, who discussed the book tirelessly on walks as I thought my way through these issues.

I could not be more fortunate than to have my book in the editorial clutches of Ian Malcolm. He believed early in *Safe Passage*, and he has been a fostering guide again on this book.

Thank you all!

ACKNOWLEDGMENTS

This book is dedicated to the memory of Tim Gray, friend of my childhood, devoted husband and father, taco truck customer, and the best critic of my work. I'm heartsick he's not here to read it and tell me where I'm wrong.

Notes

Epigraphs

1 John Muir, quoted in Jim Morrison, "How the US Army Saved Our National Parks," *Smithsonian Magazine*, September 8, 2015; www.smithsonianmag.com/history/how-army-saved-our-national-parks-180956840/#ky3xcgZbus342gxe.99.
2 Eisenhower Library, Whitman File, NSC Records, Top Secret: *Foreign Relations of the United States, 1955–1957, National Security Policy*, Volume XIX, Document 61, p. 202; https://history.state.gov/historicaldocuments/frus1955-57v19/d61.
3 Phil Klay, "Psychological Operations," in *Redeployment* (New York: Penguin Press, 2014), p. 203.

Chapter 1 Introduction

1 Samuel E. Finer, *The Man on Horseback: The Role of the Military in Politics* (London: Pall Mall Press, 1962).
2 The other four are military institutions and American society, military leaders and their professions, civilian elite interactions, and influential civilian elites and American society. Suzanne C. Nielsen and Don M. Snider, "Introduction," in Nielsen and Snider, eds, *American Civil–Military Relations: The Soldier and the State in a New Era* (Baltimore: Johns Hopkins University Press, 2009), p. 3.
3 Laura Santhanam, "Here's Who Americans Blame for US Failure in Afghanistan," *PBS News*, September 2, 2021 (www.pbs.org/newshour/politics/most-americans-think-u-s-failed-in-afghanistan).
4 Peter D. Feaver, *Thanks for Your Service: The Causes and Consequences of Public Confidence in the US Military* (New York: Oxford University Press, 2023), p. 1.
5 Pauline Shanks Kaurin, "An 'Unprincipled Principal': Implications for Civil-Military Relations," *Strategic Studies Quarterly*, www.airuniversity.af.edu/Portals/10/SSQ/documents/Volume-15_Issue-2/Kaurin.pdf.
6 Bismarck's quotation is the springboard for Walter Russell Mead's *Special Providence: American Foreign Policy and How it Changed the World* (New York: Routledge, 2002).
7 George Washington to Alexander Hamilton, April 4, 1783 (National Archives, Founders Online, https://founders.archives.gov/documents/Washington/99-01-02-10993).
8 Dwight Eisenhower, quoted in H. R. McMaster, *Dereliction of Duty* (New York: HarperCollins, 1997), p. 26.
9 Feaver, *Thanks for Your Service*, p. 2.
10 Mohamed Younis, "Confidence in US Military Lowest in Over Two Decades," Gallup, July 31, 2023 (https://news.gallup.com/poll/509189/confidence-military-lowest-two-decades.aspx).
11 Feaver, *Thanks for Your Service*, p. 3.

12 McMaster, *Dereliction of Duty*, p. 117.
13 Eliot A. Cohen, "The Unequal Dialogue: The Theory and Reality of Civil–Military Relations and the Use of Force," in *Soldiers and Civilians: The Civil–Military Gap and American National Security*, ed. Peter D. Feaver and Richard H. Kohn (Cambridge, MA: MIT Press, 2001), p. 449.
14 Ibid., p. 457.
15 Ibid., p. 432.
16 Peter D. Feaver, *Armed Servants: Agency, Oversight, and Civil–Military Relations* (Cambridge, MA: Harvard University Press, 2005).
17 Maxwell Taylor, quoted in McMaster, *Dereliction of Duty*, p. 36.

Chapter 2 Origin Story

1 Thomas Jefferson, "I am a sect by myself," quoted in Jon Meacham, *American Gospel: God, the Founding Fathers, and the Making of a Nation* (New York: Random House, 2007), p. 4.
2 Joseph Ellis, *His Excellency George Washington* (New York: Alfred A. Knopf, 2004), p. xiv.
3 Garry Wills, *Cincinnatus: George Washington and the Enlightenment* (New York: Doubleday, 1984), p. xxi.
4 Christopher Logue, *War Music* (Chicago: University of Chicago Press, 2003), p. 91.
5 Robert Middlekauff, *Benjamin Franklin and His Enemies* (Berkeley: University of California Press, 1996), p. 1.
6 Ellis, *His Excellency George Washington*, p. 65.
7 Barbara W. Tuchman, *The First Salute* (New York: Alfred A. Knopf, 1988), p. 183.
8 Ellis, *His Excellency George Washington*, p. 68.
9 Lindsay Chervinsky, *Making the Presidency: John Adams and the Precedents that Forged the Republic* (New York: Oxford University Press, 2024), p. 3.
10 Samuel Adams to James Warren, Samuel Adams Heritage Society (www.samuel-adams-heritage.com/documents/samuel-adams-to-james-warren-1776.html).
11 George Washington to Thomas Gage, August 19, 1775, in *The Papers of George Washington*, Revolutionary War Series, Vol. 1: *June – Sept. 1775*, ed. W. W. Abbott and Dorothy Twohig (Charlottesville: University Press of Virginia, 1985), pp. 326–8.
12 Don Higginbotham, *George Washington and the American Military Tradition*, Mercer University Lamar Memorial Lectures No. 27 (Athens: University of Georgia Press, 1985), p. 38.
13 Barbara W. Tuchman, *The First Salute* (New York: Alfred A. Knopf, 1988), pp. 182–3; Wills, *Cincinnatus*, p. 4.
14 Ellis, *His Excellency George Washington*, pp. 82–3.
15 George Washington, Letter to Samuel Huntington, George Washington Papers, Series 3, Varick Transcripts, 1775–1785, Subseries 3A, Continental Congress, 1775–1783, Letterbook 4 (alt. Vol. 23, p. 622).
16 Tuchman, *The First Salute*, p. 183.
17 George Washington to Henry Laurens, December 23, 1777, *The Papers of George Washington*, Revolutionary War Series, vol. 12: *October–December 1777*, ed. Frank E. Grizzard, Jr., and David R. Hoth (Charlottesville: University Press of Virginia, 2002), pp. 683–7.

NOTES TO PP. 18–22

18 General Friedrich Wilhelm von Steuben, quoted in John C. Miller, *Triumph of Freedom, 1775–1783* (Boston: Little, Brown, 1948), p. 562.
19 Ellis, *His Excellency George Washington*, p. 98; Higginbotham, *George Washington and the American Military Tradition*, p. 76.
20 George Washington to John Hancock, December 31, 1775, *The Papers of George Washington*, Revolutionary War Series, vol. 12, p. 623.
21 Douglas Southall Freeman describes Washington's military leadership as nine-tenths administrator and only one-tenth fighting general. Freeman, *Washington* (New York: Simon & Schuster, 1985), p. 512.
22 George Washington, quoted in Ellis, *His Excellency George Washington*, p. 85.
23 The language is Ellis's; ibid., pp. 91, 100–2.
24 Wills, *Cincinnatus*, pp. 3–16.
25 Henry Knox et al., "The address and petition of the officers of the Army of the United States," Dec. 1782, in *Journals of the Continental Congress, 1774–1789*, Vol. XXIV, pp. 291–3.
26 Richard H. Kohn, "The Inside History of the Newburgh Conspiracy: America and the Coup d'Etat," *William and Mary Quarterly*, Third Series, 27/2 (1970), p. 190.
27 Both Kohn and Fleming put Hamilton as the link between disgruntled soldiers and the financiers backing their play. Kohn, "The Inside History of the Newburgh Conspiracy," pp. 191–3; Thomas Fleming, *The Perils of Peace: America's Struggle for Survival after Yorktown* (Washington, DC: Smithsonian Institution, 2007), p. 261. And Hamilton later admitted as much to Washington, writing: "It was essential to our cause that vigorous efforts should be made to restore public credit – it was necessary to combine all the motives to this end, that could operate upon different descriptions of persons in the different states. The necessity and discontents of the army presented themselves as a power engine." Hamilton to Washington, April 8, 1783, in *The Papers of Alexander Hamilton* (New York: Columbia University Press), Vol. III, pp. 318–19.
28 James Madison, the Congress's secretary, records that the anti-Federalists "smiled at the disclosure . . . that Mr. Hamilton had let out the secret." James Madison, "Notes on Debates," January 28, 1783, in *The Writings of James Madison*, ed. G. G. Hunt (New York: G. P. Putnam's Sons, 1900–10), vol. I, pp. 335–6, 336n.
29 The quotation from the letter is used by Washington in his rebuttal. George Washington, Newburgh Address (https://constitutioncenter.org/the-constitution/historic-document-library/detail/george-washington-newburgh-address-1783).
30 George Washington to Alexander Hamilton, April 4, 1783 (National Archives, Founders Online, https://founders.archives.gov/documents/Washington/99-01-02-10993).
31 Knox reported to the advocates of insurrection that he would not circumvent the military chain of command but would insist on "proper authority," meaning Washington. Henry Knox to Gouverneur Morris, February 21, 1783, Newburgh records, Henry Knox Papers, LIII, i6.
32 George Washington, Newburgh Address.
33 Kohn, "The Inside History of the Newburgh Conspiracy," p. 211.
34 Robert K. Wright, Jr., *The Continental Army* (Washington, DC: Center of Military History, United States Army, 1983), pp. 177–9.

35 George Washington, Circular letter to the States, June 8, 1783 (National Archives, Founders Online, https://founders.archives.gov/documents/Washington/99-01-02-11404).
36 Alexander Hamilton to John Laurens, August 15, 1782 – the last letter known between them before Laurens's death (National Archives, Founders Online, https://founders.archives.gov/documents/Hamilton/01-03-02-0058).
37 George Washington, December 23, 1783 (National Archives, Founders Online, https://founders.archives.gov/documents/Jefferson/01-06-02-0319-0004).
38 Wills, *Cincinnatus*, p. 18.
39 Richard Kohn, *Eagle and Sword: The Beginnings of the Military Establishment in America* (New York: Free Press, 1975), p. 2.
40 Quoted in Higginbotham, *George Washington and the American Military Tradition*, pp. 45–6.
41 William Hogeland, "Why the Whiskey Rebellion Is Worth Remembering Now" (University of Richmond, History News Network, http://hnn.us/articles/27341.html).
42 Michael J. Hillyard, *Cincinnatus and the Citizen-Servant Ideal: The Roman Legend's Life, Times, and Legacy* (Philadelphia: Xlibris, 2001). Livy is the original source, casting Cincinnatus as the ideal of civic virtue.
43 Benjamin Franklin to Sarah Bache, January 26, 1784, included in *The Works of Benjamin Franklin: Containing Several Political and Historical Tracts Not Included in Any Former Edition, and Many Letters, Official and Private, Not Hitherto Published; with Notes and a Life of the Author*, ed. Jared Sparks (Boston: Hillard Gray, 1836–40), vol. 10, p. 58.
44 Ellis, *His Excellency George Washington*, p. 114.
45 Higginbotham, *George Washington and the American Military Tradition*, p. 103.
46 Kohn, *Eagle and Sword*, p. 13.
47 Richard Kohn writes in his magisterial history of the US military that "eighteenth-century Americans considered navies and naval force so different from armies and military force that the two must logically be treated separately." Ibid., p. xii.
48 *Federalist* nos. 8, 11, 22, 23, 24, 25, 26, 27, 28, 29, 41, 67, and 74 all address concerns about creating federal military forces and how to prevent them becoming a tool of tyranny.
49 Brutus IX, *New York Journal*, January 17, 1788, in *The Documentary History of the Ratification of the Constitution, Digital Edition*, pp. 617–18.
50 *Federalist* no. 41 (https://avalon.law.yale.edu/18th_century/fed41.asp).
51 *Federalist* no. 25 (https://avalon.law.yale.edu/18th_century/fed25.asp).
52 Brutus IX, *The Complete Anti-Federalist*, ed. Herbert J. Storing (Chicago: University of Chicago Press, 1981), Vol. 2, Part 2, pp. 408–13.
53 *The Anti-Federalist: Writings by the Opponents of the Constitution*, ed. Herbert J. Storing (Chicago: University of Chicago Press, 1985), p. 293.
54 Herbert J. Storing, Speeches of Patrick Henry in the Virginia State Ratifying Convention, 9 June 1788 (*The Anti-Federalist*, Chicago: University of Chicago Press, 1985), p. 316.
55 Gerry's position is recorded by James Madison in his secretarial reporting, July 25, 1787. James Madison, *Notes of Debates in the Federal Convention of 1787* (Athens: Ohio University Press, 1987).
56 Thomas Jefferson to George Washington, May 23, 1792, National Archives, Founders Online (https://founders.archives.gov/documents/Jefferson/01-23-02-0491).

57 Hogeland, *The Whiskey Rebellion*, p. 9.
58 David P. Szatmary, *Shays' Rebellion: The Making of an Agrarian Insurrection* (Amherst: University of Massachusetts Press, 1984), pp. 10–15.
59 Thomas P. Slaughter, *The Whiskey Rebellion: Frontier Epilogue to the American Revolution* (New York: Oxford University Press, 1986), p. 108.
60 The state of Kentucky's prominence in the whiskey industry gained advantage at this time because the tax was never collected there, as no local authorities could be persuaded to enforce collection or bring legal action against evaders. See David M. Gross, *99 Tactics of Successful Tax Resistance Campaigns* (San Luis Obispo, CA: Picket Line Press, 2014), pp. 77–8.
61 George Washington, Proclamation, September 15, 1792, National Archives, Founders Online (https://founders.archives.gov/documents/Washington/05-11-02-0058).
62 Alexander Hamilton, published under the pseudonym Tully No. 1, *American Daily Advertiser*, August 23, 1794, National Archives, Founders Online (https://founders.archives.gov/documents/Hamilton/01-17-02-0102).
63 George Washington, "August 7, 1794: Proclamation against Opposition to Execution of Laws and Excise Duties in Western Pennsylvania" (University of Virginia Miller Center, https://millercenter.org/the-presidency/presidential-speeches/august-7-1794-proclamation-against-opposition-execution-laws).
64 Washington complained that militia were no more effective than efforts "to raize the Dead." Cited in Higginbotham, *George Washington and the American Military Tradition*, p. 24.
65 Slaughter, *The Whiskey Rebellion*, pp. 210–14.
66 Stanley M. Elkins and Eric L. McKitrick, *The Age of Federalism* (New York: Oxford University Press, 1993), pp. 474–88.
67 Hogeland, *The Whiskey Rebellion*, p. 238.
68 George Washington, Seventh Annual Address to Congress, December 8, 1795 (www.presidency.ucsb.edu/documents/seventh-annual-address-congress).
69 George Washington, quoted in Robert Feer, "Shays's Rebellion and the Constitution: A Study in Causation," *New England Quarterly*, 42/3 (1969), p. 396.
70 Carol Berkin, *A Sovereign People: The Crises of the 1790s and the Birth of American Nationalism* (New York: Basic Books, 2017), p. 7.
71 Thomas Jefferson to William Stephens Smith, November 13, 1787, quoted in Eric Foner, *Give Me Liberty! An American History* (New York: W. W. Norton, 2006), p. 219.
72 Hogeland, *Whiskey Rebellion*, p. 241. Samuel Elliot Morrison shared the view that Hamilton's motives were social control rather than revenue. See S. E. Morison, *The Oxford History of the United States, 1783–1917* (New York: Oxford University Press, 1927), p. 182.
73 The charge was made by one of the insurrectionists' defenders, Congressman William Findley, in *History of the Insurrection*, cited in Hogeland, *Whiskey Rebellion*, pp. 245–6.
74 Ellis, *His Excellency George Washington*, p. 151.
75 Don Higginbotham, *George Washington and the American Military Tradition*, pp. 41–3.
76 Ibid., p. 104.
77 George III, quoted by Benjamin West (Library of Congress, https://blogs.loc.gov/manuscripts/2022/12/george-washington-the-greatest-man-in-the-world/).

Chapter 3 Bad Examples

1 Richard Kohn, *Eagle and Sword: The Beginnings of the Military Establishment in America* (New York: Free Press, 1975), p. 41.
2 Samuel E. Finer, *The Man on Horseback: The Role of the Military in Politics* (London: Pall Mall Press, 1962), p. 3.
3 Bertha Ann Reuter, *Anglo-American Relations during the Spanish–American War* (New York: Macmillan, 1924), p. 2.
4 Joseph Ellis, *Founding Brothers* (New York: Alfred A. Knopf, 2001), p. 197.
5 Dennis C. Rasmussen, *Fears of a Setting Sun: The Disillusionment of America's Founders* (Princeton, NJ: Princeton University Press, 2021).
6 Francis A. Boyle, *Protesting Power: War, Resistance, and Law* (Lanham, MD: Rowman & Littlefield, 2007), p. 78.
7 Larry Sechrest, "Privately Funded and Built US Warships in the Quasi-War of 1797–1801," *Independent Review*, XII/1 (2007), p. 103.
8 Donald R. Hickey, "The Quasi-War: America's First Limited War, 1798–1801," *Northern Mariner/Le marin du nord*, XVIII/3–4 (2008), pp. 67–77 (www.cnrs-scrn.org/northern_mariner/vol18/tnm_18_3-4_67-77.pdf).
9 Michael A. Palmer, *Stoddert's War: Naval Operations during the Quasi-War with France, 1798–1801* (Columbia: University of South Carolina Press, 1989), p. x; Jon Paul Eclov, *Informal Alliance: Royal Navy and US Navy Co-operation against Republican France during the Quasi-War and Wars of the French Revolution* (dissertation, University of North Dakota, 2013), pp. 223–4.
10 John Keats, *Eminent Domain: The Louisiana Purchase and the Making of America* (New York: Charterhouse, 1973), pp. 269–70.
11 Stanley Elkins and Eric MacKitrick, *The Age of Federalism: The Early American Republic, 1788–1800* (New York: Oxford University Press, 1993), pp. 55–73.
12 Gregory E. Fehlings, "America's First Limited War," *Naval War College Review*, 53/3 (2000), p. 18. The issue was referred to the Supreme Court in *Bas* v. *Tingy* and *Talbot* v. *Seeman*, which affirmed unanimously that, although not formally declared, a state of war had existed between France and the US. The ruling established the constitutionality of "police actions," although the Constitution did not expressly give the legislature that intermediate power short of declaring war. Justice Bushrod Washington wrote: "every contention by force, between two nations, in external matters, under the authority of their respective governments, is not only war, but public war."
13 Palmer, *Stoddert's War*, pp. 30–1.
14 E. Wilson Lyon, "The Franco-American Convention of 1800," *Journal of Modern History*, 12/3 (1940), p. 313.
15 James Madison, quoted in Kohn, *Eagle and Sword*, p. 221.
16 William Murphy, "John Adams: The Politics of the Additional Army, 1798–1800," *New England Quarterly*, 52/2 (1979), pp. 234–49.
17 Abigail Adams, July 10, 1798 (Adams Papers, Massachusetts Historical Society).
18 Ellis, *Founding Brothers*, p. 194; Kohn, *Eagle and Sword*, p. 253. Presidential historian Lindsey Chervinsky attests Adams's suspicions were well-founded (personal interview, September 8, 2024). Abigail frequently expounded in their letters on her distrust of Hamilton, whom she described as "A Man ambitious as Julius Ceasar [sic]. A subtle

intriguer, his abilities would make him dangerous if he was to espouse a wrong side. His thirst for Fame is insatiable" (letter from Abigail Adams to John Adams, December 31, 1796, Massachusetts Historical Society) (www.masshist.org/digitaladams/archive/doc?id=L1796 1231aa&bc=%2Fdigitaladams%2Farchive%2Fbrowse%2Fletters_1796_1801.php).

19 Kohn, *Eagle and Sword*, pp. 247–8.
20 Andro Linklater, *An Artist in Treason: The Extraordinary Double Life of General James Wilkinson* (New York: Walker, 2009), p. 86.
21 Alan D. Gaff, *Bayonets in the Wilderness: Anthony Wayne's Legion in the Old Northwest* (Norman: University of Oklahoma Press, 2004), pp. 22–33.
22 Howard Cox, *American Traitor* (Washington, DC: Georgetown University Press, 2023), pp. 277–85.
23 The case went to the Supreme Court, Justice John Marshall writing for the majority that treason must be narrowly defined.
24 Buckner F. Melton, Jr., *Aaron Burr: Conspiracy to Treason* (New York: John Wiley & Sons, 2001), p. 66.
25 Douglas O. Linder, *The Treason Trial of Aaron Burr: An Account* (www.famous-trials.com/burr/156-home).
26 Melton, *Aaron Burr*, p. 92.
27 Linder, *The Treason Trial of Aaron Burr*.
28 Alan Pell Crawford, "Founding Traitor," *American Conservative*, December 1, 2010. Wilkinson published the letter in his 1816 memoir; James Wilkinson to Thomas Jefferson, 12 November 1806 (National Archives, Founders Online, https://founders.archives.gov/documents/Jefferson/99-01-02-4537).
29 Ciphered letter from Aaron Burr to James Wilkinson, http://law2.umkc.edu/faculty/projects/ftrials/burr/burrletter.html. Incidentally, the provisioner and supporter of Burr's efforts in Tennessee was Andrew Jackson.
30 Crawford, "Founding Traitor."
31 Aaron Burr, quoted in Linder, *The Treason Trial of Aaron Burr*.
32 John Randolph, quoted in Nancy Isenberg, "The 'Little Emperor': Aaron Burr, Dandyism, and the Sexual Politics of Treason," in *Beyond the Founders: New Approaches to the Political History of the Early American Republic*, ed. Jeffrey L. Pasley, Andrew W. Robertson, and David Waldstreicher (Chapel Hill: University of North Carolina, 2004), p. 148.
33 William Gardner Bell, "Commanding Generals and Chiefs of Staff, 1775–2005," US Army Center of Military History, 1983 (https://web.archive.org/web/20210306044230/https://history.army.mil/books/cg&csa/Wilkinson-J2.htm).
34 Linklater, *An Artist in Treason*, p. 133.
35 David O. Stewart, *American Emperor* (New York: Simon & Schuster, 2011), p. 299. See also Robert Brammer, "General James Wilkinson, the Spanish Spy Who was a Senior Officer in the US Army during Four Presidential Administrations," Library of Congress, April 21, 2020 (https://blogs.loc.gov/law/2020/04/general-james-wilkinson-the-spanish-spy-who-commanded-the-u-s-army-during-four-presidential-administrations/).
36 James Wilkinson, "Colonel Thomas Butler and General Wilkinson's 'Roundhead Order,'" *Pennsylvania Magazine of History and Biography*, 17/4 (1893), pp. 501–12.
37 Andrew Lambert, *The Challenge: Britain against America in the Naval War of 1812* (London: Faber & Faber, 2012), p. 26.

38 H. W. Brands, *Andrew Jackson: His Life and Times* (New York: Random House, 2005), p. 163. An estimated ten thousand Americans were impressed into Royal Navy service between 1795 and 1812. Donald R. Hickey, *Don't Give Up the Ship! Myths of the War of 1812* (Champaign: University of Illinois Press, 2006), p. 21.

39 David S. Heidler and Jeanne T. Heidler, *Manifest Destiny* (Westport, CT: Greenwood Press, 2003), p. 9.

40 The Northwest Territory encompassed all land west of Pennsylvania, east of the Mississippi River, and northwest of the Ohio River, an expanse of over 300,000 square miles. It constituted a full third of US territory, what are now the states of Ohio, Indiana, Illinois, Michigan, and Wisconsin, and the northeastern part of Minnesota.

41 Kori Schake, "Strategic Excellence: Tecumseh and the Shawnee Confederacy," in *The New Makers of Modern Strategy*, ed. Hal Brands (Princeton, NJ: Princeton University Press, 2023), pp. 369–90.

42 Carl Benn, *The War of 1812* (London: Osprey, 2002), pp. 20–1.

43 Michael O. Wise, "Watch What We Do, Not What We Say – Executive War-Making Powers in 1818," *Florida State University Law Review*, 1/3 (1973), p. 477.

44 Herbert Bruce Fuller, *The Purchase of Florida* (Gainesville: University Press of Florida, 1964), p. 254; John Spencer Bassett, *A Short History of the United States* (New York: Macmillan, 1915), pp. 261–2.

45 James Parton, *Life of Andrew Jackson* (London: Wentworth Press, 1861), p. 555.

46 James D. Richardson, ed., *A Compilation of the Messages and Papers of the Presidents*, Vol. II, Part 1 (New York: Bureau of National Literature and Art, 1897), p. 31.

47 Jackson wrote that suggestion to Secretary of War John C. Calhoun, who recommended against. Parton, *Life of Andrew Jackson*, p. 335.

48 Andrew Jackson to James Monroe, January 6, 1818, *The Papers of Andrew Jackson*, http://thepapersofandrewjackson.utk.edu/wp-content/uploads/2014/04/AJ-to-Monroe_January-6_1818.pdf.

49 Jackson's objections to Gaines's instructions are detailed in the notes for Jackson to Monroe, ibid.

50 John Quincy Adams, *Memoirs of John Quincy Adams, comprising Portions of his Diary from 1795 to 1848* (Philadelphia: J. B. Lippincott, 1874–7), pp. 108–15.

51 The assessment of public reaction is from Parton, *Life of Andrew Jackson*, pp. 506–56.

52 Lacock Committee Report, Mr Lacock, from the committee appointed in pursuance of the resolution of the Senate, of the 18th of December last, that the message of the President, and documents relative to the Seminole War (US Congress, 1819) (https://digital.library.pitt.edu/islandora/object/pitt%3A31735054848670/viewer#page/1/mode/2up).

53 Russell Weigley, "The American Civil–Military Culture Gap," in *Soldiers and Civilians: The Civil–Military Gap and American National Security*, ed. Peter D. Feaver and Richard H. Kohn (Cambridge, MA: MIT Press, 2001), pp. 224–5.

54 Parton, *Life of Andrew Jackson*, p. 463.

55 John S. D. Eisenhower, *Zachary Taylor* (New York: Time Books, 2008), pp. 7–8.

56 Ibid., p. 31. The Whig Party in America opposed territorial expansion, favored congressional over executive power, and advocated economic protectionism and domestic subsidies.

57 Ulysses Grant, *The Personal Memoirs of Ulysses S. Grant: The Complete Annotated Edition* (Cambridge, MA: Belknap Press, 2017), p. 43.
58 Robert W. Merry, *A Country of Vast Designs: James K. Polk, the Mexican War, and the Conquest of the American Continent* (New York: Simon & Schuster, 2010), pp. 240–2.
59 K. Jack Bauer, *Zachary Taylor: Soldier, Planter, Statesman of the Old Southwest* (Baton Rouge: Louisiana State University Press, 1985), pp. 116–23; Joseph Reese Fry, *A Life of Gen. Zachary Taylor* (Carlisle, MA: Applewood Books, 2009), pp. 186–7; Holman Hamilton, *Zachary Taylor: Soldier of the Republic*, Vol. 1 (Indianapolis: Bobbs-Merrill, 1941), pp. 198–9.
60 Zachary Taylor quoted in Zachary Taylor, The White House, https://bidenwhitehouse.archives.gov/about-the-white-house/presidents/zachary-taylor/.
61 Robert Morgan, *Lions of the West* (Chapel Hill, NC: Algonquin Books, 2011), p. 243; Lewis H. Garrard, *Wah-to-yah and the Taos Trail; or, Prairie Travel and Scalp Dances, with a Look at Los Rancheros from Muleback and the Rocky Mountain Campfire* (1850, repr. Norman: University of Oklahoma Press, 1955), pp. 214–15.
62 Dale L. Walker, *Bear Flag Rising: The Conquest of California, 1846* (New York: Forge Books, 1999), pp. 143–4.
63 Francis B. Heitman, *Historical Register and Dictionary of the United States Army* (2 vols, Urbana: University of Illinois Press, 1965), Vol. 1, p. 949.
64 Peter D. Feaver, "Crisis as Shirking: An Agency Theory Explanation of the Souring of American Civil–Military Relations," *Armed Forces & Society*, 24/3 (1998).
65 J. C. Fremont, Proclamation of martial law, August 30, 1861, www.ohiocivilwarcentral.com/fremonts-declaration-of-martial-law/.
66 Eugene Morrow Violette, *A History of Missouri* (Lexington, MA: Heath & Co., 1918), p. 363.
67 Doris Kearns Goodwin, *Team of Rivals: The Political Genius of Abraham Lincoln* (New York: Simon & Schuster, 2005), p. 391.
68 James M. McPherson, *Battle Cry of Freedom: The Civil War Era* (New York: Oxford University Press, 1988), p. 356.
69 John C. Fremont, "Geographical Memoir upon Upper California, Map of Oregon and California" (House of Representatives, 30th Congress, 2nd Session, 1848, Miscellaneous, No. 5, 40pp.), www.goldengate.org/bridge/history-research/statistics-data/whats-in-a-name/.
70 Fremont was exonerated of mutiny but convicted of several other charges and dishonorably discharged. Theodore Grivas, *Military Governments in California, 1846–1850; with a Chapter on Their Prior Use in Louisiana, Florida, and New Mexico* (Glendale, CA: A. H. Clark, 1963), p. 77.
71 Allen C. Guelzo, *Lincoln's Emancipation Proclamation: The End of Slavery in America* (New York: Simon & Schuster, 2004), p. 55.
72 This version of the oath was formulated in 1860. Oath of Enlistment (Veteran.com).
73 Robert E. Lee, quoted by Charles Anderson, in Douglas Southall Freeman, *R. E. Lee: A Biography* (4 vols, New York: Charles Scribner's Sons, 1936), Vol. 1, p. 429.
74 Herbert J. Storing, ed., *The Anti-Federalist: Writings by the Opponents of the Constitution* (Chicago: University of Chicago Press, 1985), pp. 13–20, 145–58.

75 US Constitution, Article VI; Vic Snyder, "You've Taken an Oath to Support the Constitution, Now What? The Constitutional Requirement for a Congressional Oath of Office," *University of Arkansas at Little Rock Law Review*, 23/4 (2001), p. 909.
76 George Washington, quoted in Matthew J. Pauley, *I Do Solemnly Swear: The President's Constitutional Oath* (Lanham, MD: University Press of America, 1999), p. 115.
77 Snyder, "You've Taken an Oath to Support the Constitution, Now What?," p. 907.
78 Robert E. Lee, quoted in Ron Chernow, *Grant* (New York: Penguin Books, 2018), p. 514.
79 Marguerite Merington, *The Custer Story: The Life and Intimate Letters of George A. Custer and His Wife Elizabeth* (Lincoln: University of Nebraska Press, 1987); Jeffry Wert, *Custer* (New York: Simon & Schuster, 2015), p. 21.
80 George Armstrong Custer, quoted in Ralph Kirschner, *The Class of 1861: Custer, Ames, and Their Classmates after West Point* (Carbondale: Southern Illinois University Press, 1999), p. 3.
81 Tom Carhart, *Lost Triumph: Lee's Real Plan at Gettysburg and Why it Failed* (New York: G. P. Putnam's Sons, 2003), pp. 132–3.
82 James S. Robbins, *Last in Their Class: Custer, Pickett and the Goats of West Point* (New York: Encounter Books, 2006), p. 268.
83 Lawrence A. Frost, *The Court-Martial of General George Armstrong Custer* (Norman: University of Oklahoma Press, 1968), pp. 81, 88–9, 99–100, 245–6.
84 Edgar J. Stewart, Introduction, *My Life on the Plains, or Personal Experiences with Indians* (Norman: University of Oklahoma Press, new edn, 1962), p. xxiv.
85 David Nevin, *The Old West: The Soldiers* (New York: Time Life Books, 1973), p. 202.
86 Stephen E. Ambrose, *Crazy Horse and Custer: The Parallel Lives of Two American Warriors* (New York: First Anchor, 1996), pp. 400–8.
87 Gregory F. Michno, *Lakota Noon: The Indian Narrative of Custer's Defeat* (Missoula, MT: Mountain Press, 1997), p. 168.
88 Joseph M. Marshall, III, *The Day the World Ended at Little Bighorn: A Lakota History* (New York: Viking Press, 2007), p. 121; Richard Hardoff, *The Custer Battle Casualties: Burials, Exhumations, and Reinterments* (El Segundo, CA: Upton and Sons, 1989), p. 21.
89 Citizenship was not extended to Native Americans until the 1924 Indian Citizenship Act.
90 Louise Barnett, *Touched by Fire: The Life, Death, and Mythic Afterlife of George Armstrong Custer* (New York: Henry Holt, 1996), p. 311.
91 William A. Graham, *Colonel* (Mechanicsburg, PA: Stackpole Books, 1953), pp. 115–17.

Chapter 4 A Standing Army

1 Joseph Nunn, "Martial Law in the United States: Its Meaning, its History, and Why the President Can't Declare it," Brennan Center for Justice, August 20, 2020.
2 Amanda Tyler, "*Habeas Corpus in Wartime* and Larger Lessons for Constitutional Law," *Harvard Law Review*, April 15, 2019.
3 Daniel E. Sutherland, "Abraham Lincoln and the Guerrillas," *Prologue Magazine*, 42/1 (2010); www.archives.gov/publications/prologue/2010/spring/lincoln-and-guerrillas.
4 Doris Kearns Goodwin, *Team of Rivals: The Political Genius of Abraham Lincoln* (New York: Simon & Schuster, 2006), p. 355; William H. Rehnquist, *All the Laws but One: Civil Liberties in Wartime* (New York: Alfred A. Knopf, 1998), pp. 26–39.

5 Anthony Gregory, *The Power of Habeas Corpus in America: From the King's Prerogative to the War on Terror* (Cambridge: Cambridge University Press, 2013), pp. 91–105.
6 Major W. W. Morris, quoted in Benson John Lossing, "The Capital Secured – Maryland Secessionists Subdued – Contributions by the People," *Pictorial Field Book of the Civil War*, Vol. I (Baltimore: Johns Hopkins University Press, [1866] 1997), pp. 449–50.
7 Ron Chernow, *Grant* (New York: Penguin Books, 2018), p. 486.
8 Papers of Ulysses S. Grant, 10:380, Letter from Abraham Lincoln, April 30, 1864.
9 Ibid., Letter to Abraham Lincoln, May 1, 1864.
10 Chernow, *Grant*, pp. 357–8.
11 Bruce Carton, *Never Call Retreat* (New York: Doubleday, 1965), p. 265. Lincoln's quote comes from "The President's Habeas Corpus Proclamation and the Act of Congress on the Subject," *New York Herald*, September 18, 1863, p. 6.
12 Ulysses S. Grant, *The Personal Memoirs of Ulysses S. Grant: The Complete Annotated Edition* (Cambridge, MA: Belknap Press, 2017), p. 276.
13 Abraham Lincoln, City Point Conference, quoted in Goodwin, *Team of Rivals*, p. 713.
14 Andrew Johnson, quoted in Chernow, *Grant*, p. 549.
15 Both the initial and final terms of surrender can be found at www.bennettplacehistoricsite.com/history/surrender-negotiations/.
16 Chernow, *Grant*, p. 537.
17 Washington DC's Memorial Bridge was built for the parade, crossing the Potomac River below Arlington House, the home of Robert E. Lee, whose property had been used as a burial ground for Union soldiers killed by the army Lee commanded. When Sherman paraded his troops in the 1865 Grand Review of the Armies, he had marching at its front Dr Mary Walker, a surgeon who had treated his force and who is the only female recipient of the Medal of Honor. Fort A. P. Hill was renamed in her honor by the secretary of defense in 2023 on recommendation of the Naming Commission.
18 Grant, *The Personal Memoirs of Ulysses S. Grant*, chap. LXX.
19 "General Grant and the Fight to Remove Emperor Maximilian from Mexico," National Park Service, www.nps.gov/articles/000/general-grant-and-the-fight-to-remove-emperor-maximilian-from-mexico.htm.
20 "French Intervention in Mexico and the American Civil War, 1862–1867," Office of the Historian, https://history.state.gov/milestones/1861-1865/french-intervention.
21 Philip Sheridan, *Personal Memoirs of P. H. Sheridan* (New York: Charles L. Webster, 1888), vol. 2, p. 206 (quoted in Chernow, *Grant*, pp. 555–6).
22 Jean Edward Smith, *Grant* (New York: Simon & Schuster, 2001), pp. 369–97.
23 Chernow, *Grant*, pp. 550–3.
24 William S. McFeeley, *Grant: A Biography* (New York: W. W. Norton, 1981), p. 257.
25 Jean Edward Smith, p. 434.
26 Chernow, *Grant*, pp. 582–3.
27 Papers of Ulysses S. Grant, 16:330–331, Letter to Maj. Gen. Philip H. Sheridan, October 12, 1866.
28 Ibid., 17:95, Letter to Maj. Gen. Philip H. Sheridan, April 5, 1867.
29 Chernow, *Grant*, p. 589.
30 Ibid., pp. 596–7.
31 General Grant's testimony, *Harper's Weekly*, December 14, 1867.

32 The Supreme Court decision in *Myers* v. *United States* established on separation of powers grounds that the president has sole authority to remove executive branch officials. The decision also expressly declared the Tenure in Office Act unconstitutional. Jerry L. Mashaw, "Of Angels, Pins, and For-Cause Removal: A Requiem for Passive Virtues," *University of Chicago Law Review Online*, August 27, 2020.

33 Chernow, *Grant*, p. 603.

34 Ibid., p. 606.

35 Elbert B. Smith, *The Presidencies of Zachary Taylor & Millard Fillmore* (Lawrence: University Press of Kansas, 1988), pp. 40–2, 244–7; Jared Cohen, *Accidental Presidents: Eight Men Who Changed America* (New York: Simon & Schuster, 2019), p. 51; John S. D. Eisenhower, *Agent of Destiny: The Life and Times of General Winfield Scott* (Norman: University of Oklahoma Press, 1999), pp. 202–3, 324–7.

36 Chernow, *Grant*, p. 594.

37 Historically, Reconstruction commences with President Lincoln's Emancipation Proclamation in 1863. Eric Foner, *Reconstruction: America's Unfinished Revolution, 1863–1877* (New York: HarperPerennial, 2014).

38 "Grant, Reconstruction, and the KKK," *PBS: The American Experience*, www.pbs.org/wgbh/americanexperience/features/grant-kkk/.

39 Legislation originally constrained only the Army, as it was the force utilized during Reconstruction. The Air Force was added in 1956; the Navy, Marine Corps, and Space Force (!) were added in 2021. The Coast Guard is not subject to Posse Comitatus because it is not part of the Department of Defense and its purpose is explicitly customs and maritime law enforcement.

40 Robert W. Coakley, *The Role of Federal Military Forces in Domestic Disorders, 1789–1878* (Washington, DC: Center of Military History, United States Army, 1989), p. 89.

41 Jennifer K. Elsea, *The Posse Comitatus Act and Related Matters: The Use of the Military to Execute Civilian Law*, Congressional Research Service, November 6, 2018. The District of Columbia is under congressional supervision because it is not a state; because there is no governor, DC National Guard forces are under the command of the president, who delegated that authority in 1949 to the secretary of the Army by Executive Order 10030, cited in District of Columbia National Guard (https://dc.ng.mil/About-Us/Heritage/History/#:~:text=Supervision%20and%20control%20of%20District,Establishment%20to%20administer%20affairs%20of).

42 Kelly Magsamen, "4 Ways Congress Can Amend the Insurrection Act," *Center for American Progress*, June 12, 2020 (www.americanprogress.org/article/4-ways-congress-can-amend-insurrection-act/).

43 Democratic governors of several states initially refused President Reagan's 1985 call-up for deployments to Central America, but in 1986 Congress passed the Montgomery Amendment upholding the federal government's supremacy over the foreign deployment of Guard forces. The Supreme Court ruled in 1990 that states cannot withhold Guard deployments for overseas missions. David Evans, "Supreme Court Confirms US Control Over Guard," *Chicago Tribune*, June 12, 1990 (www.chicagotribune.com/1990/06/12/supreme-court-confirms-us-control-over-guard/).

44 Title 10, US Code, section 275, Restriction on Direct Participation by Military Personnel (www.law.cornell.edu/uscode/text/10/275).

45 Elsea, *The Posse Comitatus Act and Related Matters*, pp. 35–6.

46 In the immediate aftermath of the Kent State University shootings, 58 percent of Americans blamed the students, while only 11 percent blamed the National Guard for the deaths. David Lawrence, "Campus Protests Linked to Drugs," *Palm Beach Post*, May 28, 1970, p. 14.
47 HR 5122, National Defense Authorization Act 2007.
48 Elsea, *The Posse Comitatus Act and Related Matters: The Use of the Military to Execute Civilian Law*, summary.
49 Ulysses S. Grant, *The Complete Personal Memoirs of Ulysses S. Grant* (New York: Library of America, 1990), p. lxx.
50 Kori Schake, *Lessons from the Indian Wars*, Hoover Institution, February 1, 2013; www.hoover.org/research/lessons-indian-wars.
51 Allan Lee Hamilton, "Remolino Raid," *Texas State Historical Association*, May 1, 1995 (www.tshaonline.org/handbook/entries/remolino-raid).
52 Mackenzie to Sherman, June 15, 1871, quoted in William Sturtevant Nye, *Carbine and Lance: The Story of Old Fort Sill* (Norman: University of Oklahoma Press, 1983), p. 191.
53 While the description of Sheridan's outburst comes only from later accounts, it is substantiated by participants in the raid and Army requisitions of ammunition. Robert G. Carter, *On the Border with Mackenzie* (New York: Antiquarian Press, 1935), pp. 429–30.
54 Charles M. Robinson III, *Bad Hand: A Biography of General Ranald S. Mackenzie* (Austin, TX: State House Press, 1993), p. 143.
55 Peter D. Feaver, *Thanks for Your Service: The Causes and Consequences of Public Confidence in the US Military* (New York: Oxford University Press, 2023), p. 270.
56 The phrase comes from Patricia Y. Stallard, *Glittering Misery: Dependents of the Indian Fighting Army* (Norman: University of Oklahoma Press, 1978).
57 1Lt T. F. Vaill, quoted in Robinson, *Bad Hand*, p. 23.
58 Samuel P. Huntington, *The Soldier and the State: The Theory and Politics of Civil–Military Relations* (Cambridge, MA: Belknap Press, 1957).

Chapter 5 Dogs That Mostly Didn't Bark

1 "The US Army in the 1890s," US Army Center of Military History (https://history.army.mil/Unit-History/Force-Structure-Support/The-US-Army-in-the-1890s/).
2 For an excellent history of US policy, see Charles Quince, *Resistance to the Spanish–American and Philippine Wars: Anti-Imperialism and the Role of the Press, 1895–1902* (Jefferson, NC: McFarland & Co., 2017).
3 Graham A. Cosmas, *An Army for Empire: The United States Army and the Spanish–American War* (Columbia: University of Missouri Press, 1971), chs 3–4.
4 *American Military History*, US Army Center of Military History, Vol. 1, chap. 15, "Emergence to World Power 1898–1902," p. 344 (https://history.army.mil/Portals/143/Images/Publications/Publication%20By%20Title%20Images/A%20Titles%20PDF/CMH_Pub_30-21.pdf?ver=6PXj48wX_Fb12hJPSor4yQ%3d%3d).
5 Ibid., p. 346.
6 Admiral George Dewey, "The Battle of Manila Bay," *War Times Journal* (www.wtj.com/archives/dewey2.htm).
7 *American Military History*, p. 349.
8 Ibid., p. 343.
9 The history of institutional resistance to innovations in accuracy is brilliantly recounted in

Michael L. Tushman and Charles O'Reilly III, *Winning through Innovation: A Practical Guide to Leading Organizational Change and Renewal* (Cambridge, MA: Harvard Business School, 2002).
10. *American Military History*, p. 373.
11. John Coatsworth, "United States Interventions: What For?," *ReVista*, 4/2 (2005) (https://revista.drclas.harvard.edu/united-states-interventions/). Coatsworth tabulates figures of both direct and indirect interventions through 1998.
12. Samuel Harrington, *The Strategy and Tactics of Small Wars* (1921).
13. US Marine Corps, *Small Wars Manual* ([1940] 1990) (www.marines.mil/Portals/1/Publications/FMFRP%2012-15%20%20Small%20Wars%20Manual.pdf).
14. *American Military History*, p. 365.
15. Hugh Rockoff, *Until It's Over, Over There: The US Economy in World War I*, National Bureau of Economic Research Working Paper #10580, 2004, p. 4 (www.nber.org/papers/w10580); Mark Jefferson, "Our Trade in the Great War," *Geographical Review*, 3/6 (1917), p. 474 (www.jstor.org/stable/207691).
16. Matthew S. Muehlbauer and David J. Ulbrich, *Ways of War: American Military History from the Colonial Era to the Twenty-First Century* (New York: Routledge, 2013), p. 295.
17. Jim Garamone, "World War I: Building the American Military," *DOD News*, April 3, 2017 (www.army.mil/article/185229/world_war_i_building_the_american_military).
18. U.S. Army Center for Military History, *The US Army in World War I* (https://www.govinfo.gov/content/pkg/GOVPUB-D114-PURL-gpo86034/pdf/GOVPUB-D114-PURL-gpo86034.pdf).
19. F. Gunther Eyck, "Secretary Stimson and the Army Reforms, 1911–1913," *Parameters*, 1/1 (1971), pp. 20–1.
20. *American Military History*, pp. 381–2.
21. Craig L. Symonds, *The US Navy: A Concise History* (New York: Oxford University Press, 2016), p. 73.
22. D'Ann Campbell, "Servicewomen of World War II," *Armed Forces & Society*, 16/2 (1990), pp. 251–70.
23. Joseph E. Persico, "Nov. 11, 1918: Wasted Lives on Armistice Day," *Military History Quarterly*, repr. in *Army Times*, November 7, 2017; www.armytimes.com/veterans/salute-veterans/2017/11/10/nov-11-1918-wasted-lives-on-armistice-day/.
24. Tara Finn, "The War That Did Not End at 11am on 11 November," National Archives blog, 9 November 2018 (https://history.blog.gov.uk/2018/11/09/the-war-that-did-not-end-at-11am-on-11-november/).
25. House of Representatives, Select Committee on Expenditures in the War Department, www.loc.gov/resource/gdcmassbookdig.expendituresinwa00unit/?st=gallery.
26. Political leaders wanted an independent contribution in order to have influence over the terms of post-war peace, while the military did not want to subordinate operations to a foreign commander (an exception was made for Black American soldiers, to whom Pershing refused to assign combat roles and who fought instead – with great valor – as part of the French force). This politically and militarily satisfying posture was incredibly costly because, rather than fitting US soldiers into existing French and British units that had the experience of already fighting for three years, Pershing's forces suffered casualties from inexperience.
27. Symonds, p. 70.

28 Navy Secretary Josephus Daniels, quoted in Branden Little, "Tarnishing Victory? Contested Histories and Civil–Military Discord in the US Navy, 1919-24," *Defense and Security Analysis*, 36/1 (2020), p. 1.
29 Tushman and O'Reilly, *Winning through Innovation*, pp. 4–6. Roosevelt not only required the technology adoption, he promoted Sims to the post of inspector of naval gunnery.
30 Little, "Tarnishing Victory?," p. 3.
31 While Theodore Roosevelt initiated the practice of presidentially directed gag orders, Roosevelt's purpose was to discipline his civilian appointees, whereas Wilson's was the first to attempt constraint of military commentary.
32 William S. Sims and Burton J. Hendrick, *Victory at Sea* (New York: Doubleday, 1920), p. 375.
33 Robert L. O'Connell, *Sacred Vessels: The Cult of the Battleship and the Rise of the US Navy* (New York: Oxford University Press, 1993), pp. 215–16, 236.
34 Woodrow Wilson, quoted in Josephus Daniels, *Our Navy at War* (New York: Pictorial Bureau, 1922), p. 146.
35 Daniels to Sims, June 26, 1919, included in Sims and Hendrick, *Victory at Sea*, pp. 371–2.
36 Josephus Daniels, *The Wilson Era*, Vol. 2: *Years of War and After, 1917–1923* (Chapel Hill: University of North Carolina Press, 1946), p. 504.
37 William Sims, quoted in Little, "Tarnishing Victory?," p. 13.
38 Josephus Daniels, *The Cabinet Diaries of Josephus Daniels, 1913–1921*, ed. Edmund David Cronon (Lincoln: University of Nebraska Press, 1963), p. 531.
39 "Closing Chapter Naval Squabble," *Palm Beach Post*, July 18, 1921, cited in Little, "Tarnishing Victory?," p. 16.
40 Little, "Tarnishing Victory?," p. 22.
41 William Sims to Julian Street, August 18, 1921, quoted ibid., p. 18.
42 Daniels's book *Our Navy at War* blamed Sims for the greatest error of the war, shifted the locus of decision-making from Sims back to Washington, quoted Sims's own testimony to reinforce his case, and generally outmaneuvered Sims and his supporters. *Our Navy at War* came to be considered the official history.
43 Mitchell, quoted in the *New York Times*, September 7, 1925, p. 4. Mitchell was court-martialed and reduced in rank for insubordination. In reporting on the verdict, the *Times* asserted: "The verdict is a vindication of Army discipline, and the deliberation with which it was arrived at deprives Colonel Mitchell of the pose of martyrdom." *New York Times*, December 18, 1925, p. 22.
44 Williamson Murray and Allan R. Millet, eds, *Military Innovation in the Interwar Period* (Cambridge: Cambridge University Press), p. 2.
45 Kellogg–Briand Pact 1928, Article 1 (https://avalon.law.yale.edu/20th_century/kbpact.asp).
46 Allan R. Millett elegantly writes: "even after Japan repudiated the Washington Conference treaties in 1936, hope and bankruptcy combined to keep the Royal Navy and the United States Navy under the treaty limits." Millett, "Assault from the Sea," in *Military Innovation in the Interwar Period*, ed. Williamson Murray and Allan R. Millett (Cambridge: Cambridge University Press, 1996), p. 51.
47 Geoffrey Till, "Adopting the Aircraft Carrier," ibid., pp. 191–227.
48 Holger H. Herwig, "Innovation Ignored: The Submarine Problem," ibid., pp. 227–64.

49 Millett, "Assault from the Sea," ibid., pp. 50–95.
50 For a more critical view of Army innovation, see Dave Shunk, "The Failure to Adapt and Innovate after a Drawdown: The US Army in the Interwar Years," *Small Wars Journal*, June 14, 2013 (https://archive.smallwarsjournal.com/jrnl/art/the-failure-to-adapt-and-innovate-after-a-drawdown-the-us-army-in-the-interwar-years-1919-1).
51 Williamson Murray, *Transformation and Innovation: The Lessons of the 1920s and 1930s*, Institute for Defense Analysis Paper P-3799, December 2002 (https://apps.dtic.mil/sti/pdfs/ADA423507.pdf).
52 The only significant civilian interference was establishing that aircraft carrier commanders needed to be aviators, and that was important in shaping the culture conducive to carrier development. See Williamson Murray, "Innovation: Past and Future," in *Military Innovation in the Interwar Period*, p. 316.
53 "The 1931 Bonus Army," National Park Service (www.nps.gov/articles/the-1932-bonus-army.htm); Herbert Hoover, "Statement about the Bonus Marchers," July 28, 1932 (text of a press conference with MacArthur included) (www.presidency.ucsb.edu/documents/statement-about-the-bonus-marchers).
54 Donald J. Lisio, *The President and Protest: Hoover, MacArthur, and the Bonus March* (New York: Fordham University Press, 1994), p. 210; Paul Dickson and Thomas B. Allen, "Marching on History," *Smithsonian Magazine*, February 2003 (www.smithsonianmag.com/history/marching-on-history-75797769/).
55 Stephen R. Ortiz, *Beyond the Bonus March and GI Bill: How Veteran Politics Shaped the New Deal Era* (New York: New York University Press, 2012), pp. 1–3.
56 Smedley Butler, quoted in Dan Kovalik, *Nicaragua: A History of US Intervention and Resistance* (Atlanta: Clarity Press, 2023), p. 38.
57 Hans Schmidt, *Maverick Marine: General Smedley D. Butler and the Contradictions of American Military History* (Lexington: University Press of Kentucky, 1998), p. 212.
58 Ibid., p. 218.
59 Smedley Butler, quoted in "Butler for Bonus Out of Wall Street," *New York Times*, December 10, 1933. See also Stephen R. Ortiz, "The 'New Deal' for Veterans: The Economy Act, the Veterans of Foreign Wars, and the Origins of the New Deal," *Journal of Military History*, 70 (2006), pp. 434–45.
60 Smedley Butler, *War is a Racket*, chap. 4 (www.ratical.org/ratville/CAH/warisaracket.html).
61 "Credulity Unlimited," *New York Times*, November 22, 1934 (https://timesmachine.nytimes.com/timesmachine/1934/11/22/93653760.html?pageNumber=20).
62 Richard H. Kohn, "Building Trust: Civil–Military Behaviors for Effective National Security," in *American Civil–Military Relations: The Soldier and the State in a New Era*, ed. Suzanne C. Nielsen and Don M. Snider (Baltimore: Johns Hopkins University Press, 2009), p. 271.
63 Mark A. Stoler, "US Civil–Military Relations in World War II," *Parameters*, 21/1 (1991), p. 61 (https://press.armywarcollege.edu/cgi/viewcontent.cgi?article=1610&context=parameters).
64 Dean Acheson, *Sketches from Life of Men I Have Known* (New York: Harper & Bros., 1959), pp. 163–4.
65 George Marshall, quoted in Forrest C. Pogue, *George C. Marshall: Organizer of Victory, 1943–1945* (New York: Viking Press, 1973), p. 315.

66 Kent Roberts Greenfield, *American Strategy in World War II: A Reconsideration* (Malabar, FL: Robert E. Krieger, 1963), pp. 52, 80–4.
67 Franklin Delano Roosevelt, quoted in Mark A. Stoler, "The 'Pacific-First' Alternative in American World War II Strategy," *International History Review*, 2/3 (1980), pp. 436–42, 451; Geoffrey C. Ward, *The Roosevelts: An Intimate History* (New York: Knopf Doubleday, 2014), p. 402.
68 The three quotations in this paragraph are all from Greenfield, *American Strategy in World War II*, p. 50.
69 Kori Schake, *Safe Passage: The Transition from British to American Hegemony* (Cambridge, MA: Harvard University Press, 2017), p. 267.
70 Report of the Joint Chiefs of Staff Special Committee for Reorganization of National Defense, JSC 3/1, April 1945, cited in *Organizational Development of the Joint Chiefs of Staff* (Joint History Office, Office of the Chairman of the Joint Chiefs of Staff, 2013), (www.jcs.mil/Portals/36/Documents/History/Institutional/Organizational_Develop ment_of_the_JCS.pdf), pp. 11–16.
71 Anand Toprani, "Budgets and Strategy: The Enduring Legacy of the Revolt of the Admirals," *Political Science Quarterly*, 134/1 (2019), pp. 126–8.
72 Steven L. Rearden, *History of the Office of the Secretary of Defense*, Vol. 1: *The Formative Years, 1847–1950* (Washington, DC: Office of the Secretary of Defense Historical Office, 1984), p. 12; https://apps.dtic.mil/sti/pdfs/ADA150543.pdf.
73 Jeffrey G. Barlow, *Revolt of the Admirals: The Fight for Naval Aviation, 1945–1950* (Washington, DC: Naval Historical Center, 2001), pp. 207–10.
74 The extent of Denfield's encouragement can be seen in reassigning to an admiral's billet a joint staff captain who'd been relieved for holding a press conference criticizing policy. The incident resulted in an official instruction that all public statements had to be cleared by the Office of the Navy Secretary.
75 Radford is quoted in Kenneth W. Condit, *The Joint Chiefs of Staff and National Policy*, Vol. II: *1947–1949* (Washington, DC: Office of Joint History/Office of the Chairman of the Joint Chiefs of Staff, 1996), p. 181; www.jcs.mil/Portals/36/Documents/History/ Policy/Policy_V002.pdf); Vandenberg quoted in "Revolt of the Admirals," *Time*, October 17, 1949.
76 Hanson W. Baldwin, "Unification Has Become an End, Instead of a Means – Navy Fears Borne Out in Part," *New York Times*, October 28, 1949.
77 House Armed Services Committee findings, cited in Condit, *The Joint Chiefs of Staff and National Policy*, pp. 187–8.
78 Peter C. Luebke, H-078-1: "The Revolt of the Admirals," Naval History and Heritage Command, March 2023, www.history.navy.mil/about-us/leadership/director/directors -corner/h-grams/h-gram-078/h-078-1.html.
79 Condit, *The Joint Chiefs of Staff and National Policy*, pp. 180–1.
80 The phrase is from Paul M. Sparrow, "'I Have Returned!' – General MacArthur and FDR," https://fdr.blogs.archives.gov/2015/10/20/i-have-returned-general-macarthur -and-fdr/#:~:text=As%20early%20as%201932%2C%20when,for%20the%20First%20 World%20War.
81 Omar Bradley, quoted in H. W. Brands, *The General vs. the President: MacArthur and Truman at the Brink of Nuclear War* (New York: Doubleday, 2016), p. 78.
82 Franklin D. Roosevelt, quoted in Sparrow, "'I Have Returned!'"

83 Secretary of Defense to the Commander in Chief, Far East, September 29, 1951, *Foreign Relations of the United States, 1950*, Vol. VII: *Korea*, ed. John P. Glennon (Washington, DC: Government Printing Office, 1976), p. 826.
84 D. Clayton James, "Command Crisis: MacArthur and the Korean War," USAFA Harmon Memorial Lecture, November 12, 1981, pp. 1–2; www.usafa.edu/app/uploads/Harmon24.pdf.
85 Harry S. Truman, quoted ibid., p. 5. James makes a strong case that MacArthur's firing exhibits civilian and military mistakes on the Washington side of the ledger as well, in particular his initial selection and the deference to his operational decisions given the political strategy of limiting the war. James also exonerates MacArthur of intelligence failure, placing responsibility on the CIA and State Department for failing to perceive Chinese intentions.
86 Lawrence Freedman, *Command* (New York: Oxford University Press, 2022), p. 22.
87 Harry S. Truman, Diary entry on April 6, 1951, in *Memoirs by Harry S. Truman: Years of Trial and Hope, 1946–1952* (New York: Doubleday, 1956), pp. 441–2, 444.
88 Freedman, *Command*, p. 25.
89 Supporting documentation included the December 6 joint chiefs' order not to speak publicly without State Department clearance; the March 20 joint chiefs' memorandum informing MacArthur of negotiations; MacArthur's op-ed in the *New York Times* of March 24 opposing negotiations; the March 24 joint chiefs' message to MacArthur reiterating the December 6 instruction; and MacArthur's letter of March 20 to Rep. Joseph W. Martin, Jr., published in the *Congressional Record*, April 5, 1951.
90 "Statement and Order by the President on Relieving General MacArthur of his Commands," April 11, 1951, www.trumanlibrary.gov/library/public-papers/77/statement-and-order-president-relieving-general-macarthur-his-commands.
91 Douglas MacArthur, "War Cannot Be Controlled, it Must Be Abolished," speech before the Massachusetts Legislature, July 25, 1951, cited in Freedman, *Command*, p. 520, n. 32.
92 Freedman, *Command*, p. 16.
93 Eliot Cohen terms this the "unequal dialogue." Cohen, *Supreme Command: Soldiers, Statesmen, and Leadership in Combat* (New York: Anchor, 2003), chap. 1.
94 Walter Lippman, *New York Herald Tribune*, April 30, 1951.
95 Harry S. Truman, quoted in "Historical Notes: Giving Them More Hell," *Time*, December 31, 1973, https://time.com/archive/6842059/historical-notes-giving-them-more-hell/.
96 Rebecca Livingston, "Sailors, Soldiers, and Marines of the Spanish–American War: The Legacy of USS *Maine*," *Prologue Magazine*, 30/1 (1998); www.archives.gov/publications/prologue/1998/spring/spanish-american-war.
97 Samuel J. Cox, H-023-1: "The Contribution of the US Navy during World War I," Naval History and Heritage Command, November 2018, www.history.navy.mil/about-us/leadership/director/directors-corner/h-grams/h-gram-023/h-023-1.html#:~:text=The%20Naval%20Act%20of%201916%20authorized%20the%20construction%20of%2010,be%20constructed%20in%20three%20years.

Chapter 6 The Modern Military

1 Harry S. Truman, "Our Armed Forces Must Be United," *Collier's Magazine*, August 26, 1944.

2 "President's Program to Unify the Services, With Army-Navy Views," *New York Times*, June 16, 1946, https://timesmachine.nytimes.com/timesmachine/1946/06/16/113134160.html?pageNumber=34.
3 The Marine Corps was in many ways the biggest beneficiary of the inter-service maneuvering because its size and composition were established by law. So concerned was the Corps, however, that Major General Merritt Edson, who led the Marine Corps study group on the legislation, submitted his resignation papers in order to testify against the legislation. Marine Corps Commandant Vandegrift declined to accept Edson's resignation; Edson proceeded to testify while on active duty, the only active-duty officer to do so, triggering his retirement. Gordon W. Keiser, *The US Marine Corps and Defense Unification, 1944–1947: The Politics of Survival* (Washington, DC: National Defense University Press, 1982).
4 "Army-Navy Dispute Back at White House," *New York Times*, June 1, 1946, https://timesmachine.nytimes.com/timesmachine/1946/06/01/93112866.html?pageNumber=7.
5 "Black Americans in the US Army," www.army.mil/blackamericans/timeline.html.
6 Walt Napier, "A Short History of Integration in the US Armed Forces," July 1, 2021, www.af.mil/News/Commentaries/Display/Article/2676311/a-short-history-of-integration-in-the-us-armed-forces/.
7 Adrian Lentz-Smith, *Freedom Struggles: African Americans and World War I* (Cambridge, MA: Harvard University Press, 2010), pp. 1–11.
8 "The Negro in the Navy," in *Kelly Miller's History of the World War for Human Rights* ... (Washington, DC: Austin Jenkins, 1919), pp. 555–99; www.history.navy.mil/content/history/nhhc/research/library/online-reading-room/title-list-alphabetically/n/negro-navy-by-miller.html.
9 Ranald Slidell Mackenzie, January 7, 1875, Mackenzie Papers, West Point Library.
10 Morris J. MacGregor, Jr., *Integration of the Armed Forces, 1940–1965* (Washington, DC: Center of Military History, 2001), pp. 399–401, 405.
11 Army Corps of Engineers, "Historical Vignette 011 – Former Chief Played a Part in Army Integration," www.usace.army.mil/About/History/Historical-Vignettes/Women-Minorities/011-Army-Integration/.
12 Robert B. Edgerton, *Hidden Heroism: Black Soldiers in America's Wars* (New York: Barnes & Noble, 2009), p. 165.
13 MacGregor, *Integration of the Armed Forces, 1940–1965*, p. 317.
14 Two laudable exceptions were retired General George Marshall, G-3 of the Army Lieutenant General Maxwell Taylor, and 8th Army Commander General Matthew Ridgway, who in May of 1951 formally requested the authority to abolish segregation in his command. Ibid., pp. 442–3.
15 James Burk and Evelyn Espinoza, "Race Relations within the US Military," *Annual Review of Sociology*, 38 (2012), pp. 401–22; MacGregor, *Integration of the Armed Forces, 1940–1965*, pp. 432–4.
16 Ibid., p. 456.
17 Ibid., p. 333.
18 Ibid., p. 336.
19 This was particularly true of the officers of the First Marine Division, one proclaiming, "never once did any color problem bother us ... It just wasn't any problem. We had one

Negro sergeant in command of an all-white squad and there was another – with a graves registration unit – who was one of the finest Marines I've ever seen." Ibid., p. 460.
20 Ibid., p. 465.
21 Chairman of the Personnel Policy Board Thomas Reid, quoted ibid., p. 347.
22 Ibid., pp. 389–90.
23 Ibid., p. 389; National Park Service, "Executive Order 9981, Desegregating the Military" (www.nps.gov/articles/000/executive-order-9981.htm#:~:text=On%20July%2026%2C%201948%2C%20President,desegregation%20of%20the%20U.S.%20military).
24 Peter D. Feaver, "Crisis as Shirking: An Agency Theory Explanation of the Souring of American Civil–Military Relations," *Armed Forces & Society*, 24/3 (1998), p. 408.
25 MacGregor's detailed study concludes: "Congress played only a minor role." MacGregor, *Integration of the Armed Forces, 1940–1965*, p. 380.
26 "Diary: Notes dictated by President Eisenhower on October 8, 1957, concerning meeting with Governor Faubus at Newport, Rhode Island, September 14, 1957 [Eisenhower Papers, Administration Series, Box 23, Little Rock Ark (2); NAID #186622]; www.eisenhowerlibrary.gov/sites/default/files/research/online-documents/civil-rights-little-rock/1957-10-08-diary-notes-faubus-meeting.pdf.
27 Press release, "Executive Order 10730, Providing Assistance for the Removal of an Obstruction of Justice within the State of Arkansas," September 24, 1957 [Kevin McCann Collection of Press and Radio Conferences and Press Releases, Box 20, September 1957; NAID #17366749]; www.eisenhowerlibrary.gov/sites/default/files/research/online-documents/civil-rights-little-rock/press-release-eo-10730.pdf.
28 Handwritten notes by President Eisenhower on decision to send troops to Little Rock, September 1957 [Eisenhower Papers, Administration Series, Box 23, Little Rock, Arkansas (2)]; https://crdl.usg.edu/record/dde_ddetimeline_130.
29 James F. Schnabel and Robert J. Watson, *The Joint Chiefs of Staff and National Policy*, Vol. III: *1950–1951, The Korean War, Part One* (Washington, DC: Office of Joint History, Office of the Chairman of the Joint Chiefs of Staff, 1998), p. 21; www.jcs.mil/Portals/36/Documents/History/Policy/Policy_V003_P001.pdf. George Kennan, author of the policy of containment, participated in the Solarium exercise and concluded it represented continuity, although he would subsequently decry what he considered its militarization. See Kori Schake, "Trump Doesn't Need a Second 'Solarium,'" *The Atlantic*, October 30, 2018; www.theatlantic.com/ideas/archive/2018/10/what-eisenhower-could-teach-trump-about-strategy/574261/.
30 NSC 5707/8 Basic National Security Policy, 3 June 1957 (supersedes NSC 5602/1), *Foreign Relations of the United States 1955–1957*, Vol. XIX, National Security Policy, #120, p. 511.
31 Franklin C. Miller, "Establishing the Ground Rules for Nuclear Operations," in Charles Glaser, Austin Long and Brian Radzinsky, eds, *Managing US Nuclear Operations in the 21st Century* (Washington, DC: Brookings Institution Press, 2022), p. 53.
32 Memorandum of Discussion at the 312th Meeting of the National Security Council, Washington, February 7, 1957, #108, "The Human Effects of Nuclear Weapons Development," *Foreign Relations of the United States [FRUS]*, p. 414.
33 Diary entry by the President's Press Secretary (Hagerty), January 4, 1955, *FRUS*, p. 5.

34 Diary entry by the President's Press Secretary (Hagerty), February 1, 1955, *FRUS*, #8, p. 40.
35 Secretary of Defense Wilson characterized their rejection in a Memorandum of Discussion at the 293rd and 294th Meetings of the National Security Council, in Washington, on August 16 and August 17, 1956: #86, "Fiscal and Budgetary Outlook through FY 1959," *FRUS*, p. 349.
36 Hanson W. Baldwin, "Local Atom War Held Improbable; War Games Said to Show that Tactical Nuclear Arms Lead to Wide Conflict," *New York Times*, December 5, 1955, p. 12.
37 Diary entry by the President's Press Secretary (Hagerty), January 3, 1955, *FRUS*, p. 3; Testimony by General Ridgway to the Senate Armed Services Committee, January 31, 1955; Diary entry by the President's Press Secretary (Hagerty), February 1, 1955, p. 59; Supplementary Notes of the Legislative Leadership Meeting, March 1, 1955, *FRUS*, p. 57; Memorandum of Discussion at the 244th Meeting of the National Security Council, Washington, April 7, 1955, "Status of United States Programs for National Security as of December 1954: The Military Program," *FRUS*, p. 76; Memorandum of Discussion at the 267th Meeting of the National Security Council, November 21, 1955, editorial note #41, *FRUS*, p. 152; Memorandum from the Joint Chiefs of Staff to the Secretary of Defense (Wilson), March 12, 1956, *FRUS* #64, pp. 235–6; Memorandum of Discussion at the 280th Meeting of the National Security Council, Washington, March 22, 1956, *FRUS*, #67, p. 270.
38 S. Everett Gleason, Minutes of Meeting of the National Security Council, May 2.
39 Miller, "Establishing the Ground Rules for Nuclear Operations," p. 57.
40 Alain Enthoven, quoted in Fred Kaplan, *The Wizards of Armageddon* (Stanford, CA: Stanford University Press, 1983), p. 254.
41 Francis Gavin argues that Kennedy's efforts produced almost no actual change. Francis J. Gavin, "The Myth of Flexible Response: United States Strategy in Europe during the 1960s," *International History Review*, 23/4 (2001), pp. 847–75.
42 Miller, "Establishing the Ground Rules for Nuclear Operations," p. 73.
43 Lawrence Freedman describes General LeMay as "infuriated" he wasn't included. Freedman, *Kennedy's Wars: Berlin, Cuba, Laos, and Vietnam* (New York: Oxford University Press, 2000), p. 180.
44 Arthur Schlesinger, *A Thousand Days: John F. Kennedy in the White House* (Boston: Houghton Mifflin, 1965), pp. 804, 808.
45 Jonathan Colman, "Toward 'World Support' and 'The Ultimate Judgment of History': The US Legal Case for the Blockade of Cuba During the Missile Crisis, October–November 1962," *Journal of Cold War Studies*, 21/2 (2019), p. 173.
46 Freedman, *Kennedy's Wars*, "A Crisis Managed," chap. 24, pp. 218–24.
47 Nor were the military leadership the only ones embittered: those in the State Department were also aggrieved at their marginalization. See ibid., p. 170.
48 John F. Kennedy, as quoted in Benjamin C. Bradlee, *Conversations with Kennedy* (New York: W. W. Norton, 1975), p. 122.
49 Lyndon Johnson, Speech at Akron University, October 21, 1964, quoted in Susan Ratcliffe, *Oxford Essential Quotations* (Oxford University Press, 2016); www.oxfordreference.com/display/10.1093/acref/9780191826719.001.0001/q-oro-ed4-00005939. Figures from "Military Advisors in Vietnam, 1963," JFK Library,

www.jfklibrary.org/learn/education/teachers/curricular-resources/military-advisors-in-vietnam-1963.
50 "Vietnam War US Military Fatal Casualty Statistics," Electronic Records Reference Report, US National Archives, www.archives.gov/research/military/vietnam-war/casualty-statistics#:~:text=April%2029%2C%202008.-,The%20Vietnam%20Conflict%20Extract%20Data%20File%20of%20the%20Defense%20Casualty,and%20Records%20Administration%20in%202008.
51 Maxwell Taylor, quoted in H. R. McMaster, *Dereliction of Duty* (New York: HarperCollins, 1997), p. 36.
52 The administration soon replaced the chairman of the joint chiefs of staff, the Army chief of staff, and the chief of naval operations. The two remaining hold-overs, Air Force chief General Curtis LeMay and Marine Commandant David Shoup, were never reconciled to the administration's belief in limited war. Nor was Shoup's successor, General Wallace Greene.
53 McMaster demonstrates this in both the Cuban missile crisis and the Berlin crisis; *Dereliction of Duty*, pp. 47, 53.
54 While President Johnson is derided for picking bombing targets, McMaster's study demonstrates it was already established under Kennedy. Ibid., p. 60.
55 Ibid., pp. 114, 123, 188, 198.
56 Johnson's recriminations are captured in Lewis Sorley, *Honorable Warrior: General Harold K. Johnson and the Ethics of Command* (Lawrence: University of Kansas Press, 1998).
57 McMaster, *Dereliction of Duty*, p. 150.
58 Ibid., p. 333.
59 Kori Schake, "Dereliction of Duty Reconsidered: The Book That Made the National Security Advisor," *War on the Rocks*, March 28, 2017; https://warontherocks.com/2017/03/dereliction-of-duty-reconsidered-the-book-the-made-the-national-security-advisor/.
60 McMaster, *Dereliction of Duty*, p. 539.
61 Peter D. Feaver, "Resign in Protest? A Cure Worse Than Most Diseases," *Armed Forces & Society*, 43/1 (2017), pp. 29–40; and Richard H. Kohn, "On Resignation," ibid., pp. 41–52.
62 Peter D. Feaver, "Right or Wrong? The Civil–Military Problematique and *Armed Forces & Society*'s 50th," *Armed Forces & Society*, May 2024, https://journals.sagepub.com/doi/10.1177/0095327X241255642?icid=int.sj-full-text.citing-articles.1.
63 Peter D. Feaver and Richard H. Kohn, "Civil–Military Relations in the United States: What Senior Leaders Need to Know (and Usually Don't)," *Strategic Studies Quarterly*, 15/2 (2021), p. 20.
64 Richard Kohn recounts Marshall remaining silent as President Roosevelt publicly misrepresented the US posture toward Germany and US support for Britain during World War II. Kohn, "Building Trust: Civil–Military Behaviors for Effective National Security," in *American Civil–Military Relations: The Soldier and the State in a New Era*, ed. Suzanne C. Nielsen and Don M. Snider (Baltimore: Johns Hopkins University Press, 2009), p. 289.
65 McMaster, *Dereliction of Duty*, pp. 185–6.
66 Alexis de Tocqueville, *Democracy in America* (4th edn, New York: J. & H. G. Langley, 1841), Vol. 1, p. 246.

67 Selective Service head Lewis Hershey, in Congressional testimony 1958, Independent Offices Appropriation Bill for 1959, Vol. 1, p. 215; https://books.google.com/books?id=bXg0AAAAIAAJ&pg=PA215#v=onepage&q&f=false.
68 Richard Nixon, "Remarks on the CBS Radio Network: 'The All-Volunteer Armed Force,'" October 17, 1968, The American Presidency Project, www.presidency.ucsb.edu/documents/remarks-the-cbs-radio-network-the-all-volunteer-armed-force.
69 Ibid.
70 These arguments form the basis of Eliot Cohen's book *Citizens and Soldiers: The Dilemmas of Military Service* (Ithaca, NY: Cornell University Press, 1985). In particular, Cohen condemns selective service, which, "by its adoption of 'channeling,' helped subvert its moral authority, for it treated compulsory service as a useful threat rather than as an appeal to honor and duty" (p. 164).
71 *The Report of the President's Commission on an All-Volunteer Armed Force* (Washington, DC: US Government Printing Office, 1970) p. 157; www.nixonfoundation.org/wp-content/uploads/2012/01/The-Report-Of-The-Presidents-Commission-On-An-All-Volunteer-Armed-Force.pdf.
72 Ibid., pp. 143–5.
73 Ibid., pp. 19–20.
74 Robert K, Griffith, Jr., *The US Army's Transition to the All-Volunteer Force, 1968–1974* (Washington, DC: Center of Military History, United States Army, 1997) pp. 40–1.
75 Samuel Hubbard Hays, "A Military View of Selective Service," in *The Draft: A Handbook of Facts and Alternatives*, ed. Sol Tax (Chicago: University of Chicago Press, 1967), p. 10.
76 Quoted in Beth Bailey, *America's Army: Making the All-Volunteer Force* (Cambridge, MA: Harvard University Press, 2009), p. 51.
77 Vincent Shaw and Theodore MacDonald, "Committing to the All-Volunteer Force: The Role of Economics in its Adoption and Implementation," *Military Review*, January/February 2024, pp. 66–78; www.armyupress.army.mil/Journals/Military-Review/English-Edition-Archives/January-February-2024/All-Volunteer-Force/.
78 Greg Schneider and Renae Merle, "Reagan's Defense Buildup Bridged Military Eras," *Washington Post*, June 8, 2004, www.washingtonpost.com/archive/business/2004/06/09/reagans-defense-buildup-bridged-military-eras/ec621466-b78e-4a2e-9f8a-50654e3f95fa/.
79 Loren Thompson, "A Reagan Moment Arrives for America's Military," *Forbes*, January 23, 2017, www.forbes.com/sites/lorenthompson/2017/01/23/a-reagan-moment-arrives-for-americas-military/.
80 James R. Anderson, "Bankrupting America: The Impact of President Reagan's Military Budget," *International Journal of Health Services*, 11/4 (1981), p. 623.
81 *Packard Commission Report*, 1986, p. 1, www.documentcloud.org/documents/2695411-Packard-Commission.html.
82 Goldwater–Nichols DOD Reorganization Act, 10 USC 162, Combatant Commands; Assigned Forces; Chain of Command, Section (b), Chain of Command.
83 James R. Locher, Senate Committee on Armed Services, *Defense Organization: The Need for Change, Staff Report to the Committee on Armed Services*, S.Rept 99-86, October 16, 1985 (SEC809-RL-85-0150.pdf).
84 James R. Locher, III, *Victory on the Potomac: The Goldwater–Nichols Act Unifies the Pentagon* (College Station: Texas A&M University Press, 2002), p. 153.

85 John J. Hamre, "Reflections: Looking Back at the Need for Goldwater–Nichols," Center for Strategic and International Studies, January 27, 2016; https://defense360.csis.org/goldwater-nichols-2016/; David C. Jones, "Why the Joint Chiefs of Staff Must Change," *Presidential Studies Quarterly*, 12/2 (1982), p. 138.
86 Among the many good accounts of the war, one of the very best is Lawrence Freedman and Efraim Karsh's *The Gulf Conflict, 1990–1991: Diplomacy and War in the New World Order* (Princeton, NJ: Princeton University Press, 1993).
87 General Michael Dugan, quoted in Rick Atkinson, "US to Rely on Air Strikes if War Erupts," *Washington Post*, September 15, 1990; www.washingtonpost.com/archive/politics/1990/09/16/us-to-rely-on-air-strikes-if-war-erupts/6d3110ea-8425-468a-9546-10c911c90acd/.
88 The Goldwater–Nichols legislation made the chairman the president and secretary of defense's principal military advisor and the vice chairman as deputy, pulled from the service chiefs numerous responsibilities, including establishing weapons development requirements (in that case, shifted to the Office of the Secretary of Defense with a joint staff role), and strengthened the combatant commander roles.
89 Ronald Reagan, *An American Life* (New York: Pocket Books, 1990), p. 466.
90 Nathan S. Lowrey, *The Chairmanship of the Joint Chiefs of Staff, 1949–2019* (Washington, DC: Joint History and Research Office, 2020), p. 33; www.jcs.mil/Portals/36/Documents/History/Dec21/Chairmanship%20of%20the%20JCS%201949-2019.pdf?ver=5Bghr__dy6kkWoDvFv9FQw%3d%3d.
91 Colin L. Powell, "US Forces: Challenges Ahead," *Foreign Affairs*, 71/5 (1992), pp. 32–45; www.foreignaffairs.com/articles/1992-12-01/us-forces-challenges-ahead?check_logged_in=1.
92 Hew Strachan, *The Direction of War: Contemporary Strategy in Historical Perspective* (Cambridge: Cambridge University Press, 2014), quoted in Jim Gourley, "Gourley's Strachan Files (II): Was Colin Powell the Worst General of the GWOT?," *Foreign Policy*, February 18, 2014; https://foreignpolicy.com/2014/02/18/gourleys-strachan-files-ii-was-colin-powell-the-worst-general-of-the-gwot/.
93 Colin L. Powell, "Why Generals Get Nervous," *New York Times*, October 8, 1992; https://timesmachine.nytimes.com/timesmachine/1992/10/08/207892.html?pageNumber=35.
94 Frank Hoffman, "A Second Look at the Powell Doctrine," *War on the Rocks*, February 20, 2014; https://warontherocks.com/2014/02/a-second-look-at-the-powell-doctrine/.
95 Russell F. Weigley, "The American Military and the Principle of Civilian Control from McClellan to Powell," *Journal of Military History*, 57/5 (1993), Special Issue: Proceedings of the Symposium on "The History of War as Part of General History" at the Institute for Advanced Studies, p. 29.
96 Lawrence Freedman, *Command* (New York: Oxford University Press, 2022), p. 8.
97 Weigley, "The American Military and the Principle of Civilian Control from McClellan to Powell," p. 56.
98 Kori Schake and Jim Mattis, eds, *Warriors and Citizens: American Views on Our Military* (Stanford, CA: Hoover Institution Press, 2016).
99 Weigley, "The American Military and the Principle of Civilian Control from McClellan to Powell," pp. 28, 30.

100 "Public Trust in Government: 1958–2024," Pew Research Center, June 24, 2024, www.pewresearch.org/politics/2024/06/24/public-trust-in-government-1958-2024/.
101 Jeffrey M. Jones, "Americans Trust Local Government Most, Congress Least," October 13, 2023, https://news.gallup.com/poll/512651/americans-trust-local-government-congress-least.aspx.
102 Mohamed Younis, "Confidence in US Military Lowest in Over Two Decades," July 31, 2023, https://news.gallup.com/poll/509189/confidence-military-lowest-two-decades.aspx.
103 Weigley, "The American Military and the Principle of Civilian Control from McClellan to Powell," p. 30.
104 Thomas E. Ricks, "Rumsfeld on High Wire of Defense Reform," *Washington Post*, May 20, 2001; www.washingtonpost.com/wp-dyn/articles/A45657-2001May18.html.
105 Rick Atkinson and Thomas E. Ricks, "Audacious Mission, Awesome Risks," *Washington Post*, March 16, 2003; www.washingtonpost.com/wp-dyn/articles/A30774-2003Mar15.html.
106 Senator Dick Durbin recounting Eric Shinseki, *Congressional Record*, Vol. 152, pp. 6537–9; www.govinfo.gov/content/pkg/CRECB-2006-pt5/html/CRECB-2006-pt5-Pg6537-2.htm.
107 Thomas E. Ricks, "Rumsfeld Stands Tall after Iraq Victory," *Washington Post*, April 20, 2003; www.washingtonpost.com/wp-dyn/articles/A58343-2003Apr19.html.
108 Thomas E. Ricks and Vernon Loeb, "Iraq Takes a Toll on Rumsfeld," *Washington Post*, September 14, 2003; www.washingtonpost.com/wp-dyn/articles/A6695-2003Sep13.html.
109 David Cloud and Eric Schmitt, "More Retired Generals Call for Rumsfeld's Resignation," *New York Times*, April 14, 2006; www.nytimes.com/2006/04/14/washington/more-retired-generals-call-for-rumsfelds-resignation.html.
110 George W. Bush, interviewed for Timothy Andrews Sayle, Jeffrey A. Engel, Hal Brands, and William Inboden, eds, *The Last Card: Inside George W. Bush's Decision to Surge in Iraq* (Ithaca, NY: Cornell University Press, 2019). Chairman of the Joint Chiefs of Staff General Peter Pace also advised that his boss not be fired because the veterans' activism was a civil–military danger.
111 Peter D. Feaver, "The Right to Be Right: Civil–Military Relations and the Iraq Surge Decision," *International Security*, 35/4 (2011), pp. 88–9; www.belfercenter.org/publication/right-be-right-civil-military-relations-and-iraq-surge-decision.
112 Kori Schake, "Civil–Military Relations and the 2006 Iraq Surge," in Timothy Andrews Sayle, Jeffrey Engel, Hal Brands, and William Inboden, eds, *The Last Card: Inside George W. Bush's Decision to Surge in Iraq* (Cornell University Press, 2019), p. 444 (electronic).
113 Thomas E. Ricks, *Fiasco: The American Military Adventure in Iraq, 2003–2005* (New York: Penguin Books, 2007), p. 399.
114 Stephen Biddle, Jeffrey A. Friedman, and Jacob N. Shapiro, "Testing the Surge: Why Did Violence Decline in Iraq in 2007?," *International Security*, 37/1 (2012), pp. 7–40.
115 The magazine article about Fallon that doomed him stated that the admiral "may soon be unemployed because he's doing what a generation of young officers in the U.S. military are now openly complaining that their leaders didn't do on their behalf in the run-up to the war in Iraq: He's standing up to the commander in chief, whom

he thinks is contemplating a strategically unsound war . . . How does Fallon get away with so brazenly challenging his commander in chief?" Mattis's challenge was private, in administration policy councils, not public. Thomas P. M. Barnett, "The Man between War and Peace," *Esquire*, April 2008; Thomas E. Ricks, "The Obama Administration's Inexplicable Mishandling of Marine Gen. James Mattis," *Foreign Policy*, January 18, 2013.

116 "Remarks by the President in Address to the Nation on the Way Forward in Afghanistan and Pakistan," December 1, 2009; https://obamawhitehouse.archives.gov/the-press-office/remarks-president-address-nation-way-forward-afghanistan-and-pakistan.

117 General Stanley McChrystal, *Commander's Initial Assessment*, August 30, 2009; https://nsarchive.gwu.edu/document/24560-headquarters-international-security-assistance-force-kabul-afghanistan-gen-stanley.

118 Bob Dreyfuss, "The Generals' Revolt: Rolling Stone's 2009 Story on Obama's Struggle with His Own Military," *Rolling Stone*, October 28, 2009; www.rollingstone.com/politics/politics-news/the-generals-revolt-rolling-stones-2009-story-on-obamas-struggle-with-his-own-military-200776/.

119 Eamon Javers, "Jones Pushes Back at McChrystal," *Politico*, October 4, 2009; www.politico.com/story/2009/10/jones-pushes-back-at-mcchrystal-027883.

120 James Kitfield, "How Mike Flynn Became America's Angriest General," *Politico*, October 16, 2016; www.politico.com/magazine/story/2016/10/how-mike-flynn-became-americas-angriest-general-214362/.

121 Elliot Ackerman's *The Fifth Act: America's End in Afghanistan* (New York: Penguin Random House, 2022) movingly recounts a veteran of the Afghan War reliving his combat experience, assessing policy across several administrations, and working to help Afghans to safety during the withdrawal.

122 Michael Hirsh, "Lessons From Biden's Very Bad Week," *Politico*, August 20, 2021.

123 Morgan Chalfant, "Generals Contradict Biden, Say They Advised Leaving Troops in Afghanistan," *The Hill*, September 28, 2021; https://thehill.com/policy/defense/574283-top-generals-contradict-biden-say-they-advised-leaving-2500-troops-in/.

124 Congressman Les Aspin, chairman of the House Armed Services Committee, produced a study in the run-up to the war estimating ten thousand American casualties. In actuality, the US had 146 killed in action. William E. Kaiser, *An Analysis of Chairman Les Aspin's Campaign Plan for A Gulf War* (Newport, RI: Naval War College), February 11, 1991; https://apps.dtic.mil/sti/tr/pdf/ADA236610.pdf.

Chapter 7 How Worried Should We Be?

1 Greg Jaffe and Missy Ryan, "Selling America: The Army's Fight to Find Recruits in a Mistrustful, Divided Nation," *Washington Post*, August 30, 2024; www.washingtonpost.com/politics/2024/08/30/army-recruitment-numbers-low/.

2 Peter D. Feaver, *Thanks for Your Service: The Causes and Consequences of Public Confidence in the US Military* (New York: Oxford University Press, 2023), p. 2.

3 Peter D. Feaver and Richard H. Kohn, "Civil–Military Relations in the United States: What Senior Leaders Need to Know (and Usually Don't)," *Strategic Studies Quarterly*, 15/2 (2021), p. 14.

4 Benjamin Wittes and Susan Hennessey, *Unmaking the Presidency: Trump's War on the World's Most Powerful Office* (New York: Farrar, Straus, & Giroux, 2020), pp. 3–4.

5 James Golby, Kyle Dropp, and Peter D. Feaver, *Military Campaigns: Veterans' Endorsements and Presidential Elections* (Washington, DC: Center for a New American Security, 2012) (https://s3.us-east-1.amazonaws.com/files.cnas.org/hero/documents/CNAS_Military Campaigns_GolbyDroppFeaver.pdf).
6 Drew Desilver, "The Polarization in Today's Congress Has Roots That Go Back Decades," Pew Research Center, June 12, 2014; www.pewresearch.org/short-reads/2022/03/10/the-polarization-in-todays-congress-has-roots-that-go-back-decades/.
7 Karl Vick, "The Growing Evidence That Americans Are Less Divided Than You May Think," *Time*, July 2, 2024; https://time.com/6990721/us-politics-polarization-myth/.
8 "US Foreign Policy Tracker," August 29, 2024, https://pro.morningconsult.com/trackers/public-opinion-us-foreign-policy.
9 Robbie Gramer, "Congressional Gridlock Leaves Key National Security Posts Vacant," *Foreign Policy*, September 2, 2024; https://foreignpolicy.com/2024/08/23/biden-senate-confirmations-national-security-sfrc-nominees-state-department/.
10 In the specific case of Senator Tuberville's holds, the Pentagon acted in violation of congressional restrictions on abortion funding and preventing promotions was intended to force a policy reversal; 436 military promotions were stalled for nine months before the senator relented. The policy was unchanged. Audrey Decker and Bradley Peniston, "Hundreds of Promotions Approved after Tuberville Drops Hold," *Defense One*, December 5, 2023; www.defenseone.com/policy/2023/12/tuberville-drops-hold-most-military-promotions/392485/.
11 Feaver, *Thanks for Your Service*, pp. 1–2.
12 Mohamed Younis, "Confidence in US Military Lowest in Over Two Decades," Gallup, July 31, 2023; https://news.gallup.com/poll/509189/confidence-military-lowest-two-decades.aspx. The Reagan Institute finds a slightly higher level of support but similar trends: www.reaganfoundation.org/reagan-institute/centers/peace-through-strength/reagan-national-defense-survey/.
13 With the exception of 1979, Democrats have evinced less support for the military than their Republican counterparts since 1975.
14 Rosa Brooks, "Are Civil–Military Relations in Crisis?," *Parameters*, 51/1 (2021), p. 58.
15 Feaver, *Thanks for Your Service*, p. 270.
16 Peter D. Feaver, Jim Golby, and Lindsay P. Cohn, "Thanks for Your Service: Civilian and Veteran Attitudes after Fifteen Years of War," in *Warriors and Citizens: American Views of Our Military*, ed. Kori Schake and Jim Mattis (Stanford, CA: Hoover Institution Press, 2016).
17 *The Onion*, April 16, 2003; https://theonion.com/area-man-supports-the-troops-he-didnt-go-to-high-school-1819566822/.
18 Feaver, *Thanks for Your Service*, p. 261.
19 Schake and Mattis, *Warriors and Citizens*.
20 2023 Reagan National Defense Survey, https://starrs.us/reagan-institute-2023-poll-on-confidence-in-the-military/. However, the Reagan Institute polling primed respondents (thereby putting a thumb on the scales of their reactions).
21 Feaver, *Thanks for Your Service*, p. 277.
22 The original restriction was for ten years, shortened to seven years in 2008.

23 Act of July 26, 1947 ("National Security Act"), Public Law 80-253, 61 STAT 495 (https://catalog.archives.gov/id/299856).
24 Greg Miller and Greg Jaffe, "Trump Revealed Highly Classified Information to Russian Foreign Minister and Ambassador," *Washington Post*, May 15, 2017; www.washingtonpost.com/world/national-security/trump-revealed-highly-classified-information-to-russian-foreign-minister-and-ambassador/2017/05/15/530c172a-3960-11e7-9e48-c4f199710b69_story.html.
25 Lindsay Cohn, Max Margulies, and Michael A. Robinson, "What Discord Follows: The Divisive Debate over Military Disobedience," *War on the Rocks*, August 2, 2019; https://warontherocks.com/2019/08/what-discord-follows-the-divisive-debate-over-military-disobedience/.
26 Dan Lamothe, "Pentagon, Caught by Surprise by Trump's Travel Ban, Pushes for Some Iraqis to Get Special Consideration," *Washington Post*, April 8, 2019.
27 Feaver, *Thanks for Your Service*, p. 270.
28 Helene Cooper, "How Mark Milley, a General Who Mixes Bluntness and Banter, Became Trump's Top Military Adviser," *New York Times*, September 29, 2019; www.nytimes.com/2019/09/29/us/politics/mark-milley-chairman-joint-chiefs.html.
29 "Trump Picks Gen. Mark Milley as Next Top Military Advisor," *Associated Press*, December 8, 2018.
30 Rosa Brooks, "Perspective: Trump Wants to Crush Black Lives Matter with a Law That Fought Segregation," *Washington Post*, June 2, 2020; www.washingtonpost.com/outlook/2020/06/02/trump-military-insurrection-act/.
31 Peter Baker et al., "How Trump's Idea for a Photo Op Led to Havoc in a Park," *New York Times*, June 2, 2020; www.nytimes.com/2020/06/02/us/politics/trump-walk-lafayette-square.html.
32 Srijan Shukla, "Why Australia's Defence Chief Pulled Out 3 of His Officers from a Press Conference," *The Print*, March 29, 2019; https://theprint.in/world/why-australias-defence-chief-pulled-out-3-of-his-officers-from-a-press-conference/214186/.
33 Michael A. Robinson, Lindsay P. Cohn, and Max Z. Margulies, "Dissents and Sensibility: Conflicting Loyalties, Democracy, and Civil–Military Relations," in *Reconsidering American Civil–Military Relations*, ed. Lionel Beehner, Risa Brooks, and Daniel Maurer (New York: Oxford University Press, 2020).
34 "General Mark Milley Keynote Speech Transcript: Apologizes for Photo Op with Trump," June 11, 2020, www.rev.com/blog/transcripts/general-mark-milley-keynote-speech-transcript-apologizes-for-photo-op-with-trump.
35 Jonathan Swann and Zachary Basu, "Off the Rails, Episode 9: Trump's War with His Generals," *Axios*, May 16, 2021; www.axios.com/2021/05/16/off-the-rails-trump-military-withdraw-afghanistan.
36 Grace Segers, "Esper Says He Opposes Deploying Active-Duty Troops to States to Quell Protests," *CBS News*, June 3, 2020; www.cbsnews.com/news/mark-esper-pentagon-opposes-active-duty-troops-insurrection-act-protests/.
37 Mark Milley, quoted in Phil Stewart, Nandita Bose, and Idrees Ali, "Top US General Milley Takes Apparent Jab at Trump as He Retires," *Reuters*, September 29, 2023; www.euters.com/world/us/top-us-general-mark-milley-hand-over-reins-after-four-years-2023-09-29/.
38 Danielle Kurtzleben, "Top General Defends Studying Critical Race Theory in the

Military," *National Public Radio*, June 23, 2021; www.npr.org/2021/06/23/1009592838/top-general-defends-studying-critical-race-theory-in-the-military.
39. The views of General Milley's advocates come from personal conversations with the author by formal spokespeople and informal advisors to General Milley in July of 2022.
40. Doyle Hodges, "A Duty to Disobey?," *Lawfare*, August 19, 2022; www.lawfaremedia.org/article/duty-disobey.
41. Donald Trump, quoted in Brian Klaas, "Trump Floats the Idea of Executing Joint Chiefs Chairman Milley," *The Atlantic*, September 25, 2023; www.theatlantic.com/ideas/archive/2023/09/trump-milley-execution-incitement-violence/675435/.
42. Peter Feaver and I continue to dispute which of the two of us coined the metaphor of Olympic diving as the defense General Milley should adopt. It was me. ☺
43. Jim Golby, "America's Politicized Military Is a Recipe for Disaster," *Foreign Policy*, June 18, 2020; https://foreignpolicy.com/2020/06/18/us-military-politics-trump-election-campaign/.
44. Donald Trump, quoted in Michael R. Gordon, "Trump's Mix of Politics and Military Is Faulted," February 7, 2017; www.nytimes.com/2017/02/07/us/politics/trump-macdill-air-base.html.
45. Risa Brooks, "Through the Looking Glass: Trump-Era Civil–Military Relations in a Comparative Perspective," *Strategic Studies Quarterly*, 15/2 (2021), pp. 71–2; www.airuniversity.af.edu/Portals/10/SSQ/documents/Volume-15_Issue-2/Brooks.pdf.
46. Ibid., pp. 74.
47. Phil Stewart, Idrees Ali, and Steve Holland, "How Trump Fell Out of Love with His Generals, and Why the Feeling Is Mutual," *Reuters*, September 23, 2020; www.reuters.com/article/world/how-trump-fell-out-of-love-with-his-generals-and-why-the-feeling-is-mutual-idUSKCN26E2YY/.
48. Steve Benen, "Why Trump's Vow to Fire 'Woke' US Generals Matters," *MSNBC*, June 4, 2024; www.msnbc.com/rachel-maddow-show/maddowblog/trumps-vow-fire-woke-us-generals-matters-rcna155439.
49. Ryan Browne, "Top US General Tells Congress the Military Won't Play a Role in the 2020 Election," *CNN*, August 28, 2020; https://edition.cnn.com/2020/08/28/politics/milley-2020-election/index.html.
50. Army Chief of Staff General McConville, quoted in Haley Britzky, "Army Leaders Push Back on Mike Flynn's Call for the Military to 'Re-Run' the 2020 Election," *Task and Purpose*, December 18, 2020; https://taskandpurpose.com/news/army-secretary-chief-2020-election-mike-flynn/.
51. Deana El-Mallawany, Christine Kwon, and Rachel Homer, "Trump Can't Lawfully Use Armed Forces to Sway the Election: Understanding the Legal Boundaries," *Just Security*, September 23, 2020; www.justsecurity.org/72500/trump-cant-lawfully-use-armed-forces-to-sway-the-election-understanding-the-legal-boundaries/.
52. Swann and Basu, "Off the Rails, Episode 9."
53. Ibid.
54. Paul Sonne, "Joint Chiefs Call Riot a 'Direct Assault' on the Constitutional Process, Affirm Biden as Next Commander in Chief," *Washington Post*, January 12, 2021; www.washingtonpost.com/national-security/military-statement-biden-commander-in-chief/2021/01/12/9b722200-551a-11eb-89bc-7f51ceb6bd57_story.html.

55 Michael Kunzelman, "Marine Sentenced to Community Service, Probation for Capitol Riot," *Marine Corps Times*, September 11, 2023; www.marinecorpstimes.com/news/your-marine-corps/2023/09/11/marine-sentenced-to-community-service-probation-for-capitol-riot/. Missy Ryan, Paul Sonne, and Razzan Nakhlawi, "Seeking to Combat Extremists in Ranks, the Military Struggles to Answer a Basic Question: How Many Are There?," *Washington Post*, February 9, 2021; www.washingtonpost.com/national-security/military-extremist-threat-lloyd-austin-/2021/02/09/198794c8-66f9-11eb-bf81-c618c88ed605_story.html.
56 Michael Robinson and Kori Schake, "The Military's Extremism Problem Is Our Problem," *New York Times*, March 22, 2021; www.nytimes.com/2021/03/02/opinion/veterans-capitol-attack.html.
57 Robert A. Pape, "The Jan. 6 Insurrectionists Aren't Who You Think They Are," *Foreign Policy*, January 6, 2022.
58 Arie Perlinger, *American Zealots: Inside Right Wing Terrorism* (New York: Columbia University Press, 2020).
59 Robert A. Pape, Keven G. Ruby, Kyle D. Larson, and Kentaro Nakamura, "Understanding the Impact of Military Service on Support for Insurrection in the United States," *Journal of Conflict Resolution*, 69/4 (2025), pp. 571–98.
60 Lindsay P. Cohn and Steve Vladeck, "The Election and the Military," *Lawfare*, November 2, 2020.
61 Peter D. Feaver, quoted in "Thanks for Your Service: America's High but Hollow Support for the Military," *Duke Today*, August 28, 2023; https://today.duke.edu/2023/08/thanks-your-service-americas-high-hollow-support-military.
62 Jeff Schogol, "Two Officers Were Fired for Bucking Their Chain of Command: Now They're Going to Work at the Pentagon," *Task and Purpose*, January 22, 2025.
63 Pauline Shanks Kaurin, "An 'Unprincipled Principal': Implications for Civil–Military Relations," *Strategic Studies Quarterly*, 15/2 (2021); www.airuniversity.af.edu/Portals/10/SSQ/documents/Volume-15_Issue-2/Kaurin.pdf.
64 Feaver, *Thanks for Your Service*, p. 264.
65 Barbara Starr and Ryan Browne, "Trump Launches Unprecedented Attack on Military Leadership He Appointed," CNN, September 8, 2020; www.cnn.com/2020/09/07/politics/trump-attack-military-leadership/index.html.
66 Zeke Miller and Josh Boak, "Biden at Independence Hall: Trump and Allies Threaten Democracy," Associated Press, September 1, 2022; https://whyy.org/articles/biden-philadelphia-independence-hall-speech-trump-election-2022/.
67 Risa Brooks, Jim Golby, and Heidi Urben, "Crisis of Command: America's Broken Civil–Military Relationship Imperils National Security," *Foreign Affairs*, May/June 2021 (https://www.foreignaffairs.com/articles/united-states/2021-04-09/national-security-crisis-command).
68 Russell F. Weigley, "The American Military and the Principle of Civilian Control from McClellan to Powell," *Journal of Military History*, 57/5 (1993), p. 57.
69 Ibid., p. 27.
70 Mara Karlin, *The Inheritance: America's Military after Two Decades of War* (Washington, DC: Brookings Institution Press, 2022), pp. 4–5.
71 Michael C. Desch, "Soldiers, States, and Structures: The End of the Cold War

and Weakening US Civilian Control," *Armed Forces & Society*, 24/3 (1998), p. 389.
72 Heidi R. Urben, *Party, Politics, and the Post-9/11 Army* (Amherst, MA: Cambria Press, 2021), pp. 187–9.
73 Feaver and Kohn, "Civil–Military Relations in the United States," p. 3.
74 Eric Edelman, Gary Roughead, et al., *Providing for the Common Defense: The Assessment and Recommendations of the National Defense Strategy Commission* (Washington, DC: United States Institute of Peace, 2018), p. 47; www.usip.org/publications/2018/11/providing-common-defense.
75 Jane Harman, Eric Edelman, et al., *Commission on the National Defense Strategy* (Arlington, VA: RAND, 2024).
76 Brooks, "Are Civil–Military Relations in Crisis?," pp. 59–60.
77 Richard Betts, "Are Civil–Military Relations Still a Problem?," in Suzanne C. Nielsen and Don M. Snider, eds, *American Civil–Military Relations: The Soldier and the State in a New Era* (Baltimore: Johns Hopkins University Press, 2009), p. 11.
78 Susan B. Glasser and Peter Baker, "Inside the War Between Trump and His Generals," *New Yorker*, August 8, 2022; www.newyorker.com/magazine/2022/08/15/inside-the-war-between-trump-and-his-generals.
79 Robert Mendick, "Trump Is Handing Out Top Jobs – on One Condition," *The Telegraph*, November 13, 2024; www.telegraph.co.uk/us/politics/2024/11/13/trump-transition-team-vetting-applicants-one-condition/.
80 Charlie Dunlap, "Why the 'Orders Project' Is Troubling," *Lawfire*, October 26, 2020.
81 Feaver and Kohn, "Civil–Military Relations in the United States," p. 22.
82 Peter D. Feaver, "The Civil–Military Problematique: Huntington, Janowitz, and the Question of Civilian Control," *Armed Forces and Society*, 23/2 (1996), p. 149.
83 Lawrence Freedman, *Command* (New York: Oxford University Press, 2022), p. 1.
84 Ibid., p. 8.
85 Cited with permission of Eliot Cohen.
86 Freedman, *Command*, p. 515.
87 Feaver, *Thanks for Your Service*, pp. 275–6.
88 Brooks, Golby, and Urben, "Crisis of Command."
89 Avishay Ben Sasson-Gordis, "Democratic Backsliding and the Limits of Civilian-Control of the Military" (unpublished paper, cited with permission of the author), p. 16.
90 Feaver and Kohn, "Civil–Military Relations in the United States," p. 19.
91 Richard Kohn, quoted in Thomas E. Ricks, "Richard Kohn Fires a Warning Flare about a Joint Force Quarterly Article," *Foreign Policy*, September 29, 2010; https://foreignpolicy.com/2010/09/29/richard-kohn-fires-a-warning-flare-about-a-joint-force-quarterly-article/.
92 Dennis Rasmussen, *Fears of a Setting Sun: The Disillusionment of America's Founders* (Princeton, NJ: Princeton University Press, 2021).
93 James Mattis, quoted in Melissa Leon, "Mattis' Response to a Reporter Who Asked Him about NFL Protests is Another Classic," *American Military News*, September 26, 2017; https://americanmilitarynews.com/2017/09/mattis-response-to-a-reporter-who-asked-him-about-the-nfl-protests-is-another-classic/.

94 Bryan Metzger, "Republicans Call Gen. Mark Milley 'Traitor,' and Say He Should Be Fired or Court-Martialed for a Report That He Secretly Intervened to Avoid War with China," *Business Insider*, September 21, 2021; www.businessinsider.com/republicans-milley-fired-resign-court-martialed-treason-china-trump-call-2021-9?op=1.
95 Davis Winkie, "Ex-Fort Benning Commander's Retirement Halted over Tweets," *Army Times*, September 19, 2022; www.armytimes.com/news/your-army/2022/09/19/ex-fort-benning-commanders-retirement-halted-over-tweets/.
96 Steve Beynon, "Army Secretary Fires 4-Star General Who Meddled in Promotion of Unfit Subordinate," December 10, 2024, www.military.com/daily-news/2024/12/10/army-secretary-fires-4-star-general-who-meddled-promotion-of-unfit-0.
97 Lin-Manuel Miranda, *Hamilton*, www.lyricsondemand.com/soundtracks/h/hamiltonlyrics/whatdimisslyrics.html.
98 The school solution to the question is not to get caught between a rocky coastline and a stiff onshore breeze.
99 Michael Robinson, *Dangerous Instrument: Political Polarization and US Civil–Military Relations* (New York: Oxford University Press, 2023), p. 167.
100 Suzanne C. Nielsen and Don M. Snider, "Conclusions," in Nielsen and Snider, eds, *American Civil–Military Relations*, p. 303.
101 James Golby, Kyle Dropp, and Peter D. Feaver, *Military Campaigns: Veterans' Endorsements and Presidential Elections* (Washington, DC: Center for a New American Security, 2012).
102 Colby Itkowitz, "Guns Are All Over GOP Ads and Social Media, Prompting Some Criticism," *Washington Post*, May 31, 2022; www.washingtonpost.com/politics/2022/05/31/republicans-guns-ads-posts/.

Epilogue

1 James H. Doolittle, William B. Franke, Morris Hadley, and William D. Pawley, Report on the Covert Activities of the Central Intelligence Agency, p. 2, www.cia.gov/readingroom/docs/CIA-RDP86B00269R000100040001-5.pdf.
2 Ibid., p. 3.
3 Samuel P. Huntington, *The Soldier and the State: The Theory and Politics of Civil–Military Relations* (Cambridge, MA: Belknap Press, 1957), p. 456.
4 Ibid., p. vii.
5 Huntington seems to have taken the terminology from MacArthur, whom he quotes on subjective and objective discipline of military forces; p. 304.
6 Ibid., p. 83.
7 Ibid.
8 Ibid.
9 Ibid., pp. 7–10.
10 Ibid., p. 72.
11 Ibid., pp. 87–8.
12 Ibid., p. 436.
13 Ibid., pp. 186–7.
14 Ibid., p. 95.
15 Ibid., p. 94.
16 Ibid., p. 155.

17 Ibid., pp. 76–7.
18 Ibid., p. 191.
19 Ibid., p. 190.
20 Ibid., p. 163.
21 Ibid., p. 35.
22 Ibid., p. 417.
23 Ibid., p. 163.
24 Ibid., p. 168.
25 Ibid.
26 Ibid., pp. 195–8.
27 Ibid., p. 265.
28 Ibid., pp. 286–7, 291.
29 Ibid., p. 145.
30 Ibid., p. 143.
31 Ibid., p. 158.
32 Ibid., p. 148.
33 Ibid., p. 313.
34 Huntington dismisses MacArthur as "deviant, non-military"; ibid., p. 96.
35 Ibid., p. 315.
36 Ibid., pp. 315–33.
37 Ibid., pp. 326, 329.
38 Ibid., pp. 332–3.
39 Ibid., p. 344.
40 Ibid., pp. 327–8.
41 Ibid., p. 93.
42 Ibid., p. 464.
43 Ibid., p. 3.
44 Morris Janowitz, *The Professional Soldier: A Social and Political Portrait* (New York: Free Press, 1960), p. 4.
45 Ibid., p. 253.
46 Ibid., p. 343.
47 Ibid., pp. x, 264–7. As with the "realists" of contemporary international relations theory, Huntington and Janowitz are both proficient in the demagogic expertise of term selection that biases understanding, Huntington terming his preferred civil–military relationship "balanced," and Janowitz calling his preferred military attitude "pragmatic."
48 Ibid., p. 342.
49 Ibid., p. 31.
50 Ibid., pp. 13, 14.
51 Ibid., p. 426.
52 Ibid., pp. 9–10.
53 Ibid., p. lvii.
54 Ibid., p. 21.
55 Ibid., p. 153.
56 Ibid., p. 166.
57 Ibid., pp. 161–5.
58 Ibid., pp. 233–4.

59 Ibid., p. 14.
60 Ibid., pp. 23, 34.
61 Ibid., p. 268.
62 Ibid., pp. xxx, xiv.
63 Ibid., p. xv.
64 Ibid., p. lvi.
65 Ibid., p. 311.
66 Ibid., pp. li, 418.
67 Ibid., p. lvii.
68 Ibid., p. li.
69 Ibid., p. lii.
70 Ibid.
71 Ibid., p. lvii.
72 Ibid., p. 3.
73 Suzanne C. Nielsen and Hugh Liebert, "The Utility of Janowitz's Political Awareness in Officer Education," *Armed Forces & Society*, 49/1 (2021), https://journals.sagepub.com/doi/full/10.1177/0095327X211046372.

Selected Bibliography

Scholarship

David Barno and Nora Bensahel, "How to Get Generals Out of Politics," *War on the Rocks*, September 27, 2016.

Lionel Beehner, Risa Brooks, and Daniel Maurer, eds, *Reconsidering American Civil–Military Relations* (Oxford: Oxford University Press, 2020).

Jessica D. Blankshain, "Who Has 'Skin in the Game'? The Implications of an Operational Reserve for Civil–Military Relations," in Lionel Beehner, Risa Brooks, and Daniel Maurer, eds, *Reconsidering American Civil–Military Relations* (Oxford: Oxford University Press, 2020), pp. 97–114.

Risa A. Brooks, *Shaping Strategy: The Civil–Military Politics of Strategic Assessment* (Princeton, NJ: Princeton University Press, 2008).

Risa Brooks, "Through the Looking Glass: Trump-Era Civil–Military Relations in a Comparative Perspective," *Strategic Studies Quarterly*, 15/2 (2021): 69–98.

Risa Brooks, "The Creeping Politicization of the US Military: How Republican Loyalty Tests Erode National Security," *Foreign Affairs*, March 20, 2024.

Risa Brooks and Michael A. Robinson, "Let the Generals Speak? Retired Officer Dissent and the June 2020 George Floyd Protests," *War on the Rocks*, October 9, 2020.

Risa Brooks and Avishay Ben Sasson-Gordis, "How Military Leaders Can Navigate a Crisis of Democracy: Lessons from the Reservist Protests in Israel," *Just Security*, August 17, 2023.

Risa Brooks, Jim Golby, and Heidi Urben, "Crisis of Command: America's Broken Civil–Military Relations Imperils National Security," *Foreign Affairs*, May/June 2021.

Rosa Brooks, "Thought Cloud: The Real Problem with the Civilian–Military Gap," *Foreign Policy*, August 2, 2012.

Rosa Brooks, *How Everything Became War and the Military Became Everything: Tales from the Pentagon* (New York: Simon & Schuster, 2017).

Rosa Brooks, "Are Civil–Military Relations in Crisis?," *Parameters*, 51/1 (2021): 51–64.

Susan Bryant, Brett Swaney, and Heidi Urben, "From Citizen Soldier to Secular Saint: The Societal Implications of Military Exceptionalism," *Texas National Security Review*, 4/2 (2021): 9–24.

David T. Burbach, "Partisan Dimensions of Confidence in the US Military, 1973–2016," *Armed Forces & Society*, 45/2 (2019): 211–33.

David T. Burbach, "Confidence without Sacrifice: American Public Opinion and the US Military," in Lionel Beehner, Risa Brooks, and Daniel Maurer, eds, *Reconsidering American Civil–Military Relations* (Oxford: Oxford University Press, 2020), pp. 149–76.

Phillip Carter, "Unpresidential Command: Trump is Ordering Service Members to Support the Republican Agenda. That is Terrifying," *Slate*, July 24, 2017.

Eliot A. Cohen, "The Unequal Dialogue: The Theory and Reality of Civil–Military Relations and the Use of Force," in *Soldiers and Civilians: The Civil–Military Gap and American National Security*, ed. Peter D. Feaver and Richard H. Kohn (Cambridge, MA: MIT Press, 2001), pp. 429–49.

Eliot A. Cohen, *Supreme Command: Soldiers, Statesmen, and Leadership in Wartime* (New York: Free Press, 2002).

Raphael S. Cohen, "Minding the Gap: The Military, Politics and American Society," *Lawfare*, December 17, 2017.

Lindsay P. Cohn, "The Precarious State of Civil–Military Relations in the Age of Trump," *War on the Rocks*, March 28, 2018.

Lindsay Cohn, Max Margulies, and Michael Robinson, "What Discord Follows: The Divisive Debate over Military Disobedience," *War on the Rocks*, August 2, 2019.

Jason K. Dempsey, *Our Army: Soldiers, Politics, and American Civil–Military Relations* (Princeton, NJ: Princeton University Press, 2010).

Jason Dempsey and Gil Barndollar, "The All Volunteer Force is in Crisis," *Atlantic*, March 18, 2024.

Jason Dempsey, Raphael S. Cohen, Susan Bryant, and Sonya Finley, "Book Review Roundtable: Why a Political Sensibility is Important to Successful Military Command," *Texas National Security Review*, August 28, 2024.

Martin Dempsey, "Civil–Military Relations: 'What Does it Mean?,'" *Strategic Studies Quarterly*, 15/2 (2021): 6–11.

Charlie Dunlap, "Why the 'Orders Project' is Troubling," *Lawfire*, October 26, 2020.

Peter D. Feaver, "The Civil–Military Problematique: Huntington, Janowitz, and the Question of Civilian Control," *Armed Forces & Society*, 23/2 (1996): 149–78.

Peter D. Feaver, *Armed Servants: Agency, Oversight, and Civil–Military Relations* (Cambridge, MA: Harvard University Press, 2005).

Peter D. Feaver, "The Right to Be Right: Civil–Military Relations and the Iraq Surge Decision," *International Security*, 35/4 (2011): 87–125.

Peter D. Feaver, "Resign in Protest? A Cure Worse than Most Diseases," *Armed Forces & Society*, 43/1 (2017): 29–40.

Peter D. Feaver and Michèle Flournoy, "Let's Stop Being Cavalier about Civilian Control of the Military," *Lawfare*, September 13, 2022.

Peter D. Feaver and Richard H. Kohn, "Civil–Military Relations in the United States: What Senior Leaders Need to Know (and Usually Don't)," *Strategic Studies Quarterly*, 15/2 (2021): 12–37.

Samuel E. Finer, *The Man on Horseback: The Role of the Military in Politics* (London: Pall Mall Press, 1962).

Nathan K. Finney and Tyrell O. Mayfield, eds, *Redefining the Modern Military: The Intersection of Profession and Ethics* (Annapolis, MD: Naval Institute Press, 2018).

Lawrence Freedman, *Command* (Oxford: Oxford University Press, 2023).

Alice Hunt Friend, "The Pentagon is Moving Money to Pay for Trump's Border Wall: Here Are the Consequences," *Washington Post*, September 6, 2019.

Jim Golby, "America's Politicized Military is a Recipe for Disaster," *Foreign Policy*, June 18, 2020.

Jim Golby, "Uncivil Military Relations: Politicization of the Military in the Trump Era," *Strategic Studies Quarterly*, 15/2 (2021): 149–74.

Jim Golby, Kyle Dropp, and Peter Feaver, *Military Campaigns: Veterans' Endorsements and Elections* (Washington, DC: Center for a New American Security, 2012).

Jim Golby, Lindsay P. Cohn, and Peter D. Feaver, "Thanks for Your Service: Civilian and Veteran Attitudes after Fifteen Years of War," in *Warriors and Citizens: American Views of Our Military*, ed. Kori Schake and Jim Mattis (Stanford, CA: Hoover Institution Press, 2016), pp. 97–142.

Jane Harman, Eric Edelman, et al., *Commission on the National Defense Strategy* (Arlington, VA: RAND, July 2024).

Doyle Hodges, "A Duty to Disobey?," *Lawfare*, August 19, 2022.

Ole R. Holsti, "Politicization of the United States Military: Crisis or Tempest in a Teapot?," *International Journal*, 57/1 (2002): 1–18.

James Joyner, "Trump's Generals: A Natural Experiment in Civil–Military Relations," *Strategic Studies Quarterly*, 15/2 (2021): 120–48.

Mara E. Karlin, *The Inheritance: America's Military after Two Decades of War* (Washington, DC: Brookings Institution Press, 2021).

Kenneth W. Kemp and Charles Hudlin, "Civil Supremacy over the Military: Its Nature and Limits," *Armed Forces & Society*, 19/1 (1992): 7–26.

Richard H. Kohn, "Out of Control: The Crisis in Civil–Military Relations," *National Interest*, no. 35 (Spring 1994): pp. 3–17.

Richard H. Kohn, "Building Trust: Civil–Military Behaviors for Effective National Security," in Susanne C. Nielsen and Don M. Snider, *American Civil-Military Relations: The Soldier and the State in a New Era* (Baltimore: Johns Hopkins University Press, 2009), pp. 265–7.

Richard H. Kohn, "On Resignation," *Armed Forces & Society*, 43/1 (2017): 41–52.

Ronald R. Krebs and Robert Ralston, "Civilian Control of the Military is a Partisan Issue," *Foreign Affairs*, July 14, 2020.

Ronald R. Krebs, Robert Ralston, and Aaron Rapport, "No Right to Be Wrong: What Americans Think about Civil–Military Relations," *Perspectives on Politics*, 21/2 (2023), pp. 606–24.

Carrie A. Lee, "Dear Civ-Mil Community, the (Retired) Officers Are Speaking and We Should Listen," *Duck of Minerva*, June 3, 2020.

Danielle Lupton, David T. Burbach, and Lindsay P. Cohn, "Authoritarian Tactics on US Soil," *Political Violence at a Glance*, August 5, 2020.

Susanne C. Nielsen and Don M. Snider, *American Civil–Military Relations: The Soldier and the State in a New Era* (Baltimore: Johns Hopkins University Press, 2009).

Mackubin Thomas Owens, "Maximum Toxicity: Civil–Military Relations in the Trump Era," *Strategic Studies Quarterly*, 15/2 (2021): 99–119.

Robert A. Pape, Kyle D. Larson, and Keven G. Ruby, "The Political Geography of the January 6 Insurrectionists," *Political Science & Politics*, 57/3 (2024): 329–39.

Patrick Paterson, "Civil–Military Relations: Guidelines in Politically Charged Societies," *Parameters*, 52/1 (2022): 5–20.

Michael A. Robinson, *Dangerous Instrument: Political Polarization and US Civil–Military Relations* (New York: Oxford University Press, 2022).

Michael Robinson and Kori Schake, "The Military's Extremism Problem is Our Problem," *New York Times*, March 2, 2021.

Kori Schake, "The Line Held: Civil–Military Relations in the Trump Administration," *Strategic Studies Quarterly*, 15/2 (2021): 38–49.

Sarah Sewall, "US Civil–Military Relations in the Gray Zone," in Lionel Beehner, Risa Brooks, and Daniel Maurer, eds, *Reconsidering American Civil–Military Relations* (Oxford: Oxford University Press, 2020), pp. 263–82.

Pauline Shanks Kaurin, *On Obedience: Contrasting Philosophies for the Military, Citizenry, and Community* (Annapolis, MD: Naval Institute Press, 2020).

Pauline Shanks Kaurin, "An 'Unprincipled Principal': Implications for Civil–Military Relations," *Strategic Studies Quarterly*, 15/2 (2021): 50–68.

Naunihal Singh, "Was the US Capitol Riot Really a Coup? Here's Why Definitions Matter," *Washington Post*, January 9, 2021.

Marybeth P. Ulrich, "Civil–Military Relations Norms and Democracy: What Every Citizen Should Know," in Lionel Beehner, Risa Brooks, and Daniel Maurer, eds, *Reconsidering American Civil–Military Relations* (Oxford: Oxford University Press, 2020), pp. 41–62.

Heidi A. Urben, *Like, Comment, Retweet: The State of the Military's Nonpartisan Ethic in the World of Social Media* (Washington, DC: National Defense University Press, 2017).

Heidi Urben, "Generals Shouldn't Be Welcome at These Parties: Stopping Retired Flag Officer Endorsements," *War on the Rocks*, July 27, 2020.

Contemporary Veterans' Policy Analysis, Memoir, and Fiction

Elliot Ackerman, *Dark at the Crossing* (New York: Alfred A. Knopf, 2017).

Elliot Ackerman, *Waiting for Eden* (New York: Alfred A. Knopf, 2018).

Elliot Ackerman, *Places and Names: On War, Revolution, and Returning* (New York: Penguin Press, 2019).

SELECTED BIBLIOGRAPHY

Elliot Ackerman, *The Fifth Act: America's End in Afghanistan* (New York: Penguin Press, 2022).

Matt Gallagher, *Kaboom: Embracing the Suck in a Savage Little War* (Boston: Da Capo Press, 2010).

Matt Gallagher, *Youngblood* (New York: Washington Square Press, 2016).

Matt Gallagher, *Daybreak* (New York: Atria Books, 2024).

Phil Klay, *Redeployment* (New York: Penguin Press, 2014).

Phil Klay, *The Citizen-Soldier: Moral Risk and the Modern Military* (Washington, DC: Brookings Institution Press, 2016).

Phil Klay, *Missionaries* (New York: Penguin Press, 2020).

Phil Klay, *Uncertain Ground* (New York: Penguin Press, 2022).

Phil Klay, "What Do I Owe the Dead of My Generation's Mismanaged Wars?," *New York Times*, May 26, 2024.

Peter Lucier, "Not Your Messiah," *The Revealer*, September 8, 2017.

Peter Lucier, "Remembering When the Memories Are No Longer Our Own," *War on the Rocks*, November 11, 2020.

Index

abolitionism, 57
accountability, 13, 65, 87, 137, 159, 174, 184, 188, 201
activism, political, 36, 104, 143, 154, 156, 157, 186–7
  veteran, 8, 10, 146–7
Adams, Abigail, 15, 43
Adams, John, 6, 14, 15, 16, 35, 38, 39–44, 45, 48, 51, 82, 176, 184, 188, 196
Adams, John Quincy, 50, 196
Adams, Samuel, 16, 25
Admirals' Revolt, 3, 107–10, 117, 126, 136, 188
Afghanistan, war in, 148–50, 152, 154, 163, 170–1, 181
Ainsworth, Fred, 96
Air Force, US (USAF), 107–9, 119, 121, 123, 125, 127, 128, 139, 144, 146, 173, 184
Air Service, US Army, 101
aircraft carriers, 101, 102, 108, 137
airplanes, 95, 102, 117, 160
al-Qaeda, 149
Alabama, 80, 82, 84
Alanbrooke, Viscount, 107
Alien and Sedition Acts, 42
Allegheny Mountains, 31
Allen, John, 161

Amelia Island, Florida, 50
American League against War and Fascism, 103
amphibious warfare, 101–2, 112
Annapolis, Maryland, 24
Anti-Federalists, 26–7, 29–30
Apache, 85
Appomattox, surrender at
Arapahoe, 85
Arizona, 53, 54
Arkansas, 82, 84, 124
armistice, 96–7
arms control, 101, 117, 203
Arnold, Benedict, 44
Arnold, Henry H., 200
artificial intelligence, 159
Attucks, Crispus, 120
Austin, Lloyd, 161, 162
Australia, 111, 165–6
AVF, 135

Baker, James, 139
Baker, Newton D., 100
Balkans, 140, 141, 145
Baltimore, Maryland, 65, 66
Bataan Death March, 111
Baton Rouge, Louisiana, 47
battleships, 89, 95, 99
Bay of Pigs, 130, 152
Belknap, William, 61, 62, 86

INDEX

Ben-Gurion, David, 179
bipartisanship, 120, 138, 158
Biden, Joe, 9, 84, 149, 150, 159, 161, 163, 174, 188
Bismarck, Otto von, 5
Black Americans, 7, 18, 64, 72, 73, 74, 78–82, 84, 85, 90, 120–4, 133, 134, 135, 151–2, 168, 184
Blackhawk War, 53
Board of War and Ordinance, 18
bombers, 108, 126, 127, 128, 137
bonds, war, 22, 32, 65, 104
Bonus March, 83, 102, 103, 110, 111
Border Wars, 85–8
Boston, Massachusetts, 25, 39, 44
Bowser, Harriet, 171
Bradley, Omar, 108, 111, 114, 122, 124, 184, 200
Britain, 19, 28, 33, 37, 40–1, 43, 46, 48–9, 51, 95, 96, 101, 105, 115, 116, 181
British Army, 15–16, 18–19, 25, 31, 35, 49, 97, 107
Brown, C. Q., 180, 189
Brown vs. *Board of Education*, 84
Buchanan, James, 82
budgets, military, 3, 100, 102, 107–10, 117–18, 127, 131, 137, 141, 152, 158, 167, 168, 188, 196
Buena Vista, Mexico, 53–4, 55
Buffalo Soldiers, 121
Burr, Aaron, 6, 38, 44, 45–7, 76
Busch, Anhauser, 62
Bush, George H., 138, 139, 141
Bush, George W., 145–6, 147, 176, 179, 187, 188
Business Plot, 104
Butler, Benjamin, 68
Butler, Smedley, 103–4, 117, 149, 181, 184

Caesar, 18, 51
Calhoun, John C., 50, 196
California, 53–4, 55, 56–7
Campbell, Angus, 166
Canada, 19, 48–9, 82
Caribbean Sea, 40, 42
Carlson, Tucker, 183
Carlucci, Frank, 139
Carter, Jimmy, 127, 137
Cates, Clifton, 122–3, 124
cavalry, 60–1, 62, 85, 87, 102, 121
CENTCOM, 139, 145, 146, 147, 148, 150, 161
Chauncey, Isaac, 120
Cheney, Dick, 139, 185, 188
Chesapeake River 49
Cheyenne, 61
China, 112–13, 158
Churchill, Winston, 106, 179
Cincinnati, Society of the, 25
Cincinnatus, Lucius Quinctius, 30
citizenship, 6, 62, 70, 79
civil–military relations, models of, 1–4, 10–12
civil rights, 64, 78, 79, 80, 81–2, 84, 85, 120, 133
Civil War, US, 6, 38, 54–5, 56, 58, 60, 64–7, 71, 73, 78, 85, 88–90, 92, 117, 120, 133

251

INDEX

civilian supremacy, *see* supremacy, civilian
Clausewitz, Carl von, 190, 194
Clemenceau, Georges, 179
Cleveland, Grover, 83
Clinton, Bill, 143, 188
Clinton, Hillary, 148, 149
Cold Harbor, battle of, 68
Cold War, 90, 119, 140–1, 175, 190, 201
Colfax, Schuyler, 77
Collins, Joseph Lawton, 122
color barrier, 120–5
Colorado, 53, 83
Comanche, 85, 86
commander-in-chief, US president as, 3, 6, 7, 8, 31–5, 57, 62, 66, 70, 73, 76, 78, 89, 105, 106, 110, 118, 144, 146, 147, 151, 167, 169, 174, 179, 186, 194, 197
Confederacy, 6, 7, 58–60, 65, 66, 68, 69–72, 75, 78–9, 80, 82, 85, 87, 89–90, 186
Confederation, Articles of, 19, 26, 29, 32
Congress, Confederation, 24, 32
Congress, Continental, 5, 15, 17, 18, 19–22, 25, 35, 39, 59, 117, 185, 188
Congress, US, 2, 3, 4, 5, 6, 8, 9, 13, 26, 27, 28–9, 30, 34, 36, 40, 41, 42–3, 44, 47, 49, 50, 51, 52, 53, 55, 60, 61, 64, 65, 66, 67, 69, 72, 73–8, 79, 81, 82, 84, 87, 88, 89, 90, 91, 93, 97, 98–9, 102, 105, 109–10, 117, 118, 120, 123, 125, 126, 132, 135, 136, 137, 138, 143, 145, 150, 152, 158, 162, 163, 167, 168, 170, 171, 174, 177, 179, 182, 183, 185, 186, 187–8, 194, 195, 200
Representatives, House of, 44, 103, 104, 117
Senate, 41, 55, 76, 77, 100, 103, 107, 113, 123, 143, 158, 162, 184
conscription, 8, 66, 95, 103, 116, 133–6, 142, 154, 188, 206
constabulary duties, 93, 94, 116, 203
Constitution, US, 3, 6, 8, 25, 27, 28, 30–1, 36, 37, 42, 58, 59–60, 65, 67, 77, 78, 79, 82, 113, 114, 124, 130, 160, 166, 167, 168, 175, 186, 196
Article 1 of, 26
Article 6 of, 59
Fifteenth Amendment, 79–80
Fourteenth Amendment, 74, 79–80, 83, 120
Second Amendment, 30
Third Amendment, 30
Thirteenth Amendment, 79–80
Twenty-Fifth Amendment, 163
Constitutional Convention, 6, 31
Continental Army, 17, 18, 19–20, 25, 26, 33, 38, 59, 96
continuous-aim gunfire, 93, 98
Corregidor Island, 111
counter-insurgency, 147
courts martial, 10, 20, 45, 46, 47,

INDEX

53, 57, 61, 67, 100, 103, 170, 177, 184
Crazy Horse, 62
Creek (people), 49
critical race theory, 167–8
Cuba, 50, 82, 91–2, 93, 94, 115
Cuban Missile Crisis, 8, 128–9, 130, 152, 153, 162, 189
culture wars, 183–4
Custer, George Armstrong, 6, 39, 60–3, 85, 86, 91, 103, 176, 181, 184, 188

Dakota territory, 61, 62
Daniels, Josephus, 96, 97–8, 99–100, 185
Darrow, Clarence, 168
Davis, Jefferson, 53, 70
Decatur, Stephen, 42
Defense, Department of (DOD), 83, 107, 108, 109, 113, 114, 118, 119, 123, 124, 135, 136, 138, 150, 154–5, 162, 168, 183, 184, 188
Defense Intelligence Agency, 149
demobilization, 43, 64, 70, 102
democracy, 1, 2, 5, 11, 22, 38, 40, 44, 77, 114, 160, 164, 169, 177, 179, 182, 199
Democratic-Republicans, 43, 48
Democrats, 53, 55, 61, 97, 102, 113, 115, 120, 143, 147, 158, 159, 161
Denfield, Louis, 108, 109
Depression, Great, 102
desertion, 61, 133, 185
Dewey, George, 92

Dick Act (1905), 93
diplomacy, 40, 44, 101, 139, 140, 142, 150, 153, 163, 191
District of Columbia, 102, 171
Dominican Republic, 94
Donahoe, Patrick, 183
"Don't Ask Don't Tell" policy, 142–3
Doolittle, Jimmy, 200
Doolittle Report (1954), 190–1
draft, *see* conscription
draft protests, 83, 120, 176
Dugan, Michael, 139
Dulles, John Foster, 112
Dunford, Joe, 165
duty, dereliction of, 24, 132

education, military, 92, 98, 116, 134, 136, 138, 142, 166, 206
Eisenhower, Dwight D., 8, 84, 108, 124, 125–6, 127, 130, 152, 188, 190, 197, 200, 203
elections, supervision of, 74, 80, 81
emancipation, 6, 56, 64, 79, 80, 90
Enforcement Acts (1870–1), 80, 84
enslavement, 6, 18, 50, 53, 54, 56, 57, 78, 80
  abolition of, 38, 63, 79
Erie, Lake, 49, 120
Esper, Mark, 165, 167
espionage, 45
Executive Branch, 72, 109, 114, 200
extremism, 40, 168, 172, 174, 204

Fallen Timbers, battle of, 45
Fallon, William, 147–8

253

Fallujah, Iraq, 147
Faubus, Orval, 84, 124, 125
Federalist Papers, 27–9, 59, 196
Federalists, 26, 41, 43, 48, 176, 196
Fish, Hamilton, 86
Flournoy, Michèle, 148
Floyd, George, 165
Flynn, Michael, 149, 154, 161
France, 40, 43, 48, 70–1, 95, 96, 101, 176
   quasi-war with, 38, 41–2, 45
Franklin, Benjamin, 14, 25
Florida, 6, 49–50, 51–2, 63, 70, 80, 81, 82, 87
Foch, Ferdinand, 97
Forrestal, James, 121
Fort Necessity, Pennsylvania, 18
Fort Riley, Kansas, 61
Founding Fathers, 3, 14, 16, 40, 90, 182, 189
Franco-American Convention (1800), 42
Franks, Tommy, 145, 146
Fremont, John, 6, 54–7, 63, 76, 184, 188
French and Indian War, 15, 18
Friedman, Milton, 135
frontier, western, 28, 30, 32, 33, 49, 85, 88
Fugitive Slave Act, 82

Gaines, Edmund P., 51
Garrison, Lindley M., 96
Gates, Horatio, 44
Gates, Robert, 147, 148, 149
Gates Commission, 134–6, 154
General Treaty for Renunciation of War as an Instrument of National Policy (1928), 101
Genêt, Edmond-Charles, 41
geopolitics, 4, 7, 40, 164
George III, king of Great Britain and Ireland, 37, 58
Georgia, 28, 80, 82
Germany, 95, 96, 101, 106, 116, 190
Gerry, Elbridge, 31
Gettysburg campaign, 60
GI Bill (1984), 136
Gogol, Nikolai, 10
Goldwater, Barry, 138
Goldwater–Nichols reforms, 138, 140, 144, 188
Governors, role of, 5, 32, 33, 35, 59, 65, 81, 82–3, 167, 171, 178
Grant, Orville, 61
Grant, Ulysses, 2, 6, 39, 53, 55, 60, 61–2, 64, 67–78, 80, 81, 82, 85, 86, 87, 88, 89, 90, 103, 110, 176, 184, 186, 188
Greene, Nathanael, 18, 44
Greenspan, Alan, 135
Grenada, 136, 139
Guam, 92, 115
guerrilla war, 33, 69
Gulf War (1991), 8, 138–9, 144, 154

habeas corpus, suspension of, 6, 65, 66, 67, 89, 186
Haiti, 94, 103, 141
Halleck, Henry, 55, 173
Halsey, William, 108, 200

INDEX

Hamilton, Alexander, 5, 6, 14, 18, 20, 22, 27–30, 32–5, 39, 41, 42–4, 45, 48, 59, 62, 63, 184, 188, 195, 196
Harding, Warren G., 83
Harlem Hellfighters (369th Infantry Regiment), 121
Harrison, William Henry, 76
Havana, Cuba, 91, 93, 94
Hayes, Rutherford B., 81, 82
Hegseth, Pete, 173
Henry, Patrick, 30
Herodotus, 190
Higgins Boats, 102
Honduras, 94
Hoover, Herbert, 83, 102, 103
Hormuz, Straits of, 147
Houston, Texas, 121
Huntington, Samuel (military historian), 7, 10, 90, 175, 178–9, 190, 191–200, 202, 203–6
Huntington, Samuel (president of the Continental Congress), 17
Hussein, Saddam, 139

Idaho, 83
Independence, Declaration of, 16, 59
Indian agencies, 85
Indian Wars, 62, 65
Indiana, 77
indiscipline, 33, 109
insubordination, 3, 8, 38, 50, 52, 57, 70, 73, 78, 98, 105, 113, 115, 118, 139, 174, 176, 178, 180, 188

insurrection, 3, 19, 20, 21, 26, 32, 34, 35, 36, 52, 59, 64, 71, 78–85, 100, 115, 171–2, 177, 186
Insurrection Act (1807), 66, 82, 83, 84, 124, 165, 167, 178
integration, racial, 8, 74, 120, 121–5, 151
inter-service rivalry, 100
Iran Contra scandal, 139, 144
Iranian hostage crisis, 136
Iraq War (2003), 144, 145, 146–9, 152, 154, 163, 176, 181, 187
Islamic State (IS), 149
Israel, 147
Italy, 101

Jackson, Andrew, 6, 53, 63, 70, 76, 82, 87–8, 120, 176, 185, 188, 196
    invasion of Florida, 48–52
Jacobinism, 33
Janowitz, Morris, 10, 178, 190, 199–206
January 6th insurrection, 171–2, 177
Japan, 101, 111–12, 190
Jay, John, 27, 30
Jay Treaty, 40–1
Jefferson, Thomas, 6, 10, 14, 25, 35, 38, 39, 41, 42, 43, 45, 46, 47, 48, 55, 82, 196
Johnson, Andrew, 61, 69, 70, 71, 72, 73, 74–5, 76, 77, 78, 84, 176, 186, 188
Johnson, Harold, 131
Johnson, Hugh S., 104

255

INDEX

Johnson, Louis, 108, 109, 121
Johnson, Lyndon B., 129, 131, 132–3, 148, 153, 181
Joint Army–Navy Board, 101, 105
Joint Chiefs of Staff (JCS), 107, 114, 131, 138, 145, 152
   chairman of, 8, 106, 108, 111, 114, 119, 128, 130, 137–8, 139, 140, 142, 144, 146, 150, 154, 165, 169, 173, 176, 180, 187, 193, 201
Jones, David, 138
Jones, James, 148, 161
Jumonville Glen, massacre at, 18
Justice Department, US, 80

Kansas, 56
Kearney, Stephen, 54
Kellogg, Keith, 161, 164
Kelly, John, 161, 164
Kennedy, John F., 84, 126, 127, 128–9, 130, 132, 146, 148, 152, 153, 162, 188
Kentucky, 44, 45
Key West Agreement (1948), 108
Kickapoo, 85–6, 87
Kinkaid, Thomas, 108
King, Alexander Ernest, 108
King, Ernest, 197
King, Martin Luther, Jr., 83
King, Rodney, 83
Kiowa, 85–6
Knox, Henry, 20
Korean War, 3, 112–13, 122, 137, 152, 184, 190, 192, 197, 206
Ku Klux Klan, 80

Lafayette, Marquis de, 18
Lakota Sioux, 61
Latin America, 103
Laurens, Henry, 17
Laurens, John, 22
law, rule of, 16
Leahy, William, 106, 126, 130, 200
Lebanon, 136, 140
Lee, Harry, 34
Lee, Robert E., 6, 56, 58, 60, 63, 69, 72
LeMay, Curtis, 126, 200
liberalism, 192, 193–4, 195, 198
liberty, 4, 16, 27, 29, 35, 37, 79, 82, 122, 133
Lincoln, Abraham, 6, 39, 53, 55, 56, 57, 66–8, 71, 76, 79, 80, 117, 173, 179, 184, 186, 188
   assassination of, 67, 69–70, 72, 89
Lipan, 87
Little Big Horn, battle of, 61–2, 63, 85, 88
Little Rock, Arkansas, 124–5
Long, Huey, 111
Long Island, battle of, 19
Longfellow, Henry Wadsworth, 62
Los Angeles, California, 54, 83
Louis XVI, king of France, 40
Louisiana, 42, 43, 45, 49, 74, 80, 81, 82
Louisiana Maneuvers, 101
Loyalists, 41

machine guns, 95
Madison, James, 14, 22, 27, 29, 30, 42, 43, 47, 49

INDEX

MAGA movement, 174
Mahan, Alfred Thayer, 92
Maine, 28
Maine, USS, 91, 94
Manchuria, 112
Manila, Philippines, 93, 111
Marcus Aurelius, 14
Marine Corps, US, 42, 54, 92, 94, 96, 97, 101, 115, 116, 117, 119, 121, 122, 123, 128, 136, 138, 140, 147, 151–2, 174, 184, 203
   commandant of, 146
Marshall, George, 105–7, 108, 112, 113, 117, 119, 121, 132, 162, 197, 200
Marshall, John, 47
Marshall Rule, 181–2
martial law, 43, 56, 57, 63, 80
Martin, Joseph W., 113
Maryland, 33, 56, 65–6
Mason–Dixon Line, 65
Massachusetts, 31, 34
Matamoros, Mexico, 53, 54
Mattis, James, 148, 161, 162, 164, 173, 177, 183
Maximillian, emperor of Mexico, 70, 71
May, Henry, 66
Mayo, Henry R., 99
MacArthur, Douglas, 3, 7, 102, 107, 110–15, 118, 130, 173, 175, 176, 181, 185, 188, 194, 196–7, 200
McCain, John, 9
McCarthyism, 191
McChrystal, Stanley, 148–9, 173

McClellan, George, 55–6, 57, 76, 173, 188
Macgregor, Douglas, 122, 170
MacGuire, Gerald P., 104
McKenzie, Frank, 150
Mackenzie, Ranald, 7, 65, 85–8, 90, 121
McKiernan, David, 149, 173
McKinley, William, 83, 91, 92, 181
McMaster, H. R., 130–1, 132, 142, 150, 153–4, 161, 162, 163, 164
McNamara, Robert, 126, 130, 131, 132, 152, 153
Medal of Honor, 103, 110, 111, 115, 121, 164
Meigs, Montgomery, 57
merchant shipping, militarization of, 40, 42
Mescalero, 87
Mexican War, 6, 38, 53–5, 188
Mexico, 7, 43, 46, 47, 55, 65, 70–1, 73, 85–7, 88, 89, 111, 116, 121, 176
   US–Mexican border, 84
Mexico, Gulf of, 49, 50
Mexico City, 53–4
Miles, Nelson, 92
militia, 1, 24, 26, 28, 30, 31, 32, 33–4, 35, 38, 43, 44, 49, 60, 82, 85, 93, 116, 171, 176, 190
Militia Act (1792), 33
Militia Act (1903), 83
Miller, Chris, 170
Milley, Mark, 9, 150, 164–9, 170, 177, 180, 183
Mississippi (state), 82, 84

INDEX

Mississippi River, 32, 42, 43, 44, 45, 46, 49
Missouri, 6, 56, 63
Mitchell, Billy, 101
Monongahela, Pennsylvania, 18
Monroe, James, 6, 38, 50–1, 87, 176, 188
Monroe Doctrine, 93, 115
Monterrey, battle of, 53
Morgan, Daniel, 46
Mormons, 82
Morristown, New Jersey, 17
Myers, Richard, 146

Napoleon I, emperor of the French, 42, 48
Natchez, Mississippi, 47
National Defense Authorization Act, 158
National Guard, 5, 59, 82–4, 93, 95–6, 116, 124, 167, 171, 178
National Recovery Agency, 104
National Security Act (1947), 8, 107, 119, 136, 161–2
National Security Agency (NSA), 167
Native Americans, 1, 6, 38, 44, 45, 49–50, 51, 52, 62, 85, 91
Naval Act (1916), 95, 116
Naval War College, 92, 98
Navy, US, 27, 28, 41, 42, 54, 92–3, 94, 95, 96, 97, 98, 99, 100, 101, 105, 107–10, 116, 118, 120, 121, 122, 123, 125, 126, 127, 128, 138, 151–2, 184, 186, 188, 195
  Department of the, 119

Nebraska, 83, 126
Netherlands, 40
Neutrality Act (1794), 40
Nevada, 53, 54, 83
New Army, 40, 43, 176, 184, 188, 196
New Jersey, 33
New Mexico, 54, 83
New Orleans, Louisiana, 45, 46, 49, 53, 120
New York City, 19, 46, 66, 133
Newbold, Greg, 146
Newburgh, New York, 19, 20, 37
Nicaragua, 94
Nichols, Bill, 138
Nimitz, Chester, 108, 111, 115
Nixon, Richard, 133–4, 135
North Carolina, 22, 35, 82
North Korea, 110, 112, 114, 191
Northern Virginia, Army of, 68, 69
Northwest Territory, 44, 49
NSC (National Security Council), 125, 139, 145, 185
nuclear weapons, 4, 84, 108, 110, 118, 125–8, 147, 152, 190, 203
  targeting, 149, 152, 189
Nueces River, 53
Nunn, Sam, 143

oaths, 6, 34, 39, 44, 58, 59, 60, 76, 79, 159, 167
Obama, Barack, 9, 84, 147, 148, 149, 153, 154, 161, 163, 173, 176, 188
Ohio, 81, 83

258

Oklahoma, 87
Omaha, Nebraska, 126
ORANGE, Plan, 101
Oregon Trail, 56

Packard Commission, 137–8
Panama, 94, 139
Paris, France, 35
partisanship, 2, 4–5, 6, 12, 36, 40, 48, 72, 76, 97, 98, 100, 113, 126, 141, 143, 156, 158, 159, 161, 170, 173, 175, 180, 182, 186, 201
Patton, George S., 200
Pawnee, 56
Payne, Adam, 121
Pearl Harbor, 106, 112, 119
Pensacola, Florida, 50
pensions, military, 19–20, 22, 24, 36
Pennsylvania, 31, 32, 33, 44, 46
Pentagon, 83, 145, 148, 149, 162, 164, 170, 171, 176
Perry, Matthew, 120
Pershing, John J., 95–7, 99, 116, 121
Peru, 43
Petraeus, David, 148, 161
Philadelphia, Pennsylvania, 15, 19, 34, 66
Philippine–American War, 94, 103
Philippines, the, 92, 93, 111, 115
Pierce, Franklin, 76
Plains of Abraham, battle of, 16
policymaking, 1, 2, 91, 115, 192, 195

politicization, 3, 9, 36, 52, 55, 78, 88, 115, 153, 156, 157, 160–1, 169, 172, 173, 178, 180, 194, 200–1
Polk, James K., 38, 53–5, 57, 188
Pompeo, Mike, 165
Porter, David, 69, 70
Posse Comitatus Act (1878), 7, 64, 81–2, 83, 84–5, 165, 166
Powell, Colin, 8, 139–44, 148, 154, 163, 175, 180, 185, 188, 201
praetorianism, 12, 156, 157, 160, 172, 191, 195, 204
privateers, 41–2
procurement, defense, 110, 137
professionalism, military, 4–5, 7, 11, 45, 49, 157, 169, 174, 180, 191, 192, 193–4, 196
Project Solarium, 125
Provisional Army, 43, 58
Prussia, 93, 131, 193, 195
Puerto Rico, 92, 115

Quebec, Canada, 19, 44
queue (hair style), 48

racism, 121, 123–4, 151
Radford, Arthur W., 108
railroads, 83, 89
Randolph, Philip, 120
Reagan, Ronald, 137, 138, 139, 140, 144, 160
Reconstruction, 64, 71–75, 77, 78, 79, 81, 82, 85, 88, 91, 121, 186
Remolino Raid, 65, 121

INDEX

Republicans, 25, 43, 55, 56, 69, 72, 74, 76, 77, 80, 81, 97, 100, 112, 113, 114, 115, 139, 141, 149, 158, 159, 161, 173, 174, 176, 178, 179, 180, 183
Reserve Officer Training Program (ROTC), 95
reservists, 116, 144, 156, 171
Reuter, Bertha Ann, 40
Revenue Service, US, 41
Revolutionary War, American, 15, 32, 33, 35, 41, 43, 48, 120
Rey Molino, Mexico, 87
Richmond, Virginia, 70
Ridgway, Matthew, 125–6, 195, 200–1
Rio Grande, 53, 71, 86
Roosevelt, Franklin D., 102–3, 104, 105–6, 107, 111, 117, 126, 176, 181, 188, 197
Roosevelt, Theodore, 47, 83, 92, 93, 98, 121, 181
Root, Elihu, 93, 116, 162
Rough Riders, 92, 121
Royal Navy, 115–16
Royall, Kenneth, 122
Rumsfeld, Donald, 144–5, 146–7, 152
Russell, Richard, 123
Russia, 106, 149, 158, 162

Saigon, fall of, 150
St Augustine, Florida, 50
St Marks, Florida, 50
San Antonio, Texas, 86
San Francisco, California, 54, 56

San Juan Hill, battle of, 121
Santa Ana, Antonio López de, 53
Saratoga, battle of, 44
Schurz, Carl, 68
Schwartzkopf, Norman, 139
Scott, Winfield, 53–4, 55, 58, 76, 173, 188
Scowcroft, Brent, 163
secession, 6, 31, 34, 38, 56, 57, 58, 59, 64, 71, 90
segregation, 119, 122, 123, 151, 184, 188, 205
Seminole, 50, 51, 87, 121
Seminole War, First, 50
Seminole War, Second, 53
Senate Committee on Military Affairs, 76, 107
Seven Years' War, 16
Seward, William H., 71
Shawnee, 49, 53
Shays's Rebellion, 31–2, 34–5
Shenandoah campaign, 61
Shepherd, Lemuel, 123
Sheridan, Philip, 61, 62, 71, 73, 74–5, 81, 86–7, 89, 184
Sherman, William Tecumseh, 62, 67, 69–70, 72, 73, 75, 76, 78, 86, 89, 196
Shiloh, battle of, 68
Shinseki, Eric, 145–6, 150, 161
shirking, 10, 41, 56, 57, 76, 105, 123, 184
Short, Jennifer, 173
Shultz, George, 140
Sims, William, 7, 97–100, 105, 116–17, 118, 176, 181, 184, 188

Single Integrated Operational Plan (SIOP), 127
Sioux campaign, 61–2
Sitting Bull, 61
Sloat, John, 54, 55
Somalia, 141
Sonoma, California, 56
South Carolina, 22, 80, 81, 82
South Korea, 110, 112
SOUTHCOM, 161
Soviet Union, 106, 112, 125, 127, 128, 190, 191, 197
Spain, 6, 28, 32, 42, 44, 45, 46, 47, 49, 50–1, 91–2, 94
Spanish–American War, 7, 91–3, 95, 115–16
Springfield, Massachusetts, 31
Spruance, Raymond, 108
Stanbery, Henry, 74
Stanton, Edwin, 69, 70, 74, 75–6, 77
Stark, Harold, 105
State Department, US, 94, 113, 114, 154
Stimson, Henry, 96
Stockton, Robert, 54
Stoicism, 14
strategy, 3, 5, 8, 19, 33, 55, 89, 94, 106–7, 108, 109, 110, 113, 114, 118, 125, 126, 127, 131, 137, 141, 142, 144, 147, 148, 149, 151, 152, 153, 169, 176, 179, 185, 189, 192, 201, 203, 206
strikes (industrial action), 83
Stuart, J. E. B., 60
submarines, 95, 98–100, 101, 116

subservience, military, 3, 12
Sullivan, John L., 108
supremacy, civilian, 5, 12, 17–22, 89, 105, 114, 157, 173, 189, 199, 201
Supreme Court, US, 9, 33, 47, 66, 67, 76, 81, 84, 121
Symington, Stuart, 121, 123

Taft, William Howard, 181
Taiwan, 112
Taliban, 149, 171
Taney, Roger, 66
tanks, 95, 101, 102, 117
taxation, 15, 31–2, 33, 34, 35, 82, 134, 136
Taylor, Maxwell, 12, 125–6, 128, 129–30, 132, 152, 188
Taylor, Zachary, 6, 52–5, 63, 76, 82
technology, 93, 95, 119, 198
Tecumseh, 49, 53
Tennessee, 80, 82
Tenure of Office Act, 74, 77
Texas, 47, 53, 71, 74, 81, 82, 85, 87
Themistocles, 14
Thomas, Lorenzo, 57
Thucydides, 190
time-phased force deployment data (TPFDD), 145
Title 10 (US Code), 83–4, 124
Tocqueville, Alexis de, 133, 205
Tonkin, Gulf of, 130
Torch, Operation, 107
treason, 20, 33, 45, 46–7, 60, 66, 72, 75, 101, 169, 170, 183

INDEX

Truman, Harry S., 3, 7, 108–15, 118, 119–20, 121, 125, 126, 127, 152, 173, 176, 184, 188, 197
Trump, Donald, 9, 84, 149, 150, 157, 161, 162, 163–5, 166–7, 169–74, 176, 177, 188–9
trust, public, 2, 7, 9, 110, 117, 119, 132, 143, 173, 188–9
Turkey, 128
Tuskegee Airmen, 121
tyranny, 16, 26, 35

United Nations (UN), 112, 138
Urban, David, 165
Utah, 53, 54, 82
Ute, 85

Valley Forge, Pennsylvania, 17
Van Buren, Martin, 82
Vandegrift, Alexander, 108
Vandenberg, Hoyt, 109, 121, 123
Veracruz, Mexico, 53, 103
Versailles Treaty, 101
veterans, 4, 8, 9, 11, 13, 24, 26, 28, 32, 36, 83, 88, 102, 103, 104, 109, 111, 117, 142, 144, 146, 150, 156–7, 161, 162–4, 170, 171–2, 174, 177, 181, 186–7, 188
Vietnam War, 8, 83, 119, 124, 129–33, 135, 137, 139, 142, 144, 147, 152–4, 175, 179, 181, 205, 206
Virginia, 15, 30, 33, 34, 43, 44, 58, 82, 196

volunteer force, US military as, 4, 12, 115, 119, 134–5, 138, 142, 144, 157, 195, 206
Von Steuben, Friedrich Wilhelm, 18

Wainwright, Jonathan M., 200
Wake Island, 113
war, secretary of, 50, 61, 65, 65, 69, 70, 74, 75, 76, 77, 83, 86, 87, 89, 92, 93, 96, 100
war crimes, 10, 111, 170
War of 1812, 48–9, 53, 120, 129
warfare, 4, 12, 15, 19, 61, 85, 95, 98, 99, 100, 101, 108, 117, 129, 132, 142, 199, 200, 202, 203, 205
  air, 102
  nuclear, 125, 127, 152
  submarine, 116
Washington, DC, 49, 65, 66, 70, 95, 102, 103, 109, 111, 113, 126, 131, 147, 163, 176
  Capitol, 39, 46, 56, 147, 171, 172
  Lafayette Square, 165–6, 170, 171, 186
  White House, 49, 72, 74, 105, 106, 126, 128, 130, 135, 139, 144, 147–9, 150, 152–3, 154, 161, 162, 164, 165, 167, 170, 174, 175
Washington, George, 2, 5–6, 12, 14–26, 29, 30, 31–7, 38, 39, 40, 41, 42, 43, 44, 45, 47–8, 53, 55, 58, 60, 63, 64, 76, 82,

89, 90, 117, 154, 155, 174, 179, 185–6, 188, 189, 196, 204
as commander in chief, 31–5
elected president, 29
resignation as president, 35
retirement from the army, 22–5
"war of posts" strategy, 19
Washington Naval Accords, 101
Wayne, Anthony, 45
Webb, Thomas, 15
Weinberger, Caspar, 136, 138, 139–40
Weinberger Doctrine, 140
West Point, New York, 60, 111
West Virginia, 83
Westmoreland, William, 135
Whigs, 53, 54, 76
Whiskey Rebellion, 31–2, 33, 35, 58, 176

Wilkinson, James, 6, 44–8, 53, 63, 184
Wilson, Woodrow, 7, 83, 95, 96, 97, 98–9, 100, 176, 181, 185, 188, 202
women in the military, 96, 121, 124, 136, 140, 143, 159, 160, 172, 173, 179, 183, 206
Wood, Leonard, 96, 196
World War I, 83, 94–7, 102, 111, 116–17, 120
World War II, 7, 8, 90, 102, 105–7, 108–9, 117, 121, 125, 126, 133, 159–60, 181, 190, 201, 202
Wyoming, 53

Yalu River, 112
Yorktown, battle of, 19, 33

Zinni, Tony, 146